John

G000244454

John Wesley

The Evangelical Revival and the Rise of Methodism in England

John Munsey Turner

EPWORTH PRESS

All rights reserved. No part of this publication may be reproduced, stored in a retrieval system, or transmitted, in any form or by any means, electronic, mechanical, photocopying or otherwise, without the prior permission of the publisher, Epworth Press.

Copyright © John Munsey Turner 2002

British Library Cataloguing in Publication Data

A catalogue record for this book is available from the British Library

ISBN 0 7162 0556 4

First published in 2002
by Epworth Press
20 Ivatt way
Peterborough, PE3 7PG

Typeset by Regent Typesetting, London
and printed in Great Britain by
Biddles Ltd, Guildford and King's Lynn

Contents

Preface

The year 2003 marks the 300th anniversary of the birth of John Wesley. There may be those who will say, 'Not another book on Wesley.' I cannot claim to offer new research, but seek to interpret John Wesley and the movement he founded to those outside and inside the Methodist tradition, who may be tempted still to imagine him as an eighteenth-century Billy Graham, but always on a horse or at a market cross! We need to see him in the context of the eighteenth century, also to make clear that the Methodist Movement was much more than a 'one person show'. We are bound to ask what effect Methodism had on ordinary people and on society at large, remembering in how many different environments characteristic Methodist styles flourished. Sheer space confines me largely to England, but there were and are 'many Methodisms'. A chapter on Primitive Methodism reminds us that Wesley's Methodism was not the only group to bear that name, although his theology was normative for that church. I have pillaged my earlier writings, but have sought to represent the latest research, not least in interpreting 'the Long Eighteenth Century' between the Revolution of 1688–9 and the Reform Act of 1832. A notable group of Methodist historians have, since 1960, revolutionized our picture of Wesley and Methodism. I have ransacked their work with, I hope, due acknowledgement. In the early days of my interest in history, two scholars taught me much – the great Anglican church historian Norman Sykes, and Rupert Davies. Gordon Wakefield, once my Principal when I was a tutor at the Queen's College, Birmingham, was another, much missed, encourager. They gave models of wise scholarship and counsel. I hope I have not departed too much from their standards in the proper interest of popularization.

John Munsey Turner
Horwich, Bolton

Abbreviations

Baker	F. Baker, *John Wesley and the Church of England*, Epworth Press, 1970; 2000
BE	*Bicentennial Edition of the Works of John Wesley*, Clarendon Press and Abingdon Press, USA
Green	V. H. H. Green, *John Wesley*, Nelson, 1964
HMGB	R. E. Davies and E. G. Rupp (eds), *A History of the Methodist Church in Great Britain*, 4 vols, Epworth Press, 1965–88
HP	*Hymns and Psalms: A Methodist and Ecumenical Hymnbook*, Methodist Publishing House, 1983
Journal	*Journal of the Rev John Wesley*, 8 vols, ed. N. Curnock, Epworth Press, 1906–16
Letters	*Letters of the Rev John Wesley*, 8 vols, ed. J. Telford, Epworth Press, 1931
Lives	*Lives of the Early Methodist Preachers*, ed. Thomas Jackson, Wesleyan-Methodist Book Room, 1865; 4th edn, Tentmaker, 1998
Poetical Works	*The Poetical Works of John and Charles Wesley*, 13 vols, ed. G. Osborn, London, 1868–72
PWHS	*The Proceedings of the Wesley Historical Society*

Rack   H. D. Rack, *Reasonable Enthusiast: John Wesley and the Rise of Methodism*, Epworth Press, 1989

Rupp   E. G. Rupp, *Religion in England 1688–1791*, Oxford University Press, 1986

Schmidt   M. Schmidt, *John Wesley: A Theological Biography*, 3 vols, Epworth Press, 1966–72

Sermons   *Wesley's Standard Sermons*, ed. E. H. Sugden, Epworth Press, 1931

Works   *Works of John Wesley*, 14 vols, ed. Thomas Jackson, London, 1829–32

The Evangelical Revival: An Overview

Every Christian denomination has its myths and legends. There is a long-standing Methodist legend that the Evangelical Revival began precisely at a quarter to nine on the evening of 24 May 1738, when John Wesley felt his heart 'strangely warmed' at a religious society meeting in Aldersgate Street in London. Methodists even celebrate 'Aldersgate Sunday' – surely the only Christian festival dedicated to a street, although Pentecostals look back to Azusa Street in Los Angeles, where 'the fire came down' on 9 April 1906.

Certainly John Wesley played a leading part in the movements of renewal. The Revival without Wesley would seem like *Hamlet* without the Prince of Denmark, but the broad movement of evangelicalism was well under way long before 1738. It was European and transatlantic with four central characteristics, emerging in many different forms and styles.[1]

New birth or conversion was the ever-present focal point. Here is George Shadford, later one of Wesley's itinerant preachers, describing his conversion in 1762. A preacher had said 'Is there any young man here about my age willing to give up all to come to Christ? I cried out . . . God be merciful to me, a sinner. No sooner had I expressed these words, but by the eye of faith (not with my bodily eyes) I saw Christ, my advocate, at the right hand of God, making intercession for me. I believe he loved me and gave himself for me. In an instant the Lord filled my soul with Divine Love. As quick as lightning . . . immediately my eyes flowed with tears and my heart with love. Tears of joy and sorrow ran mingled down my cheeks . . . As I walked home along the streets, I seemed to be in paradise. When I read my Bible, it seemed an entirely new book . . . everything appeared new, and stood in a new relation to me. I was in Christ a new creature. But no sooner had I peace within, than the devil and wicked men began to roar without . . . in order to drown the young child. But none of these things moved me for I was happy, happy in my God, clothed with the sun, and the moon under my feet . . . '[2]

This is a typical, stereotyped experience of 'New Birth', the emotional side of justification by faith and the consequent assurance of present salvation. It is the religion of the heart. It became very much at the centre of religious discourse for a century or more.

Activism was the second characteristic, in terms not only of evangelism and pastoral activity, but of missionary endeavour and social action. 'Action is the life of virtue and the world is the theatre of action', said Hannah More,[3] echoing John Calvin.

The third characteristic is the centrality of the cross in preaching and devotion. 'The Evangelical Movement', said W. E. Gladstone, 'aimed at bringing back, and by an aggressive movement, the cross and all that the cross essentially implies.'[4] A recent survey by Boyd Hilton calls the period when evangelicals were dominant in England 'the Age of Atonement',[5] pointing to a later period at the end of the nineteenth century when the incarnation was much more emphasized. It is significant that at the time around 1900, when the incarnation was central in Anglican thinking, two leading Methodist theologians, John Scott Lidgett (1854–1953) and William F. Lofthouse (1871–1965), wrote books on the atonement,[6] while also greatly stressing the incarnation. John Wesley sought to preach Christ in 'all his offices'.

The fourth characteristic, if we follow David Bebbington's analysis, is a stress on the Bible as the heart of devotion and the final authority. When John Wesley said he was 'a man of one book', he did not mean that the Bible alone mattered. This was clearly not true of him. It meant that the Bible was the source of authority and teaching, endorsed by tradition, not contradicted by reason, and confirmed by experience.[7]

The European evangelical movement must claim priority, as

has been clearly shown recently by W. R. Ward in notable summaries. First, we must note the movement in the German principalities called *Pietism*, a word which, sadly, has come to be a term of abuse. It might be the case that the Peace of Westphalia (1648) ended thirty years of war and a century of strife and that it was the end of religious wars as such, but it did not seem like that to the Protestants. They could feel besieged in Catholic principalities with the possibility of attempts at further domination by Roman Catholics. Even as late as the Seven Years War (1756–63), when England and Prussia were at war with France and Austria, an evangelical, the somewhat eccentric Howel Harris, began to create a 'Dad's Army' of volunteers to defend the east coast of England against the French, 'lest our privileges and liberties should be taken away from us, especially the liberty of the gospel which, should the Papists succeed, we should be robbed of'.[8] The whole history of Protestant religious renewal in the eighteenth century was deeply conditioned by the fear that confessional warfare was by no means at an end.

The religious wars left a legacy of bitterness in Europe contributing to what the French historian Paul Hazard called 'the crisis of the European conscience'[9] when France moved from believing with Bossuet (the great Catholic preacher) to doubting with Voltaire, who wished to 'écraser l'infâme', that is to rid the world of Catholic and any other superstition. Gordon Rupp[10] wrote of 'the great estrangement' when modern Europe bred a largely secular tradition, disentangled from religion and theology. This became true in great areas of politics, law, philosophy and science. The churches had used up vital energy in their struggle. The failure of the church to resolve the danger of secularization was not merely an intellectual failure. There was also a failure of nerve in the face of new coherent styles of formulating truth and a failure of compassion in the face of new idealism in the realm of social justice. We can point in England to a more moderate religious fragmentation, paralleled on the continent, into mystics, moralists and rationalists. This was the time when the place of reason, the nature of authority, thinking about the character of the universe, and the nature of historical evidence, were creating the world of enlightenment or 'Modernism' as we now call it in our 'post-modern' disillusionment. Herbert Butterfield suggests that the scientific revolution of the seventeenth century was the most important event since the rise of Christianity, making Renaissance and Reformation seem like 'mere internal displacements' within the system of medieval Christendom.[11] Galileo and Newton showed new ways of looking at the universe. Newton's machine needed a great mechanic, which led to changes in ways of looking at God and his creative activity.

> Nature and Nature's laws lay hid in night
> God said 'Let Newton be' and all was light.

> (Alexander Pope)

Despite the 'rage of party' at the time of Queen Anne, orderliness, law, reliability and reason were to be stressed, at least in the higher echelons of society. There was a growth of deistic views and a rational style of piety, which contrasts with the intense religiosity of the previous century.

In Europe, we dare not underestimate the effect of the migrations of religious groups – Huguenots, Silesians, the Salzburgers and Moravians, which, due to large-scale emigrations to America and elsewhere, ensured new religious pluralism outside politically dominated orthodoxies. In the German principalities, there was some revolt against the dryness of later Lutheran styles of worship and the stifling atmosphere of churches under the control of the princes, who resented any kind of synodical government, claiming to be the lay voice of the church. Theologians tended to emphasize either the 'practical' or the 'spiritual' climate of the church so strongly that policy decisions were surrendered to the prince. This later involved even the Pietists, whose earlier mentors, as we shall see, attempted to resist these tendencies. Frederick William I of Prussia was said to choose Pietists as chaplains, and later it was said that the University of Halle provided obedient, competent and responsible servants of the state. They said the same of the Methodists in Britain after initial hostility. In the age of the 'Enlightened Despots', Frederick the Great of Prussia, who had little personal faith himself, saw religion as a valuable instrument of social control, almost an opium for the people. The church became a 'cog in the bureaucratic machinery of a secular state'.[12] The Prussian Landrecht (Land Law) of 1794 – issued after Frederick's death – granted a certain amount of liberty to the church, but the church was seen as a useful agency of policy designed to inculcate the virtue of obedience and submission. The German writer Herder bitterly remarked, 'a minister is only entitled to exist now under state control and by authority of the prince as a moral teacher, a farmer, a list-maker, a secret agent of the police'. In the pulpit dry aridity, logic, pedantry and parades of learning seemed to have superseded the warmth of early Lutheranism, though we must beware of accepting the tendency of evangelicals to denigrate their contemporaries. Church of England preachers received similar complaints for their stress on morality rather than spirituality. Renewal had to come from new styles of voluntary religion. This is the background of the revival in Europe, America and Great Britain. It is a highly complex scenario.

For the origins of Pietism, we must look back a century. In Luther's later days, there were signs of a more mystical style of Christianity. Kaspar Schwenkfeld (d. 1561) a sixteenth-century nobleman who wandered all over Europe exploring inner experience rather than dogma – similar in some ways to the Quaker George Fox – can be seen as a precursor of Pietism, as can the Silesian Jakob Boehme (1575–1624). He was the shoemaker of Goelitz who asked what it would profit one to know the Bible by heart if one did not know the Spirit that inspired the book. Boehme might well seem a 'loose cannon' with his strange view of the nature of God, the Fall and human nature, but he brought the idea of new birth to the forefront of spirituality. He had a strange underground influence, not least in the next century, when William Law, the Anglican non-juror and mystic, fell under his spell. John Wesley, in contrast, was highly critical of him.[13] Wesley found Johann Arndt (1555–1621), whose *Vier Bücher vom wahren Christentum (Four Books of True Christianity,*

1606) interpreted history with a stress on spirituality and the
work of Christ in the heart of humanity, much more congenial.
He placed him strategically in *The Christian Library* of classic
texts he edited.

We can note the hymns of Martin Rinkart (1586–1649) and
Paulus Gerhardt (1607–76). Congregations still sing 'Now Thank
We All Our God' by Rinkart and 'O Sacred Head' by Gerhardt.
John Wesley discovered the rich source of German hymnody,
when in Georgia, through the influence of the Moravians.

> My Saviour, how shall I proclaim,
> How pay the mighty debt I owe?
> Let all I have, and all I am,
> Ceaseless to all thy glory show.
> Too much to thee I cannot give;
> Too much I cannot do for thee;
> Let all thy love, and all thy grief,
> Grav'n on my heart for ever be.
>
> *HP* 743

This was written in the grim days of the Thirty Years War, keeping alive a genuine Lutheran piety. The normative originator of
Pietism[14] was Philip Jacob Spener (1635–1705) of Frankfurt,
whose *Pia Desideria* (*Devotional Desires*) of 1675 laid down a
programme for the church, stressing personal and practical
needs. In 1694 the University of Halle was founded, to serve as
the centre of the movement. At the height of its influence, 1,200
pastors graduated from its faculty of theology each year.

Spener and his successor and friend August H. Franke
(1663–1727) sought to set up *Collegia Pietatis* – societies for the
mutual improvement of the members of the Lutheran church, a
clear foreshadowing of later Anglican and Methodist developments, not least the class meeting. They also instituted schools, a
Bible institute and a massive orphanage. There was an independence here from both church and state, a clear desire to supplement the normative parish institutions. The setting up of the
Halle-Danish Mission in south India was an indication of new

missionary enterprise. Another notable Pietist, J. A. Bengel (1687–1752) of Württemberg, pioneered new ways of studying the Bible. His writings, especially the *Gnomon Novi Testamenti* (1742), were pillaged by John Wesley, whose *Notes on the New Testament* (1755) – still part of the doctrinal 'standards' of the Methodist Church in Great Britain – owe much to Bengel. This is an interesting prolongation of Pietist influence, which was a stumbling block to the biblical scholar Arthur S. Peake in the twentieth-century negotiations leading to Methodist union. He thought the *Notes* to be the work of 'an outmoded exegete', especially as Wesley followed Bengel (albeit with reservations!) in suggesting the date of the second coming of Jesus as 1836![15]

The stress on the Bible, small-group spirituality and evangelistic missions were transmitted from Europe through a man greatly influenced by the Pietists – Nicolaus Count Von Zinzendorf (1700–60), though he was by no means unique in this role.[16]

Zinzendorf was a nobleman who had contact with a branch of the old Hussite groups going back before the Reformation, the *Unitas Fratrum* or 'Unity of the Brethren', driven out of Bohemia and Moravia during the Thirty Years War. Herrnhut, built on Zinzendorf's estate in Saxony, near to what is now the Polish border – Silesia then – became a kind of international headquarters of evangelical piety (even if its population was less than a thousand), extending its influence to America and Britain. The parish pastor of Berthelsdorf, J. A. Rothe (1688–1758) was a notable Pietist. His hymn from the *Herrnhut Gesangbuch* is typical.

> Now I have found the ground wherein
> Sure my soul's anchor may remain –
> The wounds of Jesus, for my sin
> Before the world's foundation slain;
> Whose mercy shall unshaken stay,
> When heav'n and earth are fled away.

HP 684

This is John Wesley's translation, much sung in Methodism until recent times.

Wesley visited Herrnhut in 1738, immediately after the 'Aldersgate Street' episode, 'to see how the Christians live'. It seems probable that he was refused communion, being considered 'homo perturbatus', a man unsure of salvation![17] As we shall see, there were grave differences on the theology of sanctification between Wesley and Zinzendorf. Indeed Reinhold Niebuhr stated that 'in the debate between Wesley and the Moravians all the important issues between Reformation and perfectionist spirituality emerge in the meetings between the two'. Wesley is primarily intent to guard against any idea that relationship with Christ does not involve pressing on to the goal of perfect love – a lack, he believed, in some Reformation thinking.[18] If C. J. Podmore[19] is right to stress the theological differences, obvious temperamental difficulties played their part too. Count Von Zinzendorf would not wish to play second fiddle to an Oxford don! The Oxford don also had his pride.

The Moravians did not intend to separate themselves from orthodox Lutheranism, rather to be a reforming 'ginger group' within, an oft-repeated tale, but they retained and developed an episcopal style of a simple type, which enabled Anglicans to enjoy some measure of communion with them, established by parliamentary statutory recognition in 1749, reaffirmed in 1995. They had an appeal to 'high church' Anglicans like the Wesleys and were the means of enabling some parts of the Church of England tradition to come to terms with Reformation emphases, which were in danger of being lost. The effect of their message that grace was not only free, but immediately accessible, that an assurance of saving faith could be instantly enjoyed, had an electric effect on some hearers, providing for many a missing episode in their spirituality. Zinzendorf – his hymnody still features in Methodist hymn books – laid great stress on Calvary, on Jesus as a living person, on personal devotion to him, sometimes in a rather sentimental manner. He took up the Pietist stress on groups within the church to induce spiritual growth. In 'bands' and 'choirs' the ages and sexes were separated. Also, he pioneered or restored love feasts, watchnights, footwashings, some of which, in a rather different style, were adopted later in Methodism.

Rupert Davies[20] pointed to certain characteristics of Methodism, which he claimed could be found also in Pietism and Moravianism. His assertion can be reversed. The priority should go to Pietism, but the characteristics are valid. 'The distinctive type of churchmanship which sets about reforming the inner life of the church, the orthodoxy which is never questioned but tends to remain in the background, the intensely personal devotion to God in Christ, the striving towards holy love, the groups which practise fellowship in the Spirit rather than formal acts of worship without neglecting the "means of grace", the desire to make known the love of Christ to those who have passed him by, and most plainly the hymns.' This is the shape of the whole Evangelical Revival (with divergence on predestination), not just Methodism.

The danger of the 'religion of the heart'[21], which was to be found in contemporary Roman Catholicism also, typified by Alfonso Liguori and the Redemptorists,[22] is the neglect of the intellect – though this was not true of Halle in its early days. It is to fail to keep spiritual vitality and intellectual vigour in proper balance, with a tendency to overstress the subjective and individualist element in religion. Conversion experiences could become more important than conversion itself, feeling more than faith. Yet as John Walsh affirmed, 'through the sentimental passion piety of the Herrnhuters, German pietism cross-fertilized High Church Anglicanism. In some ways the *Unitas Fratrum* was peculiarly fitted to attract High Churchmen, and to make more palatable doctrines which might otherwise have been brusquely dismissed as "Enthusiasm"'.[23]

In its charitable endeavours, Pietism joined Christian compassion with the humanitarianism of the Enlightenment. The Enlightenment stressed the reasonable, decried the irrationality of war, opposed the gross superstition, the hanging of witches and the treatment of the insane as demoniacs. Pietism stressed love and compassion, opposed the murder of war and took care of the victims of fate, fault and folly.[24]

Pietism began to decline in the eighteenth century. It was overshadowed in the German principalities and Prussia by the rapid growth of rationalism. But ordinary people had been made aware that God is concerned with them – 'the most forlorn beggar . . . is just as precious to God as a prince', said Gottfried Arnold. There was a tendency for the Pietists to leave the universities, and they had not got the critical tools with which to undermine the anti-religious element in the Enlightenment. By 1750 Pietism had virtually come to an end at Halle. We may summarize the Pietist movement by stating that it intensified Bible study, it provided fuller exercise by the laity of their spiritual priesthood. It emphasized the practical rather than the intellectual side of Christianity, it sought to stress charity in religious controversy, it reformed and revived preaching. In modern terms it adds up to a somewhat conservative outlook, a lay person's religious movement. There was some underrating of the academic and intellectual aspect of Christian practice, a stress on undenominational practice, a triumph of the voluntary over the constitutional, a preference for prayer over instruction and a stress on conversion. It is the style of spirituality exemplified in much evangelical religion. A concern for world mission, Christian education, service to the poor and ecumenical cooperation is characteristic of Pietism at its best.

One of the remarkable features of the Evangelical Revival was its transatlantic character. There was an amazing 'to-ing and fro-ing' across the Atlantic before the days of steam power. Today it would be called 'networking'. In New England and elsewhere, Puritanism had become virtually the established faith. Those who could point to a visible faith were church members, a perquisite of full citizenship. Church and state were one. Yet together they embraced only a minority of the community. If you did not like it, you could stake a colonial claim elsewhere. As one Puritan, John Cotton, said with some irony, 'Banishment in this country is not so much a confinement as an enlargement.'[25]

This could not last. Either citizenship must be enlarged or the whole community must be converted. This was the hope of that remarkable man Jonathan Edwards (1703–58), about whom there has been a recent renaissance of interest. In some ways a 'modern', he was influenced greatly by John Locke and Isaac

Newton. He was a fine theologian, acknowledged as such by evangelicals like John Newton. He was a classical Calvinist, yet quite aware of the philosophy of his day. There was, too, a mystical streak to his nature. 'The sense I had of divine things would often of a sudden, kindle up, as it were, a sweet burning in my heart, an ardour of soul . . . I walked abroad alone in a solitary place in my father's pasture, for contemplation. And as I was walking there, and looking up on the sky and clouds, there came into my mind so sweet a sense of the glorious *majesty* and *grace* of God as, I know not how to express . . . the appearance of everything was altered, there seemed to be, as it were, a calm, sweet cast or appearance of divine glory in almost everything . . . in the sun, the moon and stars . . . ' Here is a Protestant mystic pointing to the romanticism of Wordsworth. Edwards seems a strange mixture of the Enlightenment, Calvinism and a precursor of some styles of Romanticism.

There is here a paradox of the Evangelical Revival, which Methodists of the evangelical Arminian variety often fail to understand. Many of its leaders like Edwards, and the remarkable dramatic preacher George Whitefield, became firm believers in predestination. What makes a Neo-Calvinist an evangelist? All is of grace, they would say. God ordained preaching as a means to disclose the elect – a vital assertion which Wesley did not at first appear to understand at all. Edwards's startling but not entirely typical sermon, 'Sinners in the Hands of an Angry God', preached on 8 July 1741, was a summons to awake. To Edwards God indeed is an angry God, and he has fully as much reason to drop a rebellious man into the flames of hell as men have to fling a venomous spider into the fire. But God is holding back to give man another chance. Only his hands prevent them from falling into the flames any moment! 'O sinner! Consider the fearful danger you are in . . . It would be no wonder if some persons, that now sit here in some seats of this meeting house, in health, quiet and secure should be there before tomorrow morning.' The effect was dramatic! Before the close of the evening, it was reported that there was a great moaning and crying out through the whole house. The shrieks and cries were piercing and amazing. 'Several souls were wrought upon that night and oh the cheerfulness and pleasantness of their countenances that received comfort.'

The Great Awakening had been in full flow in Northampton, Massachusetts, from 1735. It reached its peak under George Whitefield in 1740–1. Responses to revivalist preaching represented surges in church membership rather than long-lasting proportionate gains.[26] John Wesley was greatly influenced by Edwards in 1738, whatever he may have thought of Calvinist theology. It is significant that the credibility, nature and value of alleged 'religious experiences' was often hotly debated in the eighteenth century. If Edwards in *A Faithful Narrative of the Surprising Works of God* (1737), which influenced Wesley, made clear conversion as genuine experience, he came in the later *A Treatise Concerning The Religious Affections* (1746) to a very penetrating analysis about the kind of experience found in a typical 'revival'. John Wesley would sometimes be less rigorous in assuming other people's religious claims.

Waves of revival broke out from time to time bringing together folk of all types. In areas where life was hard and where loneliness could be a desperate thing, such meetings could provide occasions for companionship and outlets for pent-up spirits. It became later part of the frontier tradition of American life, typified by the later camp meetings. That is certainly one side of it, though early revivals in settled areas, affected the whole 'parish'. Next century also, revival was an urban as well as a rural phenomenon. The 'frontier' thesis must not be overdone. Richard Carwardine, in *Transatlantic Revivalism and Popular Evangelicalism in Britain and America 1790–1865* (1978), shows how revival in the next generation became revivalism – a studied technique with men like Charles Grandison Finney and a little earlier the rather eccentric Lorenzo Dow, whose use of camp meetings was copied by the early Primitive Methodists in England. All that was still a generation in the future.

A very notable example of an early revival was in the parish of Cambuslang near Glasgow in 1742.[27] William McCulloch, the parish minister, reported many 'reawakened' in a dramatic way.

Services continued until 2 o'clock in the morning. 'The bodies of some of the awakened are seized by a trembling, fainting. Histerisms in some few women and with convulsive motions in some others.' Female converts outnumbered men two to one. George Whitefield was involved in all this – it can be called the Calvinism of the heart. John Wesley wrote – and this has some significance – 'What a glorious work of God at Cambuslang and Kilsyth from 1740 to 1744! But the war (1745) that followed tore it up by the roots and left scarce any trace of it behind inasmuch that when I diligently inquired a few years after, I could not find one that retained the life of God.'[28] We must beware of possible hidden agendas here. Though Wesley delighted in revivals he become chary of expecting too much permanent growth from them, observing later in life that for the most part, 'After that great and extraordinary work of God, there should be a remarkable decay. Some have found in almost all places a swift increase is generally followed by a decrease equally swift.' He realized that his own movement owed more to careful institutionalization than to violent bursts of collective religious excitement. Wesley's Methodism was a slow not wildfire growth. The difference here between Whitefield and Wesley is important. Wesley's was 'a patient, persistent evangelism in a myriad of dingy villages and seedy backstreets'.[29] Whitefield's unconcern with organization guaranteed that English Methodism would become almost entirely Arminian in its theology.

We have to ask of both the first Wesleyan and Calvinist stage and the second stage, often called 'the Second Evangelical Revival', why should and did this method work? Can it be linked with sexual repression, was it the proximity of death or the fear of hell or sheer release from guilt feelings and inadequate styles of religion? The revival did not spring from a religious vacuum. A careful historian, Michael Watts, asserts that 'the Methodist preachers, like the Antinomians and early Friends, brought relief and joy to men and women whose conscience was tormented by the memory of unforgiven sins and whose lives were burdened by the over-scrupulous performance of religious duties'. Was there a method in the first stage? What of strikingly similar occurrences today with the same 'networking' across the Atlantic in the so-called 'Toronto Blessing' of the early 1990s?[30] Here the corporate physical manifestations ceased after a fairly brief time with a consequence of more social outreach, but also division. Is it really an unconscious form of 'brainwashing', as William Sargant claimed in *Battle For the Mind?*[31] Sargent represented the secular view before the charismatic revival brought widespread revival style activity across the churches. Here, certainly, were recurring phenomena, to which we shall return. We need to be aware of the way in which revival gave hope to the oppressed or repressed, with a modern parallel in James Cone and recent 'black theology'. There is, too, an interesting link between revivalism and the anti-slavery movement. The role of women in the church, too, is spotlighted by the early Primitive Methodists and Bible Christians, and later notable female preachers such as Phoebe Palmer and Catherine Booth, who played a transatlantic role in the mid-nineteenth century, linking revivalism and the holiness movement.

We return to England. The ground here was prepared in much quieter ways. Various societies and groups, not unlike Pietism, developed in England. Anthony Horneck (1641–97), pastor of Savoy chapel, a German priest of the Church of England, founded, in 1678, a religious society in which the study of the Bible, prayer, self-examination and social work were the staple activities. There was a weekly subscription of sixpence with a threepenny fine for swearing. There does not seem to be much room for the poor, for whom a swear would be intolerably expensive! The group elected its own stewards, with a clerical adviser. The societies of this kind sought to keep a middle road between 'popery' and 'enthusiasm'. Such societies became widespread after 1700 and up to the time of Whitefield and Wesley, who were brought up in their tradition. Even if the heyday of the societies was largely over by 1740, there were 30 or 40 societies in London at that time – a considerable activity into which early Methodism and the parallel Anglo-Calvinist evangelicalism could tap. It was a moderate English form of Pietism. Dissent, too, was by no means without its sparks of renewal and spiritual fellowships at this time. One such was at Chinley in Derbyshire, which fostered the young John Bennet, soon to impinge on Wesley's life.[32]

The fairly rapid growth of the Evangelical Revival in its earliest phase was due not only to 'field' or open-air preaching to the religiously disinherited but also to a successful recruitment from a very different stratum of society, the devout, respectable and often high church members of the religious societies of the Church of England.

Although separate from the societies, the Society for the Promotion of Christian Knowledge (SPCK) of 1698 – still in existence – and the Society for the Propagation of the Gospel (1701),[33] intended to disseminate literature both to the colonies and in Great Britain, were societies halfway between the militant Puritanism of the seventeenth century and the benevolent Puritanism of the next century. There was also the Society for the Reformation of Manners, intended to put legal sanctions against vice into effect – a difficult task before Peel's police, sometimes productive of petty informing, militating against the poor, if unintentionally, a foreshadowing of one aspect of the later evangelicals in Wilberforce's day.

Forms of elementary education also came under the general umbrella of bodies like the SPCK. Private subscription charity schools to give religious instruction and the three Rs – reading, writing and reckoning – were coordinated by the SPCK. Looking back at them now, they can seem to be aimed at producing compliant members of the lower order – 'God bless the Squire and his relations and keep us in our proper stations' – part of a hierarchical class structure, but this implies that the poor were much more naive than was the case. Except for old grammar schools and the Dissenting Academies, there was little else. In Wales, it was claimed that by 1761, 3,498 schools had been created, largely under the umbrella of the SPCK, with over 158,000 children passing through them, though this figure seems exaggerated.[34]

These institutions and movements were creating a new climate of opinion as part of the eighteenth-century scene, as significant as Hogarth's grim pictures of *Gin Lane* and *The Rake's Progress*. Many 'jeremiads' poured out, yet positive signs were part of the scene also. In 1736 the bishop of Bristol, Joseph Butler (1692–1752) could say that 'Christianity is not so much a subject of enquiry; but that it is, now at length, discovered to be fictitious. And accordingly . . . a principal subject of mirth and ridicule, as it were by way of reprisals, for its having so long interrupted the pleasures of the world' (Advertisement of the *Analogy of Religion*).[35] The flank of the much-feared deism and reductionist religion was to be turned by something other than Butler's brilliant arguments.

We must not forget the close links between the religious societies and Wesley, such as concern for pastoral care, a stress on personal religion and devotional exercises, the endeavour to do good – the activism element – and the intention to make dull Christians articulate. A concern for education, for missions, which came out of voluntary societies later, and a devotional and biblical orientation, were all taken up by Wesley, with a much sharper cutting edge. He never showed the condescension to ordinary people which other leaders sometimes showed, though he was always the leader. He had an extraordinary gift of genuinely appealing to the poor – deserving and undeserving alike.

Wesley did not originate the Evangelical Revival in England. Contemporaries in the 1730s and 1740s regarded George Whitefield (1714–70) as the great leader of revival. He had received 'mercy from God' in 1735 and was preaching to large crowds while Wesley was in Georgia. Whitefield combined amazing oratory with the gift of an actor. He was a popular entertainer, in one sense, the first of a long line of religious 'pop-stars'. By making religion dramatic and enthralling, by promoting it in outdoor spaces alongside competing secular diversions, he led the way in showing how religion could be made popular and marketable to a dawning age of religious consumerism. Religion as personal experience is both cause and effect of a dawning religious culture created by self-selected consumers. 'Whitefield's mode of revivalism – theatrical, passion based, non-denominational, international, experience centred and self-consciously promoted through media and word of mouth, would outlive his Calvinism and prove as receptive to Arminian preachers as to Calvinist. It would transcend media and embrace television and characterize evangelicalism in the twentieth century.'[36] This may appear somewhat exaggerated, though David Garrick, the eighteenth-century actor, greatly envied Whitefield his gifts. Attending his sermons, he claimed that he could make men weep and tremble by his varied pronunciation of the word 'Mesopotamia'. Though Whitefield founded orphanages and churches, G. R. Cragg is accurate in saying: 'Wherever Whitefield went, he left an overwhelming impression of impassioned eloquence. Wherever Wesley went, he left a company of men and women closely knit together in a common life'[37] – though it must be admitted that Scotland and Wales were more congenial to Whitefield than to Wesley.

Contemporary with Whitefield was the revival in Wales. Griffith Jones (1682–1761), ordained in 1708, later rector of Llanddowror, became a significant figure in both evangelism and education. There is a language paradox here. 'A sustained campaign to assimilate Wales to English language, culture and religious establishment, generated by way of reaction a religious revival which ended by being Welsh, evangelical and dissenting, though the élite who launched the revival was almost as anglicanising as the official policy it sought to supplement.'[38] The most notable in revival styles were Howel Harris (1714–73) and Daniel Rowland (1713–80). Rowland began an itinerant ministry in 1736 – three years before Whitefield pushed Wesley into the open air in Bristol. The Calvinist wing of the revival – George Whitefield, Rowland, younger men like William Williams 'Pantycelyn' (writer of 'Guide Me O Thou Great Jehovah') owed much to the support and patronage of the 'great leaderine' Selina, Countess of Huntingdon (1709–91).[39] She drew a few of her own class in the 1750s into the revival, though not many 'wore coronets – and prayed' as William Cowper said of the Earl of Dartmouth. She set up her own private chapels, which after 1781 became registered as dissenting chapels under the title of *The Countess of Huntingdon's Connexion*. In 1768, she established a significant theological institution at Trevecka in Wales for the training of evangelical clergy, with support from Arminians who believed in universal salvation, like John Fletcher (1729–85) of Madeley. She was no narrow sectarian. Her place in society, her femininity and her faith created many problems, not least an inability to cope with John Wesley! She always expected deference to her rank – even Wesley gave her a private seat in West Street Chapel in London. Her temperament demanded continuous religious emotion. She had a tendency to misjudge people's abilities which makes the failure of the Bethesda Mission in America and of the Trevecka College, and the alienation from Wesley, a sad tale in the end. The more parish-based evangelicals like John Berridge of Everton ('You threaten me Madam, like a Pope, not like a Mother in Israel . . . my instructions you know must come from the Lamb not from the Lamb's wife') prospered in the end, free from her patronage.[40]

The Anglo-Calvinist stream of evangelicals was at first almost solely from within the Church of England. It is now, in a renewed form, very much a force within the Anglican Communion. It can appear sometimes slightly patronizing towards Methodism, suspecting it of being too 'liberal' in theology. Evangelicals began to appear almost spontaneously, being a renewing and reawakening of dormant Puritanism – Thomson of St Gennys, Samuel Walker of Truro and Henry Venn of Huddersfield were typical.[41] Difficulties of succession could occur if an 'unevangelical' vicar took the place of an avowed evangelical. Quite often – as in Huddersfield – a dissenting chapel took on the role, rather later in the day, of fostering evangelicalism. 'The clergy beat the bush, the dissenters got the game.' In the end, this led to bodies like the Elland Clerical Society, which sponsored young converts of slender means to be educated for the priesthood, the Simeon Trust and other bodies aimed at securing the purchase of 'advowsons' or titles to a living securing 'sound' churchmanship, with theological colleges to follow in the next century.

Anglican evangelicals tended to object to the itinerating method of Whitefield and Wesley. While it would be quite unfair to say that they saw their parish as their world, they tended to stress control by the clergy leading to the problem of the eloquent, extrovert convert, although William Grimshaw (1708–63), the eccentric priest of Haworth, was exceptional in this respect. For a time he had his 'round' or circuit, with allies like 'Scotch Will' – William Darney – who had been converted in the revival at Kilsyth.

Old dissent – that is the Congregationalists, Presbyterians, Baptists and Quakers[42] – were at first touched little by the revival, though the General or Arminian Baptists resembled the early Methodists in some of their methods. Certainly Philip Doddridge (1702–51), now known as a hymn writer, through his book *The Rise and Progress of Religion in the Soul* (1744) was another fertilizing influence, a key link with men like William Carey (1761–1834), the Baptist, who began the next great move of evangelicalism into world mission

That is to anticipate later developments. The purpose of this chapter has been to underline the point made long ago by William Ewart Gladstone, that the Evangelical Movement was the result of the confluence of many tributaries, quite independent of the Wesleys and the early Methodists. In the early eighteenth century we have, then, a somewhat declining dissent, a Church of England apparently declining, not able any longer to claim a monopoly of religious activity but with signs of renewal through the societies and the evangelical clergy. These presages of change prevent us from seeing the period as entirely an era of disaster. Jonathan Clark's controversial assertion that England was still an *ancien régime* has some force at this point.[43] The Church of England was still the chief element in English religion, whatever was the strength of dissent and Roman Catholicism.

Dissent began to pick up steam again. After 1770, there is a growth of itinerancy and a priority of evangelistic expansion over consolidation which might be called 'popular ecumenism'.[44] Certainly the rise of popular evangelicalism was giving English dissent a broad base in artisan groups, a clientele not unlike that of John Wesley's Methodism. By the time of the Religious Census of 1851, dissent and Methodism were to embrace 20 per cent of the population.[45]

John Wesley – Eighteenth-Century Man

The scene is the rectory at Epworth in the Isle of Axholme in Lincolnshire. 'Sukey,' said Samuel Wesley, the Rector, after concluding family prayers sometime in 1701, 'Why did you not say "Amen" to the prayer for the King?' 'Because', said his wife, 'I do not believe William III to be king.' 'You and I must part, for if we are to have two kings, we must have two beds.' The Rector left for London to attend Convocation. He later sought a naval chaplaincy. Soon afterwards William III was gathered to his Calvinist fathers, Queen Anne succeeding him. She was acceptable to Susanna, if not to all the Non-Jurors. Reconciliation was not immediate, but the Rector did return to Epworth. Some nine months afterwards on 17 June 1703, John Wesley was born.[1] Such are the contingencies of history. It is also an illustration of the way in which the non-juring and Jacobite controversies could split a family as they divided the Church of England, which had lost much of its Puritan wing in 1662, and now lost many of its 'high church' constituency.

Samuel Wesley (1662–1735) can be described as a somewhat 'high church' parson in a seventeenth-century sense, strictly non-Roman, opposed to dissent, reliant on the Book of Common Prayer, rigorous in his pastoral duties. He was disliked by some of his somewhat rough parishioners, not least for his incapacity with money. His colossal work on the *Book of Job* was presented by John, after his father's death, to Queen Caroline, who 'much admired its binding'. This man, who was forced to see his parish as his world, has a normative influence not least in his insistence on method in pastoral care and wide and relentless reading in spirituality. Psychologically Wesley was more influenced by his mother, but it was his father who insisted on 'the inward witness' as the heart of the matter, as he faced death.

Samuel had married Susanna Annesley, twenty-fifth child of one of the leading dissenting ministers, Samuel Annesley. She, like Samuel, had become a member of the Church of England early in life, through conviction. Much Puritan blood flowed in her veins. She bore nineteen children, of whom seven daughters and three sons survived. That in itself can serve, as can the even worse experience of Queen Anne, as an example of the status and role of women in any age prior to our own. A woman did not expect to rear more than half of her children. Life expectancy was about thirty-five at that time in England, with higher birth rates raising population levels later.

John Wesley grew up in a rectory much dominated by his mother and sisters. When he was six, the rectory was set on fire – possibly arson but more likely an accident. The great blaze was portrayed in many Victorian chapels as part of the 'Methodist myth' along with the saying that he was 'a brand plucked from the burning', having been rescued from an upper storey window. Wesley can easily become an icon!

Susanna Wesley was a remarkable woman. Her principles of child rearing might make the European Court of Human Rights' hair stand on end, though the girls were taught to think as much as the boys were. There was much in common with the contemporary ideas of John Locke. She sought to 'break their wills', meaning any wilful disobedience. Every hour was planned. There were serious talks with each child each week. A child might be punished if he or she ate between meals. At five years old, they had to learn the alphabet in a day – most did! There was genuine care and happiness in this frugal household. For good or ill, John Wesley owed an immense debt to it. From it, he learned the meaning of disciplined, methodical living in a home where 'that odious noise the crying of children was seldom heard'. Much simple Church of England Puritanism and churchmanship was transmitted through Samuel and Susanna Wesley to Methodism, not least the 'society' aspect of parochial church-manship.

The character of his mother gave John Wesley too high and romantic a view of women, causing him to idealize those to whom he became attracted, of whom there were not a few. Certainly psychologists have enjoyed a 'field day' at Susanna's expense, though recent studies give a sympathetic counter-balance, not least in showing Susanna's astute knowledge of theology and spirituality. 'I will continue to pay my respects to an unknown God. I cannot know him, I dare not say I love him – only this, I have chosen him for my only happiness, my all, my only God . . . and when I sound my will, I feel it adheres to its choice, though not so faithfully as it ought.' John Wesley was to echo that fluctuating religious experience many times – often forgotten when his 'conversion' in 1738 is overstressed, as if it ended all self-doubt, which it certainly did not.[2] Matthew Arnold's verse is pertinent to the man of the 'warmed heart', a Methodist legend, at least at times:

> We cannot kindle when we will
> The fire that in the heart resides;
> The spirit bloweth and is still,
> In mystery the soul abides.
> But tasks in hours of insight will'd
> Can be through hours of gloom fulfill'd.

Education for the boys was top priority in the Wesley household. At the age of eleven John Wesley was sent to Charterhouse, and in 1720 he went up to Christchurch, Oxford, with a scholarship of £40 per annum at a time when the University was moving into a period of torpor. It tended to be a centre of opposition to the Court also, which was not irrelevant to Wesley's political stance later. He was clearly a good scholar, well read for his day, though easily bowled over by the latest book. In 1725 came his first religious awakening which can be called conversion in a very real sense. The 'Caroline Divine' Jeremy Taylor's (1613–62)

Holy Living and Holy Dying and the almost inevitable *Imitation of Christ*, usually attributed to Thomas à Kempis, were positive influences, stressing purity of intention. These were followed, sometime afterwards, by the writings of the non-juror William Law (1686–1761) on *Christian Perfection* (1726) and *A Serious Call to a Devout and Holy Life* (1729). These convinced him of the absolute impossibility of being 'half a Christian'. He resolved to dedicate his whole life to God. Wesley became aware of, and remained aware of, the need for holiness, for growth in spiritual life. He sought to be 'an altogether Christian', even if he was not sure what this was to imply for him. His later somewhat harsh, and even impertinent, attitude to William Law must not lead us to underrate Law's importance for Wesley's spiritual development and his ideas about marriage and poverty. Can a direct comparison be made here with the young John Henry Newman, a century later, though Newman's 'first conversion' was more in the classic Calvinist mode? Fr Maximin Piette, a Belgian Franciscan, stressed this period more than 1738 as the period of conversion. While we may not agree with Piette in his downplaying of the events of 1738, he was right to point to the foundation of much of Wesley's thought on Christian perfection at this point. The sermon on 'The Circumcision of the Heart' preached before the university in January 1733 was later placed in the *Standard Sermons* with minor alterations, still affirmed by Wesley, fifty years later. 'Let your soul be filled with so entire a love of him that you may love nothing but for his sake' succinctly sums it up. How one was to reach this state was the continuing problem for Wesley.

In September 1725, he was ordained deacon, proceeding to the priesthood in 1728. On a later occasion Bishop John Potter,[3] who had been a Fellow of Lincoln College, like his ordinand, said, 'If you desire to be extensively useful, do not spend your time and strength in contending for and against things that are of a disputable nature but in testifying against open notorious vice and in promoting real essential holiness.' This was thought pelagian by S. T. Coleridge! Potter was judiciously sympathetic to both Wesley and the Moravians.

In 1726, to his father's delight, Wesley became a Fellow of Lincoln College, teaching classics, philosophy, divinity and New Testament Greek, to use modern terms. This gave him a modest but secure living until marriage – revival run on a £30 sinecure! Wesley's life in his Oxford period had not been grimly ascetic, to say the least. He would hold serious and romantic conversations with his attractive lady friends at Stanton in the Cotswolds. He was surely in love with Sally Kirkham and continued correspondence with her after her marriage. The mixture of spiritual direction and human attraction was to be a feature of Wesley's relationship with women throughout his ministry. One of the ladies, the glamorous Mrs Pendarves, called him 'Primitive Christianity'. For a time he was his father's curate at Wroot, a village near Epworth. He realized that he did not want to be an 'action replay' of his father at Epworth, though he affirmed it in a clumsy manner.[4]

His brother Charles came up to Christ Church in 1726. When John returned to Oxford permanently in November 1726, recalled by his college, he found a very small group of undergraduates which included his brother Charles and William Morgan (whose later death cast a cloud on the group) meeting devotionally. Wesley quickly became a virtual leader of this group, which was a few years later nicknamed by its denigrators 'Methodists', or more contemptuously 'Bible Moths', 'sacramentarians' and the 'Holy Club', though it was never a 'club' of any kind. 'Methodist', like 'Quaker' in the previous century, moved from nickname to normal designation. It could be (as Charles Wesley later affirmed) derived from the methodical style of prayer laid down by the University of Oxford, which Charles claimed he followed, or after a group of ancient physicians, or more likely some seventeenth-century religious groups similarly styled. John Wesley seized on the name, and greatly broadened its meaning, and it survived. He continued as the acknowledged leader of the group of rather diverse young men, who read the Greek New Testament and Latin classics, met for pious conversations, received Holy Communion regularly and, influenced by non-juring John Clayton, fasted twice a week.[5] They were concerned for the nurture of their souls and for some of the minutiae of liturgical practice, as were the non-jurors. Their concern for the poor and the prisoners in Oxford jail was notable. This stress remained for life with the Wesleys.

Recent research by V. H. H. Green, and by Richard Heitzenrater, who has deciphered Wesley's diaries, gives vivid pictures of the somewhat diverse manifestations and developments of the Oxford Methodists, which Wesley saw as the first beginning of Methodism. The 'society' and the cell group style have always been at the heart of the many Methodisms in different parts of the world. Leadership skills were developed in this period by Wesley.

From the Oxford Methodists, vilified by a letter in Fog's *Weekly Journal* in December 1732,[6] flowed many tributaries into the renewal of the eighteenth-century church, if one thinks of the contribution of George Whitefield, Benjamin Ingham and the Wesleys alone. There were others who contributed to a 'high church' tradition which is now known to have been far stronger in the eighteenth century than previously thought to be the case.[7]

In 1732, the philanthropist General James Oglethorpe[8] founded the colony of Georgia. The Wesley brothers were importuned under the auspices of the *Society for the Propagation of the Gospel* (SPG), to accompany Oglethorpe – John to act as chaplain, with Charles as Secretary for Indian Affairs under the Governor, which proved to be a fiasco. In their small boat *The Simmonds*, they met with an Atlantic storm, which made Wesley's heart strangely cold at the possible approach of death. He could not fail to notice the contrast with a group of serene Moravians. To communicate with them, Wesley learned German. 'Do you know Jesus Christ? Do you know he has saved you?' was the pointed question of August Gottlieb Spangenberg (1704–82), who was to become a leading Moravian. 'I do,' replied Wesley, but added in his Journal, 'But I fear they were vain words.' Here we see the impinging on Wesley of the Pietist and Moravian traditions, which conflicted, to some extent, with the more mystical style which he had also absorbed, especially from French spirituality.[9]

Wesley began to translate some of the Pietist and Moravian hymns which were, very soon, to become a rich part of the hymnody sung in Methodist worship. The new chaplain was diligent, but an ecclesiastical purist, concerned with liturgical exclusiveness including rebaptizing dissenters. It must be remembered that colonists were not by any means the cream of the exporting society. Wesley was frequently in conflict with the formidable ladies of the thousand-strong colony. He fell in love with the delectable teenage Sophia Hopkey, with whom he shared French devotional works. Unfortunately his mother and sisters were not there to warn him of the serpent in Eden. Sophia's family were leaders of a somewhat 'Micawberish' kind in the colony – the chief magistrate, Thomas Cawston, was her uncle. She eloped with and married a rival suitor. Wesley, in a mixture of sour legalism and pique repelled them from Holy Communion. He was arraigned for defamation of character, leaving Georgia under a cloud,[10] which hindered his reputation for some time. We ought not to underestimate the importance to him of the Georgia period. He had not converted the Indians, but many of the characteristics of his pastoral style became part of later Methodism – not least the stress on small groups for spiritual edification, the use of hymnody and extempore prayer, lay leaders and the love feast. Above all the pursuit of holiness, even if unattained, was central to Wesley.

Returning to England, he resumed acquaintance with the Moravians, moving away from the influence of mysticism, though French spirituality and Gregory Lopez, the eccentric Mexican mystic, remained in his mind-set. He had tried asceticism, solitude (at Wroot), works of charity with the Holy Club, and mysticism. None brought him the assurance he sought. In some dudgeon, he wrote to William Law, blaming him for not having warned him of the spiritual dangers he now faced.

Wesley was nearly thirty-five, on the edge of a mid-life crisis.[11] In February 1738 he met Peter Böhler, who raised again the personal spiritual questions which Spangenberg had asked in Georgia. 'My brother, that philosophy of yours must be purged away' – a vague statement which stuck in Wesley's throat.

William Law was not altogether helpful. Böhler's counsel 'Preach faith *till* you have it and *because* you have faith, you *will* preach faith' was accepted and acted upon immediately in preaching.[12] In this pregnant statement, wrote the Lutheran scholar Martin Schmidt,[13] lies the 'deep truth that the task of the preacher is not to bring before his hearers himself or his own spiritual attainment but the authoritative Word, the greater reality of God'. Wesley began to be excluded from some London pulpits because of the new Lutheran–Moravian stress in his preaching. Anglicans had forgotten Cranmer's *Homilies*. Böhler, and Wesley too, pushed the originally Anglican Fetter Lane Society in London into a more Moravian style, with 'bands', love feasts and days of intercession.[14]

The climax of the new assertion of justification by faith came on 24 May 1738, a day etched in Methodist mythology, sometimes misunderstood as akin to an emotional conversion from unbelief to faith, which it certainly was not. In his journal[15] (the only evidence) Wesley wrote: 'I think it was about five this morning that I opened my Testament on these words "There are given unto us exceeding great and precious promises, even that ye should be partakers of the divine nature" (2 Peter 1:4), Just as I went out I opened it again on these words "Thou art not far from the Kingdom of God." In the afternoon I was asked to go to St. Paul's. The anthem "Out of the depths have I called unto Thee, O Lord, hear my voice" . . . In the evening I went very unwillingly to a society in Aldersgate Street where one was reading Luther's *Preface to the Epistle to the Romans*. About a quarter before nine, while he was describing the change which God works in the heart through faith in Christ, I felt my heart strangely warmed, I felt I did trust in Christ, Christ alone for salvation, and an assurance was given me that he had taken away *my* sins, even mine and saved *me* from the law of sin and death. I began to pray with all my might for those who had in a more especial manner despitefully used me and persecuted me. I then testified openly to all these what I now first felt in my heart. But it was not long before the enemy suggested "This cannot be faith for where is the joy?" Then was I taught that peace and victory over sin are essential to faith in the Captain of our salvation; but that as to the transports of joy that usually attend the beginning of it, especially in those who have mourned deeply, God sometimes gives, sometimes withholdeth them according to the counsels of His own will.'

It is interesting that the random opening of the Bible (very Moravian) hit upon a text in the Second Letter of Peter much used in Eastern Orthodoxy, as holding out the promise of godliness, that we might become perfect. The 'warmed heart' was paralleled by the Cambridge Platonist John Smith, who asserted in 1673, 'That is not the best and truest knowledge of God, which is wrought out by the labour and sweat of the brain, but that which is kindled within us by an *heavenly warmth in our hearts*. As in the natural body it is the heart that sends up good blood and warm spirits into the head, whereby it is best enabled to its several functions, so that which enables us to know and understand aright in the things of God must be a living principle of holiness within us.' John Wesley's experience was less dramatic than the 'palpitation of heart' Charles Wesley experienced three days before. It was in no way the violent physical experience such as occurred often in the Revival, as a result of Wesley's preaching.

The crucial influence here is surely Martin Luther, even if John Wesley later thought Luther quite unsound in his view of sanctification. This is almost certainly part of the passage read, though whether it was read in English, Latin or German is not known.

'But the Holy Ghost is not given except in, with and by faith in Jesus Christ. And faith does not come save only through God's Word or gospel which preaches Christ, that he is God's son and a man who has died and risen again for our sakes. Hence it comes that faith alone makes righteous and fulfills the law; for out of Christ's merit it brings the Spirit and *the Spirit makes the heart glad and free* as the law required it shall be. Faith, however, is a divine work in us. It changes us and makes to be born anew of God . . . O, it is a living, busy, active, mighty thing this faith, and so it is impossible for it not to do good incessantly. It does not ask whether there are good works to do, but before the question rises, it has already done them and is always at the doing of them.

Faith is a living, daring confidence in God's grace, so pure and certain that a man should stake his life on it a thousand times. This confidence in God's grace and knowledge of it, makes a man glad and bold and happy in dealing with God and all his creatures; and this is the work of the Holy Ghost in faith. Hence a man is ready and glad without compulsion, to do good to everyone, to serve everyone, to suffer everything in love and praise of God who has shown him this grace; and thus it is impossible to separate works from faith, as impossible as to separate heat and light from fire.'[16]

It can be said that for Wesley there was an existential confirmation of what he already believed. It was an experience of the 'inward witness', assurance, though he was by no means set free from fretful self-concern. He was ready to do the work of an evangelist. It was when he began his open air preaching with people responding that his self-absorption began to disappear. In his own much later words he exchanged 'the faith of a servant' for the 'faith of a son'.[17] We may call this 'evangelical conversion' or the gift of assurance, the heart of it is a personal dealing with a living Lord not a mere emotional disturbance. Some modern writers like Gerald O'Collins speak of a 'second journey', which follows a mid-life crisis when a settled pattern is broken down by exile, sickness, bereavement, loss of job or boredom. There is a search for new meanings, different goals, renewed strength and self-knowledge. Both the Wesleys can fit this pattern, with a literal second journey from Georgia before the 'second journey' of faith.

Charles Wesley, who had been ill with pleurisy and, one suspects, suffering some kind of nervous breakdown, had a similar but more dramatic experience on Whit Sunday, three days before.[18] The two brothers could rejoice together at what for them was liberation and later a sense of purpose and power.

> Where shall my wondering soul begin?
> How shall I all to Heaven aspire?
> A slave redeemed from death and sin,
> A brand plucked from eternal fire . . .

> Outcast of men, to You I call,
> Harlots, and publicans, and thieves!
> He spreads his arms to embrace you all . . .

HP 706

It could be that Charles Wesley's version of the salvation event etched itself into Methodist spirituality more than his brother's more subtle theology. Charles wrote his hymn in that May of 1738 using the very phrase 'a brand plucked from eternal fire' which his brother could literally have said of himself. It was Charles who quickly began to minister to thieves on the scaffold.

This was, as we have seen, not the beginning of the Evangelical Revival in England. It was the 'plugging in' of the Wesleys to a movement already well under way. John Wesley certainly set out his manifesto, preaching his sermon on 'Salvation by Faith' before the University of Oxford in June 1738, which can be compared with John Keble's Assize sermon in 1833, seen by some as the beginning of the Oxford Movement in the Church of England.

Wesley journeyed soon afterwards to Herrnhut, 'to see how the Christians lived', meeting Zinzendorf on the way. He was not received with open arms. The crisis between Wesley and the English style of Moravianism and later with Zinzendorf himself in 1741 in London was looming up. Returning to England the association with the Fetter Lane Society continued for a time. On 1 January 1739 at a love feast, the Wesleys met with Whitefield, Benjamin Ingham and about sixty members of the 'society'. 'About three in the morning as we continued instant in prayer, the power of God came mightily upon us inasmuch that many cried out with exceeding joy and many fell to the ground.'[19] This is very much like the occurrence at Herrnhut in 1727. It was to be echoed frequently in the following years as, for example, at Cambuslang and Kilsyth in 1741-2. Within two years (July 1740) John Wesley and his friends had left the Fetter Lane Society, unable to stomach the teaching of the Moravian Philip J. Molther, that those seeking salvation should not make use of the means of grace such as Holy Communion. Wesley's 'Caroline' churchmanship had not deserted him. He saw, as did his mother, Holy Communion as a 'converting ordinance'.[20] A new meeting place was necessary now. The old 'Foundery', the leasehold of which was bought by Wesley in November 1739, became virtually the headquarters of a new style of religious society, masterminded by Wesley, though he clearly had, as yet, no masterplan. It was to be quite independent, both of the Church of England parish system, though Wesley saw himself as a virtual link, and of Moravianism also.

Within a year or so, there was also a breach with George Whitefield – never total – following Wesley's sermon of August 1740 on 'Free Grace'.[21] He clearly rejected double predestination, asserting at the same time the Arminian view of the absolute necessity of grace and the role, too, of human free will. It was a polemical sermon which in its dialogue between God and the devil almost makes mock of Neo-Calvinism like the rhyme:

> There once was a man who said 'Damn!
> It is borne in upon me I am
> An engine that moves
> In predestinate grooves
> I'm not even a bus, I'm a tram!'

(M. E. Hare, 'Limerick', 1905)

Wesley was beginning to make himself the odd man out in the Evangelical Revival, especially after the Countess of Huntingdon moved into the Anglo-Calvinist camp. Wesley did not perceive that preaching might be God's way of calling the elect, though in an early conference in 1745 could ask: 'Wherein do we come to the very edge of Calvinism? In denying all natural free will and power, antecedent to grace. But God will grant that grace to all.'[22] This is the essence of evangelical Arminianism or the doctrine of universal grace and the free movement of the Spirit, one of the legacies of the radical Reformation which alongside the traditions of Lutheranism and Calvinism was such a fruitful

source of religious ideas. Was Wesley, too, without realizing it
linking up with what has been called 'Arminian Enlightenment'?
D. M. Baillie naughtily quoted once an American who said, 'A
Methodist knows he's got religion but he's afraid he may lose it.
A Presbyterian knows he can't lose it but he's afraid he hasn't got
it.' But was not predestination primarily a doctrine of pastoral
comfort, not fear? Those who are truly redeemed do not need
endlessly to worry about whether they are saved or not. Energy
can be given to serving the Sovereign Lord. There is a Calvinism
of the heart as well as an Arminianism of the heart.

Wesley derived his theology not directly from Arminius, but
from one side of his own Anglican tradition.[23] Later the differences between Arminians and Calvinists marred the witness of
the Evangelical Revival, with Wesley spending much time
defending himself against James Hervey (1714–58) and later
Augustus Montague Toplady (1740–78), the writer of 'Rock of
Ages', no mean theologian despite Wesley calling him a chimney
sweep.

This is to anticipate. Wesley was on the verge of the beginning
of his itinerant style of evangelism paralleling that in Wales and
in England by Whitefield. The idea that he, like one of Stephen
Leacock's heroes, set off on horseback in six directions at once is
mythical. He did itinerate to the end of his life, but very soon his
journeys were carefully planned. The long journeys soon avoided
by and large the winter months, when he worked largely in and
around London. In March 1739, he wrote (to John Clayton or
James Hervey), 'suffer me now to tell you my principles in this
matter. I look upon all the world as my parish thus far I mean
that in whatever part of it I am, to judge it meet, right and my
bounden duty, to declare unto all who are willing to learn the
glad tidings of salvation. This is the work I know God has called
me to. And sure I am that his blessing attend it, great encourage-
ment have I therefore, to be faithful in fulfilling the work he has
given me to do.' This Wesley saw as the scriptural call of God. 'If
by Catholic principles you mean any other than scriptural, they
weigh nothing with me. I allow no rule whether of faith or practice than the Holy Scripture but on scriptural principles I do not

think it hard to justify whatever I do.'[24] It is significant that George Whitefield talked of the world as *his* parish also[25] and was assiduous in fulfilling it, crossing the Atlantic, while Wesley never left the British Isles after the Georgia episode except for two short 'sabbaticals' in Holland later in life, when he linked up with the Moravians again at Zeist.

Whitefield was already engaged in open air preaching in Bristol. It was he, in April 1739, who pushed Wesley into what came to be called 'field preaching'. Wesley writes, 'At four in the afternoon, I submitted to be more vile (2 Sam. 6:22) and proclaimed in the highways the glad tidings of salvation, speaking from a little eminence in a ground adjourning the city to about three thousand people. The scripture on which I spoke was this (Is it possible that any one should be ignorant that it is fulfilled in every true minister of Christ?) The Spirit of the Lord is upon us because he both anointed me to preach the Gospel to the poor . . .'[26]

Revival was coinciding with social change, especially increase in population. In 1733 Kay devised the 'Flying Shuttle', the first of the inventions which like the 'Spinning Jenny' and Crompton's 'Mule' revolutionized the cotton industry. In 1740 Huntsman forged steel by the 'crucible method' at Handsworth in Sheffield. In 1741 the Highways Act sought to improve the roads but with slight effect. Bristol – more typical of mercantilism and the infamous 'triangular trade' incorporating the slave trade – doubled in population in the first half of the century. New styles of religion provided structure and purpose to those who lacked both, socially, in England at this time, which began to change its face even though most people were still rural. It was the time of the beginning of industrialization, though as yet on a comparatively small scale. Large factories and 'dark satanic mills' were yet to come. What W. W. Rostow called 'the great economic take-off' was still thirty years in the future, but villages in Coalbrookdale in Shropshire or in the mining areas around Bristol, such as Kingswood, were growing without church or parish minister on the spot. The parish system could not cope with new populations. A good example is the period of the pastorate of Dr George Legh (1694–1775) at Halifax.[27] He had some Moravian sympathies. His parish covered the whole of what is now Calderdale, an area larger than Rutland. Even if 'chapelries' and 'chapels of ease' relieved some of the impossible pastoral load, it was left to the new informal or formal 'connexions' linked to Benjamin Ingham, William Darney and later John Wesley to gather the harvest of neglected people. By 1843 there were 100 nonconformist chapels in the parish of Halifax with 22 Anglican places of worship; 22,713 children attended dissenting Sunday schools. In the areas of Cornwall, where tin mining flourished, and the coalmining villages around Newcastle and Durham, Methodist societies were to flourish surprisingly quickly. Wesley's work in the early days was based on the triangle of London, Bristol and Newcastle, soon with 'headquarters' buildings in each place.

This was also a period of acute social discontent, a fact seized upon in 1906 by the French historian Elie Halévy, who exaggerated the role of Whitefield and Wesley in the area around Bristol.[28] Certainly it was there that Whitefield, before crossing the Atlantic, had begun what was for a time a joint ministry. Wesley quickly found a new confidence when the poor responded to him. He never blamed them for their poverty. With them he had surprising rapport with complete lack of condescension. How could he reach those outside the church? Given an established church with a parish system, could an itinerant evangelist be other than an irritant? Joseph Butler, the philosopher-bishop of Bristol, later of Durham, told Wesley that he had no business to preach in his diocese. He was bluntly telling the truth. Wesley's Fellowship at Lincoln College did not, as he affirmed, give him the right to preach anywhere, though he could have sought such a right as Dr Alec Vidler did when he was Dean of King's College, Cambridge, in the 1960s. Butler was critical of Whitefield. 'Sir, the pretending to extraordinary revelations and gift of the Holy Spirit is a horrid thing – yes it is a horrid thing.' Wesley would not speak for Whitefield. Reformation spirituality and Hanoverian moderation appeared to clash, though Butler was nearer to Wesley in his theology than immediately meets the eye, as his sermons on the love of God reveal. Wesley did not comply with Butler's demands, and 'strict order once broken, confusion rushes in', as Wesley's correspondent 'John Smith' wrote later. In fairness to Butler, who had three interviews with Wesley, the evangelist had been unfairly critical of one of Butler's clergy, Josiah Tucker (1712–89), who was to write one of the most trenchant critiques of Methodism, becoming later Dean of Gloucester. He was no mean economist.[29]

Significantly, it was in Bristol that the first real Methodist meeting house – the New Room in the Horsefair – was opened in 1741. By that time the term 'united society'[30] was used by the two, originally, Anglican Bristol societies. The system of 'bands', with their separation of sexes and strict rules, was in operation. 'Tickets' were beginning to be issued to society (and band) members, which became a Methodist characteristic. It was in Bristol that the 'class' system ('class' means division of people not a teaching group in this context) developed on Pietist-Herrnhut principles, but with ideas also from the French mystic Gaston Jean-Baptiste, Marquis de Renty (1611–49).[31] The detail of the system owed its practical form to a Bristol sea captain named Foy, whose idea was to raise money for the 'New Room' by dividing the society into groups, each member to give a penny a week. The 'class system' was, said Whitefield, Wesley's great master stroke, otherwise the revival would be 'a rope of sand', a phrase Wesley often used himself. We shall discuss 'class' and 'bands' as means of grace later. This was an age when the English were very clubbable. Wesley cashed in on an age of joinery.[32]

Inevitably, opposition grew as Wesley began to work on his axis between London, Bristol and Newcastle. The 'itinerant preachers', whom he fostered after 1740, began to enter parishes without prior invitation from the incumbent. Within ten years the skeleton of Wesley's system was in place, an example of evangelical pragmatism, unequalled in the eighteenth century. Societies needed leaders. 'Feasts and fasts' developed as they inevitably do when new groups emerge. The societies began to be grouped in 'rounds' or 'circuits' – seven in 1746, nine in 1748, 50 in 1770 (one in America), 64 in 1780, 114 by Wesley's death in 1791. At first the circuits were very large indeed, embracing whole counties, typified by the 'Great Haworth Round'. After 1748, pioneered by John Bennet and William Grimshaw of Haworth, quarterly meetings (a Quaker precedent?) were presided over by itinerant preachers, to supervise the circuits. These laymen became Wesley's 'assistants', to be called 'superintendents' after his demise. From 1744 an annual conference of Wesley's friends became the embryo of what became the Conference of Preachers with Wesley as supremo. Its first Agenda was to the point – (1) What to teach; (2) How to teach; and (3) What to do; that is 'how to regulate our doctrine, discipline and practice'.[33]

Opposition was diverse. At the highest level, there was theological opposition – Josiah Tucker, 'John Smith', Bishop Gibson, later Bishops Warburton, Lavington, Porteus, Horne, Hurd and Douglas are, on any reckoning, a formidable list. Wesley's replies were courteous and firm to the charge of antinomianism and 'enthusiasm' typified by John Green, later bishop of Lincoln, who complained that Methodism 'removed Christianity from the basis of just and rational proof . . . that rock of evidence whereon it had stood for ages and set it down as the shaking sands of inward impulses which may be entirely fantastical'. The idea of Christian perfection and Wesley's breaches of church order offended evangelicals as much as they did the more rationalistic groups. Martin Schmidt outlines the heart of the charges against the Methodists: 'In spite of all their variations, the attacks from the Anglican side were all characterized by a great similarity. From all the writings, speeches, and newspaper articles came the same complaints about enthusiasm, exaggerated piety, fanaticism, lust for power and tyranny, excessive austerity or unrestrained lawlessness, hypocrisy, disparagement of the regular church and its representatives and more than all and yet running through all, threats to the power of the church and disturbance of the public quiet. The memory of the Great Revolution a hundred years earlier was still living and it affected the whole controversy.'[34] Opposition was often fomented by local clergy who hardly saw Methodism as an orderly counter-revolutionary force inculcating submission.[35] Those with power in the localities found the new itinerant evangelists a challenge to public order and authority at a time when Prime Minister Walpole's motto was 'Quieta Non Movere' – let sleeping dogs lie. The fact that the 'Connexion' soon had a highly organized nature, and the youth of Wesley's 'Helpers', made the Methodism of the 1740s and 1750s seem sinister in an age with a lack of strong central organs.

Folk memories of the Civil War were still not far below the surface. The itinerant preachers whom Wesley – and others such as Benjamin Ingham – encouraged, appeared a threat to gentry and clergy alike. The preachers, too, might have an attraction for local girls which could cause the local lads to throw the preacher into the duck pond! The publican, likewise, saw a threat to his trade, though the early Methodists were not teetotallers. That was a nineteenth-century phenomenon. Clandestine society meetings, bands and classes generated paranoid feelings. The mob hysteria period of Methodist history did not last long – though it could recur well into the next century. Its peak was in the 1740s, not surprisingly at the time of the '45'. It led to great unpleasantness, as in the Wednesbury[36] and Black Country riots from 1743. There was at least one martyrdom – William Seward at Hay on Wye. Clergy like George White, the eccentric curate of Colne, were only too eager to stir up the mob. The famous meeting of Wesley with Richard ('Beau') Nash (1674–1762), the elegant leader of society in Bath in June 1739, seems tame in comparison to White's style of abuse in 1748.[37] Nash asked what was Wesley's authority. 'By the authority of Jesus Christ conveyed to me by the (now) Archbishop of Canterbury (Potter) when he laid his hands upon me and said "Take thou authority to preach the Gospel."'

Nash   This is contrary to Parliament. This is a conventicle.

Wesley Sir, the conventicles mentioned in that Act, the Preamble shows are *seditious* meetings. Yet this is not such. There is no shadow of sedition. Therefore it is not contrary to that Act.

Nash   I say it is. And beside, your preaching frightens people out of their wits.

Wesley   Sir, did you ever hear me preach?

Nash   No.

Wesley   How then can you judge of what you have never heard.

Nash   Sir, by common report.

Wesley   Common report is not enough. Give me leave to ask, Is not your name Nash?

Nash   My name is Nash.

Wesley   Sir, I dare not judge of you by common report. I think it is not enough to judge by.

Nash   I desire to know what these people come here for?

On which one replied, 'Sir, leave him to me. Let an old woman answer him – you Mr Nash, take care of your body. We take care of our souls and for the good of our souls we come here.'

Nash's point about the Conventicle Act of 1670 (22 CAR 11 c.1) haunted Wesley throughout his career. It is interesting, too, that by the end of the century the Methodists of Bath were strikingly bourgeois in style!

There were, no doubt, highly charismatic and even hysterical episodes which Wesley did not encourage, though sometimes he interpreted them naively. These were clearly part of the eighteenth-century scene from 'the French prophets' onwards. There were spurious fanatics and humbugs, like the notorious George Bell in the 1760s, which haunted Wesley.[38] He could on the other hand always point to many people who found their lives transformed – nobodies who became somebodies. This was the answer he gave to Bishop Warburton and Lavington as well as to 'John Smith'.

A few clergymen began to associate themselves with the new movement like William Grimshaw (1708–63), pastor of Haworth and later Vincent Perronet (1693–1785) of Shoreham and John

Fletcher (1729–85) of Madeley,[39] whom Wesley saw as his possible successor before his comparatively early death. Many churches closed their doors on Wesley for several decades. This meant the necessity of the use of lay preachers, about which Wesley had considerable hesitation at first. The appointment in 1740 of men like Joseph Humphreys and Thomas Maxfield (supported by Susanna Wesley), later a thorn in Wesley's flesh, was a practical move.

It very soon heralded what was an alternative voluntary pastoral ministry independent of the parish system.[40] To 'John Smith', Wesley wrote, 'And whatever may be the fruit of lay preaching when you and I are gone to our long home every serious man has cause to bless God for those he may see with his eyes, for the saving of many souls from death and hiding a multitude of sins.'[41] The creation of a system of itinerant preachers working in the first very large circuits, with 'local' preachers operating at reasonably neighbourhood level, was a typical example of Wesley's pragmatism. He frequently moved his itinerant preachers, realizing realistically their limitations. If they remained in one place too long, they could become ineffective and boring! This hardened later into a three-year itinerancy which lasted until the twentieth century except in city missions. The purpose of the system in the early days was clear:

Q. In what view may the Methodist Preachers be considered?

A. As messengers sent by the Lord out of the common way to provoke the regular clergy to jealousy (i.e. zeal) and to supply their lack of service towards those who are perishing for want of knowledge and above all to reform the nation by spreading scriptural holiness over the land.

They certainly provoked the regular clergy, though not always to zeal, sometimes to jealousy in the modern sense of the word.

What of John Wesley as preacher? The great preacher of the revival was clearly Whitefield, though Wesley mastered all the skills of the outdoor preacher, even if, after the early days, many of his sermons were preached indoors. His published sermons,

typified by those preached before the University of Oxford, such
as that on 'Salvation by Faith', were clearly different from
Wesley's open-air style, which was extempore. Most of the
sermons noted in his Register were never published and were
frequently used, though he had a large range of sermons. For him
preaching was vital. 'About noon (28 July 1757) I preached at
Woodseat in the evening at Sheffield. I do indeed live by preaching.' The avowed aim of Methodist preaching was clear. In 1744
the question was asked,

Q. What is the best general method of preaching?

A. (1) To invite, (2) To convince, (3) To offer Christ.

Lastly to build up and to do this (in some measure) in every
sermon. In 1753 it was stated that 'the most effective way of
preaching is to preach him in all his offices, and to declare his law
as well as gospel to believers and unbelievers'. An important
letter of December 1751 stated clearly the importance of preaching the law as well as 'the gospel' to avoid the worst kind of
enthusiasm and antinomianism and mere 'cordials'.

  Horace Walpole reported on hearing Wesley, 'Wondrous
clean, but as evidently an actor as Garrick. He spoke his sermon
but so fast and with so little accent that I am sure he has often
uttered it, for it was like a lesson. There were parts and eloquence
in it, but towards the end, he exalted his voice and acted very
ugly enthusiasm.' John Hampson (Junior), an early and astute
biographer, said 'His voice was not loud but clear and manly, his
style neat, simple perspicuous and admirably adapted to the
capacity of his hearers.' Sir Walter Scott said that his preaching
included 'many excellent stories'. Clearly he sought, as his
mother said, 'to unite the pair so long disjoined, knowledge and
vital piety'. Wesley was able to communicate with those far from
church life, able to make people feel that he was preaching to
them personally. John Nelson describes hearing Wesley preach
at Moorfields in 1739. 'I thought his whole discourse was aimed
at me.'[42]

  Preaching was, however, aimed at enabling people to join the

Methodist societies as well as the offer of salvation. As he wrote in 1739 in the Preface to a hymn collection 'The Gospel of Christ knows no of religion but social, no holiness but social holiness.' By social holiness in this context he did not mean social right-eousness or politics – that was another issue – but that converts must belong to a group. Whitefield realized that was Wesley's strength. 'Joining in class, he preserved the fruit of his labour. This I neglected and my people are a rope of sand.'

Can we summarize Wesley as a person? John Hampson's con-temporary estimate that he travelled 250,000 miles and preached 40,000 times[43] has been endlessly cited. It is perfectly possible – he could cover ninety miles in a day sometimes. In later years Wesley's coach was a mobile office and private chapel. His sheer energy was quite extraordinary. How did he find time to write or edit well over two hundred books and pamphlets including *The Christian Library* from 1749? This is an enterprise designed as a kind of *Reader's Digest* of the best of Christian spirituality, edited and adapted theologically by Wesley including a great deal of Puritan writing as well as the Fathers and his favourite slightly off-beat mystics. Later the *Arminian Magazine* (1778) was published for the ordinary society members, which became later the *Wesleyan Methodist Magazine* with stories, sermons and accounts of particular personal 'providences'.

Wesley's life was strict, methodical, almost obsessive, as revealed in his diaries. He would rise at 4.30am – not entirely unusual then – and be in bed by 9.30pm. He was comparatively short, about 5ft 3in. His neat black hair (no wig!) became white with age. He often wore full clerical dress even in the open air and was always scrupulously neat – 'cleanliness indeed is next to godliness' is a phrase used by Wesley. It even found its way into the Millennium Dome! Dr Samuel Johnson complained that Wesley never had time for a leisurely discussion. This was due to his total absorption in his mission, though this did not mean obsession with ecclesiastical matters. He had, as befitted a man of his age, a tremendously wide range of interest. One example can be that he opened a medical clinic in Bristol in 1746. His book *Primitive Physic* (1747)[44] is a strange mixture of old wives' tales and recent insights. For us to realize its popularity, it must be compared with the sometimes appalling crudities and signs of change with new hospital foundations in eighteenth-century medicine. He was interested in unusual electrical experiments, giving electric shocks to depressed or mentally ill people. This was a striking anticipation of ECT. In *Primitive Physic* we read, 'For one seemingly killed by lightning . . . or suffocated, plunge him immediately into cold water or blow slowly with bellows down his throat. This way revives a person seemingly drowned. It is still better if a strong man blows into his mouth.' Here is the paradox of Wesley – the combination of reason, enlightened exploration and popular beliefs. His puritanical streak is seen in his condemning of snuff, tobacco and even the downright poison – tea! Beer was much to be preferred, doubtless safer than water at that time, though the reasons were then unknown. Wesley forbade his class members to drink 'spirits', which was wise advice at the time of the gin plague.

What of relationships with women after the romantic episodes of his Oxford days and in Georgia? Wesley met the woman – a widow Grace Murray – who might have made the kind of wife he needed, when he was forty-five.[45] It is a curious tangled story, not least in its legal aspects, which before Hardwick's Marriage Act of 1753 were not clear. She had another suitor, John Bennet, who like Wesley had been nursed by Mrs Murray at the Newcastle Orphan House of which she was Matron. She nursed their bodies and broke their hearts. Charles Wesley considered Grace to be well below his brother's social position. 'All our preachers will leave our societies if John married so mean a woman.' By Charles Wesley's swift interference, assisted by Christopher Hopper while George Whitefield attempted some kind of mediation, Grace Murray was married to Bennet. It left Wesley 'in great heaviness, his heart sinking in him like a stone'. This is the human Wesley! For the sake of propriety in 1751, he married Mrs Mary Vazeille, the widow of a London merchant, a Huguenot. She was wealthy and could be quite independent of her new husband. V. H. H. Green[46] does not exaggerate when he calls it the worst mistake of his life. Mrs Wesley had no desire to

be part of a travelling caravan, though she did accompany
Wesley at first, indeed, behaving like a Hogarthian virago in a
rumpus with Bennet over legal matters at Bolton. Letters from
female friends and converts, especially those from Sarah Ryan,
the housekeeper at Kingswood School, who had a dubious past,
aroused Mrs Wesley's jealousy. The breakdown of the marriage
seemed almost inevitable. From 1758 to 1781, when Mary died,
they had periods of separation punctuated by attempts at reconciliation and unpleasantness, even of a physical nature, with
Mrs Wesley once pulling out her husband's hair, according to
Hampson, an early biographer. In the end it was like the bizarre
antics of elderly folk.[47] John Wesley heard of his wife's death only
after her funeral. The episode is a striking example of Lawrence
Stone's[48] contention that the middle of the century roughly
marked the transition from marriage of convenience to marriage
of love. It is a very broad generalization, but Wesley's 'last love'
(Grace Murray) and marriage illustrate it well. Wesley was quite
clear that he would be 'boss' of his household. In 1771 when
separation seemed final, he said, 'Non eam reliqui, Non dimissi,
Non revocabo'[49] – 'I did not leave her, I did not send her away,
I did not call her back.' While not condoning Mary Wesley's
behaviour, sometimes John Wesley's insensitiveness on marital
matters was great, as when he told Christopher Hopper that he
would be able to give more time to his work after his first wife
died.[50] We cannot ignore the attraction he had for women nor his
patient skill in pastoral and spiritual counselling, so long as he
was in the commanding position.

By 1780, Wesley's Methodism was widespread in the West
Country as well as in the North, in Ireland, particularly in the
'textile triangle', and to a much lesser extent in Scotland and
South Wales. At City Road Chapel, London, which in 1778
replaced 'the Foundery', Wesley presided over a significant
'Connexion' with 470 meeting houses by 1791, equalling in
numbers the Roman Catholic Community in England. He was
now a revered if eccentric figure in British Society. 'I am become
I know not how an honourable man,' he wrote in 1785. On his
last visit to Cornwall, he recalled at Falmouth,[51] 'The last time I

was there forty years ago [at eighty-six he had forgotten he had been twice there] I was taken prisoner by an immense mob, gaping and roaring like lions, But how is the tide turned! High and low men lined the streets from one end of the town to another out of love and kindness, gaping and staring as if the King was going by.' Churches once closed to him were now open. On his deathbed, cared for by a bevy of pious ladies, he quoted Isaac Watts. 'I'll praise my Maker while I've breath.' His last words were, 'The best of all is God is with us.'

The *Gentleman's Magazine* in March 1791 had a long obituary.[52] It ended, 'His history if well written, will certainly be important for in every respect as the founder of the most numerous sect in the Kingdom as a man and as a writer, he must be considered as one of the most extraordinary characters that this or any age ever produced.' At the end of the twentieth century A. L. Rowse, no particular friend of Methodism, could state that 'No Oxford man has ever accomplished more.'[53]

It is clear that he was revered by his followers, who went to extraordinary lengths in their mourning. Some of his more astute adjutants like John Pawson[54] were almost relieved at his dying – a matter which the 'Methodist myth' conveniently forgets! Certainly Wesley stamped his character on Methodism in a way comparable with Ignatius Loyola and the Jesuits and William Booth and the Salvation Army. He has been typecast in many ways by propagandists lining him up for their Christian styles – Anglo-Catholic, evangelical, social reformer. Certainly, he was a great lover of Holy Communion in an age of comparatively low observance.[55] To others, he was an evangelical par excellence, who had shaken off 'the graveclothes of popish superstition' after 1738 – a view which did not take account of his rejection of Neo-Calvinism and his assertion of the centrality of Christian perfection, which made him different from the generality of the Evangelical Revival. To the late Dr Frank Baker, one of the leading Wesley scholars of the last generation, he became a 'doctrinally liberal iconoclast who had little use for many traditional beliefs and a somewhat low view of church, ministry and sacraments'.[56]

So often, he has been torn out of the eighteenth-century context and set alongside Newman or Pusey or Keble rather than Hoadly, Butler or Warburton of his own century. Without doubt, he is to be seen as an eighteenth-century man who saw his task as 'spreading scriptural holiness throughout the land'. He, somehow, could be an Oxford don and the man for 'Christ's poor' at the same time. He was a man of great charm but also lonely, with no one, after his brother Samuel's death, who could challenge him in a way which his other brother Charles and his unfortunate sisters could not.

Vivian Green is not far off the mark when he states, 'His charm and grace cloaked an iron will, he was granite in aspic.' Nothing, says Green, could justify the wild attacks of the Neo-Calvinists and the mockers in the *Gospel Magazine*, but their fury, like his wife's rages, may have been provoked by his untouchability, the hard core of his personality.[57] This may seem harsh, but it is near the bone. It is confirmed by the first Life of any consequence, by his former preacher John Hampson (Junior), who had become an Anglican clergyman. This was before Wesley became an 'icon'. 'Mr Wesley', the Methodists would always call him, just as Victorian Liberals were to call W. E. Gladstone 'Mr Gladstone' a century later, with his portrait on their mantelpieces.

We must now explore several major questions: What was Wesley's essential strategy and spirituality? How did his brother's hymns fit into that picture? Was Wesley essentially a 'folk theologian'? What folk were attracted to his method? What was his social and political position? What effect did it have on his followers before and after his death? Why and how did his movement become separate from the Church of England? Did it save England from revolution? If not, what effect did it have on society?

3

John Wesley's Strategy, Spirituality and Charles Wesley's Hymns

Wesley was an astute organizer, though Ronald Knox's view that he could cope only with 'Yes men' needs to be taken seriously.[1] It is also notable that he was prepared to sweep other small 'Connexions' into his well-disciplined system. 'In John Wesley', said Bernard Manning, the Cambridge historian, with pardonable exaggeration, 'the Methodists had a leader who, by a stroke of divine genius that puts him in the same rank as Hildebrand, St. Dominic and Ignatius Loyola combined the evangelical passion and experience of Luther with Calvin's ecclesiastical system.'[2] Of few Christian leaders can it be said that so many of his usages and institutions began as inspired improvisations and borrowings – unless it be the early Christian communities. The consequence, however, was that the new styles became a rigid constitution which became inflexible in the next generation, although the heart of it was exported to Ireland, America and other parts of the world.

The Methodist *societies* were the basic unit. Then almost from the beginning there were the 'bands'[3], whose members, recruited from the larger societies, met in a kind of mutual confessional with the clear aim of pressing on to perfection. Methodists of an older generation sometimes use the phrase 'this is in band', meaning 'hold your tongue'. A question asked in the bands was, 'Do you desire to be told all your faults and that plain and home?' Then, 'Do you desire that every one of us should tell you from time to time whatever is in his heart concerning you? Do you desire that in doing this we should come as close as possible, that we should cut to the quick and search your heart to the bottom?'

This was laid down in December 1738, modified in 1744. The bands, which were expected to meet each week, and the slightly later 'select societies' – those from the bands pressing further on to perfection – became too intense, élitist and almost sectarian in effect, slowly dying away at the end of the century. Methodism could not remain a holiness group. Its constituency became too broad for that. Wesley came to terms with this – his obsession with developing more styles of sub-group ended. By 1780 John Pawson, one of the somewhat later itinerants, can still speak of a scandal in a 'select society'. His wife, Frances, wrote in her journal of problems with 'enthusiasm' at that time.

Two elements in Wesley's thinking – perfection as instant gift and experience and also as a steady progress through devotional means to holiness (the 'bands' were part of this process) tended to split apart into two different versions of thinking about holiness. As Gordon Wakefield puts it, 'Wesley went on to claim that entry into perfection might be instantaneous like first conversion. The doctrine not only aroused opposition, it led to some scandals within the Methodist societies, extreme claims and fanatical scenes. Wesley never claimed perfection, always standing at some distance from his own movement. What must not be forgotten is that for him "perfection" was perfect love, the keeping of the great commandment. The test was whether one loved one's enemies with the heart cleansed of hatred. But who would determine these matters?'[4] The *class meetings* became the means to ensure that there was genuine growth in discipleship, a means of evangelism and discipline which could be very rigorous. Earlier models and pragmatism went together. By 1783, in Bristol, there were 57 classes with nine to eighteen members in each. In Sunderland, by contrast, the classes were much larger. Classes needed lay leaders – men and women who were to be the pioneers of growth, though Wesley himself and later his 'assistants', took on themselves the task of purging the classes of those who did not live up to expectations. Entry into a class was on the basis of seeking salvation, but consequent discipline was involved. Expulsions were frequent. This was never seen as expulsion from the church but from the 'society'. This style had a long innings. By the middle of the nineteenth century, it was beginning to lose its popularity while it was still considered a criterion of membership. What was proper to a society was under too much strain to be the basis for membership of a denomination. This resulted in a loss of close supervision and discipline.

The class style had a remarkable renaissance in universities and colleges, beginning with Oxford and Cambridge in the 1920s. These 'Methodist Societies' were organized on the class style with leaders who would be responsible to the chaplain. In the early 1950s Cambridge University 'Meth Soc' had more groups than letters in the alphabet. The groups were pastoral, not merely discussion groups, a format which had direct links with Wesley's method.[5]

Another long-lasting style was the training of *local preachers*,[6] who became vital to the maintenance and growth of the circuit system. Wesley adopted the apprenticeship system familiar to artisans – those who later became the 'labour aristocracy'. The neophyte preacher would accompany an experienced preacher with a 'note' from the 'assistant' granting permission to preach. He would, then, later be 'on trial' on his own, like a journeyman. If he had the necessary 'faith, grace and fruit', he would be received as a 'fully accredited' local preacher who could, if he moved house, preach anywhere in the connexion. In the twenty-first century, remarkably, this is still the basic style, though the training is far more sophisticated. A large number of local preachers, men and women, come now from the teaching profession.

The itinerants and the assistants who headed up the circuits – those prepared to be full-time – were, at first, youthful, needing to possess great physical stamina and energy. These men were not dissenting pastors, although 53 of them, like John Bennet, became such. Forty-seven became Anglican clergymen before Wesley's death in 1791. Numbers of members of the societies were 25,911 when statistics began to be collected in 1767, with

72,467 in 1791, including Ireland. In 1781 there were 178 itinerant preachers with 63 circuits. By Wesley's death there were 300 full-time itinerants. This was not wildfire revival. We must note that over half the members were women, some of whom served as class leaders, with some being permitted to 'exhort', i.e. to speak without a text or preach.

For worship, Wesley was in no doubt that his people should have the '*instituted*' means of grace[7] at the parish church. This would include Holy Communion, which in the average parish would be celebrated at least quarterly. The Methodist leaders, like Wesley himself, thought highly of the Eucharist, but many of the ordinary members, like most churchgoers then, did not give it the priority Wesley desired, though we must not forget the huge numbers at Holy Communion conducted by the Wesleys and others like Grimshaw and Whitefield. These were occasional if outstanding occasions. The other 'instituted' means of grace were *prayer* – private, family and public – *searching the Scriptures* by reading and meditating, for which the methods of Bishop Hall and Richard Baxter were 'models'. It is not clear how much these were used. Then there was *fasting* on Fridays. This was resumed in Methodist ministerial training colleges in the next century. *Christian conference* was vital, i.e. meeting in pursuance of those 'means'. Clearly the Church of England liturgy was supposed to be central here. This was an ideal not always realized in practice at parish level. In Bishop John Ross's Exeter returns of 1779, the Vicar of Launceston mentioned 'a conventicle belonging to a sect called Methodists, but as they, at times, frequent the parish church, I suppose they can't properly be called dissenters'.[8] This was Wesley's constant plea, as illustrated in the brush with Nash.

In addition there were what Wesley called 'the *prudential means*' which gave Methodists their own particular ethos – bands, classes and the very significant *preaching service*. This may have been partly derived from the university sermon familiar to the Wesley brothers or perhaps the medieval 'prone' or 'bidding of the bedes', a devotion including a sermon. More likely, it was an adaptation of Puritan and dissenting models which would be not unfamiliar to some of the members of the societies. The Methodist preaching service was much briefer than the typical meeting house service, the timing at 5am and 5pm being a factor.[9] Wesley insisted on men and women sitting apart.

Hymns from Charles (and John) would provide a 'drip-feed' of theology. At first the hymns were lined out by the leader, which enabled illiterate people to remember the words and 'own' them in a way which proved to be very important indeed. Owen Chadwick claims that the 'modern flowering of the hymn changed the feel of Christian worship'.[10] Theology came alive in hymnody. 'Lining out' has revived in China in recent years.

The straightforward expository sermon would be part of the short preaching service of 5am or on Sunday after Evensong at the parish church. Later, after the lighting of chapels (and pubs!) by gas mantles, evening worship could be encouraged. The servant class benefited greatly by this, but it was in the generation after Wesley. Wesley tells us that he preached for half an hour at the Foundery. Most sermons were preached by itinerant or local preachers. They were not confined to Sundays.[11]

A generation later Charles G. Finney described their American successors, but the reference can be to the whole period. 'Look at the Methodists. Many of their ministers are unlearned in the common sense of the term, many of them straight from the shop or farm and yet they have gathered congregations and pushed their way and won souls everywhere. Wherever the Methodists have gone, their plain, pointed and simple but warm and animated mode of preaching has always gathered congregations – we must have exciting, powerful preaching or the devil will have the people, except what the Methodists can save.'[12]

Then there was the *Love Feast*, another borrowing from the Moravians. It was a service of testimony with prayer and hymn-singing. Cakes and water were the elements. It was a 'democratized folk eucharist' in effect. It was not an open meeting, one required a class ticket to attend. This style survived well into the twentieth century in village chapels[13] in Wesleyanism and Primitive Methodism.

The *Watchnight Service* was held as a kind of popular vigil,

not necessarily on New Year's Eve. Often it was held on the night
of the full moon to avoid getting mugged on the way home. *The
Covenant Service*[14] was borrowed from the Puritans. In Wesley's
time clergymen or ministers like William Grimshaw and John
Fletcher still used impressive personal covenants, suggesting a
continuity going back a century. Wesley adapted a style based on
Joseph and Richard Alleine, which was used from 1755 onwards
as a corporate means of rededication of an exacting personal
kind – very much the Methodist style of combining the individual and the 'society'. The Covenant Service has recently been
adopted in modern style by the Church of South India in 1956
and in the Book of Common Order of the Church of Scotland in
1994. The modern form includes the heart of the service: 'Christ
has many services to be done: some are easy, others are difficult;
some bring honour, others bring reproach; some are suitable to
our natural inclinations and material interests, others are contrary to both: in some we may please Christ and please ourselves;
in others we cannot please Christ except by denying ourselves.
Yet the power to do all these things is given to us in Christ, who
strengthens us' (*Methodist Worship Book* 1999). The modern
forms are less starkly demanding compared with . . . 'I come
Lord, I believe Lord. I throw myself upon thy Grace and Mercy;
do not refuse me! I have not whither else to go; Here will I stay,
I will not stir from thy door; on thee will I trust and rest and venture myself. God hath laid my help on thee and on thee I lay for
hope, for pardon, for life, for salvation; if I perish, I perish on thy
shoulder; if I sink, I sink in thy vessel; if I die, I die at thy door;
bid me not go away for I will not go.' Christ's service might mean
'sailing against the wind, swimming against the tide, steering
contrary to the tide, parting with our ease, our liberties and
accommodations for the Name of our Lord Jesus' (1780). Was
that what Wesley meant by scriptural holiness?

The astute Roman Catholic commentator Clifford Longley
said in 1988, 'Wesley did not leave behind a systematic theology
. . . His memorial was the Methodist Movement itself, a living
thing rather than a set of ideas. It took its deepest inspiration not
from him, however, but from his brother . . . Wesleyanism, at its

simplest definition, is a choir founded by John to sing the
hymns of Charles and to live accordingly. This is its heart, its
spirituality.'[15] There was, of course, more than Charles Wesley's
hymns as carriers of theology. We must not underestimate 'field
preaching', which greatly influenced the ethos of Methodist
worship, since it generated the concept that the chief function of
the sermon is the offering of the gospel to those outside the
fellowship of the society. This gave a cutting edge to Methodist
preaching which has been made increasingly difficult in the
second part of the twentieth century except in the ministry of
Donald Soper at Tower Hill and Hyde Park. The claim made is
that Methodism was 'born in song'. Its spirituality cannot be
understood without looking at how theology can be conveyed
both in public worship and in private devotion through 'irregular dogmatics' in hymnody.

Since about 1960 there has been an extraordinary production
of new hymns and 'worship songs' right across the Christian
spectrum, with some material of the highest quality. At the same
time there has been a realization of the literary merit of the
classical hymn exemplified by the writing of Donald Davie,
Isabel Rivers, Ian Bradley and Richard Watson of Durham.[16]
Hymns are the folk music of the church militant. David Martin,
the sociologist, went so far as to say that 'the hymn is the most
central item in the religion of Britain'.[17] Could the Methodist
Revival have been possible without the hymns of Charles
Wesley?

On any account Charles Wesley's hymns are a major contribution to Christian spirituality. He may have been a lesser figure,
historically, than his brother John, who was himself no mean
poet and translator, but it is possible that Christian congregations will be singing Charles Wesley's hymns when his brother's
Forty Four Sermons are read only by the historically minded
theologian, and the Methodist organization has passed into the
museum of history. 'This little book', said the Congregationalist
historian Bernard Lord Manning, with his usual love of the striking phrase, speaking of the 1780 Collection, 'ranks in Christian
literature with the Psalms, the Book of Common Prayer, the

Canon of the Mass . . . It is a work of supreme devotional art by a religious genius.' Some might jib now at the reference to the Latin Mass! Another Congregationalist and hymnologist Erik Routley once suggested that Charles was too introverted, knew nothing of the social gospel and that his monumental output stifled hymn-writing in his own communion. He admitted exaggeration, but it is the case that it is the more objective hymns for the Christian year that have been most used in non-Methodist circles. It is interesting to note how many of these were not in the Collection of 1780, which was intended for the devotional exercises of the Methodist societies, and for the private prayers of the individual Methodist, perhaps something unique to them.[18]

If we look at the contents page of the *Collection of Hymns for the Use of the People called Methodists*,[19] we may note how John Wesley arranged and edited his brother's hymns, and some of his own, with a sprinkling of Isaac Watts, and others as a kind of spiritual autobiography in 'a little book of experimental and practical divinity'. It was re-issued, with supplements, throughout the nineteenth century. So in Part I we have exhorting and beseeching sinners to return to God, followed by describing the pleasantness of religion, the goodness of God, death, judgement, heaven, hell, praying for a blessing. Part II describes formal and inward religion. Part III gives praying for repentance, for mourners convinced of sin, brought to the birth, convinced of backsliding and recovered – not an infrequent matter! Part IV moves to believers – rejoicing, fighting, praying, watching, working, suffering, groaning for full redemption, brought to the birth, saved, interceding for the world. Part V has the society – meeting, giving thanks, praying, parting.

We can compare this with any modern hymn book based on the Christian year or Christian doctrine, but the contextual parallel should be made with the *Olney Hymns* of 1779, produced by John Newton and William Cowper. Here we can compare what we have called 'the Calvinism of the heart' with Wesley's 'Arminianism of the heart'. Newton's arrangement eschews any perfectionism as we might expect. Bruce Hindmarsh[20] points out that it is less elaborate than the Wesleys and follows the basic pattern of his letters on growth in grace. There are eight sections, the last added by request and not found at all in the Wesley collection.

1 Solemn Addresses to Sinners.
2 Seeking, Hearing, Hoping.
3 Conflict.
4 Comfort.
5 Dedication and Surrender.
6 Cautions.
7 Praise (focused upon Christ).
8 Short liturgical hymns.

So here, the sinner is first awakened to contrition and spiritual desire before experiencing testing which, intermingled with divine assistance, leads to a more perfect obedience and resignation to God, leading in time to a more contemplative mind focused on Christ.

Wesley's Collection, with 480 hymns by Charles, has a passionate sense of personal experience and a Christian mysticism which is neither absorption into God – though Charles comes near to it sometimes – nor a 'flight of the alone to the alone', for there is always the stress on deep fellowship with other Christians. The whole is charged with orthodox Christian doctrine, for which the best word is doxology. One should add J. E. Rattenbury's[21] more controversial assertion that the Collection is a 'personation' of the heights and depths of Christian experience. Charles Wesley is thus both writing of himself and projecting himself on to others, seeking to share his pilgrimage with them.

What is more mystical than this?

> Ah, show me that happiest place,
> The place of thy people's abode,
> Where saints in an ecstasy gaze,
> And hang on a crucified God.

Thy love for a sinner declare,
Thy passion and death on the tree;
My spirit to Calvary bear,
To suffer and triumph with thee.

HP 750. *Short Hymns on Select
Passages of the Holy Scriptures* (1762)

As with the Book of Psalms, the poet is in turn convert, preacher, pastor, controversionalist, expositor, theologian.[22] In his hymns Charles Wesley somehow lives in the experience of the early Methodists and interprets them to themselves. It is as if he pushes them beyond their wildest dreams:

Changed from glory into glory
Till in heaven we take our place,
Till we cast our crowns before thee
Lost in wonder, love and praise!

HP 267. BE 7, no. 374

If we are to compare the contribution of Isaac Watts and the Wesleys to English hymnody, then we can say that Watts is stronger on the sovereignty of God, creation and the cosmic aspect of redemption. This is so in the most sung of his hymns by every denomination.

Were the *whole realm of nature* mine,
That were a present far too small
Love so amazing, so divine
Demands my soul, my life, my all.

HP 180

Charles Wesley is stronger on the personal aspect of the faith with the cross at the heart of it all. His hymns are based on his own experience of redemption and his passionate desire to share it.

What man, what experience underlay the hymns?[23] Like his brother John, Charles sought to do all he could for God. 'How do you hope to be saved?' said Peter Böhler, the Moravian, to Charles. 'Because I have used my best endeavour to serve God.' Liberation from self-concern came significantly on Whit Sunday, 21 May 1738 – three days before his brother's 'Aldersgate Street experience'. Charles, sick in body, tormented in mind, was staying with a man named John Bray. Brooding on Martin Luther's *Commentary on Galatians*, he realized that Christ loved him as if there was no one else in the universe, and had died for him. There, not in his best endeavours, was his salvation. His heart was not 'strangely warmed' but 'palpitating'! The symptoms he describes seem to be a classic anxiety state as well as pleurisy. Torment and release are illustrated in the 'Wrestling Jacob' hymn. The lonely soul searches for God and wrestles with him in an agony:

> Wrestling, I will not let thee go,
> Till I thy name, thy nature know . . .

He is in despair. Who is God? What is God like?

> Speak or thou never hence shall move
> And tell me if thy name is Love.

HP 434. BE 7, no. 136

Yes it is –

> 'Tis Love! 'tis Love! Thou diest for me!
> I hear thy whisper in my heart.
> The morning breaks, the shadows flee,
> Pure, universal love thou art,
> To me, to all, thy mercies move;
> Thy nature and thy Name is Love.

Here is the great discovery of the love of God – 'for all the fallen race and me'. It was Dr Scott Lidgett – first President of the Methodist Conference in 1932 – who said that the meaning of

Methodism is that it recovered by experience and set forth by its preaching and teaching the supremacy of the love of God.[24] That discovery had to be shared. Within 48 hours Charles Wesley had written the conversion hymn in which we can see enshrined the very essence of Methodism.

> Where shall my wondering soul begin? . . .
> That I, a child of wrath and hell –
> I should be called a child of God.

> *HP* 706. *BE* 7, no. 29

> Shall I, the hallowed cross to shun
> Refuse his righteousness to impart
> By hiding it within my heart?

> No – God's love was for all

> Outcast of men, to you I call
> Harlots, and publicans, and thieves
> He spreads his arms to embrace you all.

Charles's personal ministry to felons was notable, but above all he taught the Methodists to sing their faith. Through the hymns, creed and culture were passed on to the great variety of folk who sang them. In the hymns the distinctive emphases of Methodism were set down to become part of the fibre of the church. The spirituality of 'the Arminianism of the heart' is better expressed in hymns than anywhere else.

> O for a trumpet voice
> On all the World to call
> To bid their hearts rejoice
> In him who died for all!
> For all, my Lord was crucified
> For all, for all my Saviour died!

> *HP* 226. *BE* 7, no. 33

The 'all' was constantly stressed –

> Its streams, the whole creation reach
> So plenteous is the store,
> Enough for all, enough for each,
> Enough for evermore.

> HP 48. BE 7, no. 241

This conviction arose in Wesley's mind from the fact that he knew himself to be saved by Christ. Of the grace of God he can say that it is

> So wide it never passed by one,
> Or it had passed by me

> HP 46. BE 7, no. 207

From this stems the assurance which seemed like rank 'enthusiasm' to his opponents.

> He owns me for his child . . .
> I can no longer fear;
> With confidence I now draw nigh
> And Father – Abba – Father cry

> HP 217. BE 8, no. 164

The Wesleys never stopped with the beginning of the Christian life, as we have seen Charles asserts this in two fascinating lines:

> We all shall commend the love of our Friend
> For ever beginning what never shall end

> *Methodist Hymn Book 66.*
> *Hymns and Sacred Poems, 1749*

or again –

> Thy Nature, Gracious Lord impart
> Come quickly from above:
> Write thy new name upon my heart
> Thy new best name of love.

Again and again the hymns bring together pardon, holiness and heaven. Despite the difficulties of conceiving sin as rather like a rotten tooth, the following is a gem-like summary of Charles Wesley's doctrine of perfection:

> Jesus, the First and Last,
> On thee my soul is cast:
> Thou didst thy work begin
> By blotting out my sin;
> Thou wilt the root remove,
> And perfect me in love.
> Yet when the work is done,
> The work is but begun:
> Partaker of thy grace,
> I long to see thy face;
> The first I prove below,
> The last I die to know.

HP 735. From *Short Hymns on Select
Passages of the Holy Scriptures*, 1762

This gospel is to be offered to the world –

> O let me commend my Saviour to you,
> I set to my seal that Jesus is true;
> You all may find favour who come at his call;
> O come to my saviour! His grace is for all.

HP 805. *Hymns on God's Everlasting Love*, 1741

John Wesley advised his preachers, 'You have nothing to do but to save souls, therefore spend and be spent in this work. And go always not only to those that want you but to those that want (i.e. need) you most.'[25] Wesley hymns are contextual theology.

Despite the formidable combination of parson, squire and mob to whom Methodism seemed a threat, a return to king-killing Commonwealth days, the gospel was preached – miners, farm labourers, soldiers, ordinary folk were claimed from degradation to a more wholesome life and were enabled to sing

> My heart is full of Christ, and longs
> Its glorious matter to declare

> *HP 799. Collection of Psalms*
> *and Hymns, 1743*

As the brickbats of opposition flew around their heads they could burst out:

> Though the sons of night blaspheme
> More there are with us than them
> God with us – we cannot fear;
> Fear ye fiends – for Christ is near.

> *HP 811. Hymns and Sacred Poems,*
> *1742. To be sung in a Tumult*

Thus the story of Elisha is relevant to eighteenth-century life! Imagine a group of Methodists interrupted, as they worship, by a mob. The house in which they worship is not licensed for preaching, so out they go to the jeers of the crowd, walking or running to a place where they could worship legally in peace. They sing

> Jesus – the name high over all,
> In hell, or earth or sky!
> Angels and men before it fall
> And devils fear and fly.

> *HP 264. Hymns and Sacred Poems, 1745*

The gospel was preached to the quarry workers of Portland

> Come O thou all victorious Lord,
> Thy power to us make known.
> Strike with the hammer of the word
> And break these hearts of stone.

Amid all the political tension of 1745, when Bonnie Prince Charlie threatened civil war, the old Methodist message was proclaimed. A series of hymns *To be Sung in a Tumult* were written, the tumult being the threatened war. 'Ye servants of God, Your master proclaim' (*HP* 278) was written for this occasion when to some it seemed as if the Protestantism of England was threatened.

Nothing better illustrates Wesley's love of souls than his *Hymn for a Local Preacher* sung by congregations in alliance with the preacher.

> Give me the faith which can remove
> And sink the mountain to a plain . . .
> Enlarge, inflame and fill my heart
> With boundless charity divine;
> So shall I all my strength exert,
> And love them with a zeal like thine;
> And lead them to thy open side,
> The sheep for whom their shepherd died.

> *HP* 767

Charles Wesley was a wholehearted churchman. He loved the Christian year with its annual presentation of the truths of Christ. Hymns were written for all the great festivals. These are the hymns by and large that are popular outside Methodist circles. For Advent there is 'Come Thou long expected Jesus' (*HP* 81) and 'Lo! He comes with clouds descending' (*HP* 241). No Christmas carol service would be complete without 'Hark! the herald angels sing' (*HP* 106). Charles Wesley wrote originally

'Hark! How all the welkin rings, Glory to the King of Kings' (*Hymns and Sacred Songs*, 1749). George Whitefield's Collection of 1753 altered it as did Martin Madan later. Henry Bett avowed that the original was better for the angels did not praise the holy babe but God.[26] Urchins still sing high christology through our letter boxes

> Veiled in flesh the Godhead see!
> Hail, the incarnate Deity!
> Pleased as man with men to dwell
> Jesus our Immanuel.

> *HP* 106

If we look at the hymns on the incarnation we can delect a rich incarnational theology. Here is Charles Wesley at his toughest and most paradoxical theologically

> Our God contracted to a span
> Incomprehensibly made man.

> *HP* 109. *Hymns for the*
> *Nativity of the Lord*, 1744

The 'span' is taken from George Herbert. Wesley was an unrepentant borrower of other poets' gems. Note the ending: This is the Eastern view of humanity, finally at one with the Deity.

> Made perfect first in love,
> And sanctified by grace,
> We shall from earth remove,
> And see his glorious face;
> His love shall then be fully showed
> And man shall all be lost in God.

How better can the 'kenotic' or 'self-emptying' theory of the incarnation be expressed than in 'Glory to God on high'?

> Emptied of his Majesty,
> Of his dazzling glory shorn
> Being's source begins to be
> And God himself is born.

> *HP 101. Hymns for the*
> *Nativity of our Lord, 1744*

The poet Donald Davie called this earthiness or carnality.[27]

> Our God ever blest
> With oxen doth rest
> Is nurst by his creatures
> And hangs at the breast.

John Wesley rejected this! He was not at ease with babies and breasts, with a horror of what he called the 'namby-pamby'.

We move to the Passion. Here we are at the heart of the matter:

> Come then, and to my soul reveal
> The heights and depths of grace
> The wounds which all my sorrows heal,
> That dear disfigured face.

> *HP 184. Hymns in the use of Families*
> *and on Various Occasions, 1767*

Charles Wesley, with supreme art, offers the crucified Christ as redeemer. He is the poet of redemption, liberation, cleansing, said W. F. Lofthouse in a brilliant summary of the Passion hymns. The Greeks spoke of 'catharsis', purging of the passions, making clean. The Christian, pushing beyond the Aristotelian 'purging of pity and fear', looks to purity and holiness in those cleansed from sin. Charles Wesley asks:

> What meant the suffering Son of Man.
> The streaming blood divine?

> *HP 184*

At Calvary, says Lofthouse, we not only look into the misery of the world's broken heart, but are aware of the approach of God, of humanity as God's creation, of human estrangement from God and of God who rises as the sun with healing in his wings. 'My God who suffers there' (*HP* 166). Calvary is the place of suffering and triumph.[28]

Wesley's christology is remote from any idea of God as not able to suffer. Instead he seems to verge on the very brink of patripassianism – the Father suffering in the son.

> Endless scenes of wonder rise
> From that mysterious tree,
> Crucified before our eyes
> Where we our Maker see;
> Jesus Lord, what hast thou done
> Publish we the death divine . . .

> *HP* 166. *Hymns for the*
> *Lord's supper*, 1745

And

> Faith cries out, 'tis he, 'tis he
> My God that suffers there.

Or

> O Love divine, what hast thou done!
> The immortal God hath died for me!
> The Father's co-eternal son,
> Bore all my sins upon the tree.
> The immortal God for me hath died!
> My Lord, my Love is crucified.

> *HP* 175. *Hymns and*
> *Sacred Poems*, 1742

It was Bernard Manning[29] who spotted that this was not patripassianism – 'crucifying the Father and putting to flight the spirit', as Tertullian mocked at Praxeas, but the patristic device, which was later used by Martin Luther, called the 'communicatio idiomatum', the 'transference of the attributes', so that what can be predicated of the humanity of Jesus can also be predicated of his divinity. If Manning pointed this out first, Professor Geoffrey Wainwright, in *Doxology*,[30] has woven Charles Wesley into his presentation of the atonement which stresses the involvement of God in his creation, facing the music of his own creation, the granting of freedom to humankind. Professor Frances Young[31] in a series of studies makes the point even more sharply: 'But I would still maintain that a properly Christian response to the problem of evil has to begin with the cross, with an understanding of atonement. We do not begin by explaining evil away, justifying God, excusing him for the mess he has made of his creation. We begin by contemplating the story, which tells of God taking responsibility for the evil of his world, entering it himself, taking it upon himself in all its horror, cruelty and pain.' This is a christology which can use Charles Wesley's hymns in worship. *Lex orandi est lex credendi* – the law of praying is the law of believing.

No Easter service is thinkable in Methodism, even now, without 'Christ the Lord is risen today', with its tremendous note of exaltation.

> Love's redeeming work is done,
> Fought the fight, the battle won,
> Vain the stone, the watch, the seal;
> Christ hath burst the gates of hell:
> Hallelujah.

> *HP* 193. *Hymns and*
> *Sacred Poems*, 1739

For Ascensiontide – so often left out of the Protestant and Methodist calendar – we have a whole clutch of hymns, of which 'Rejoice the Lord is King' (*HP* 243) was given its own tune by G. F. Handel. For Pentecost there are hymns rich in imagery and evangelical reality; 'O Thou who camest from above' (*HP* 745) and 'Father of everlasting grace' (*HP* 300) are typical:

> Jesus confirm my heart's desire
> To work, and speak and think for thee;
> Still let me guard the holy fire
> And still stir up thy gift in me.

> *HP* 745

No hymn for Trinity Sunday in the English language is greater than

> Hail! holy, holy, holy Lord!
> Whom One in Three we know
> By all thy heavenly host adored
> By all thy Church below.

> *HP 6. Hymns of the Trinity*, 1767

The festivals of the church year lead to the fellowship of the church. The Wesleys were never undenominational freelance evangelists, but always sought a corporate expression of the faith. Deep, prayerful fellowship seemed, to those who knew it, a real anticipation, a foretaste of heaven.

> And if our fellowship below
> In Jesus is so sweet,
> What height of rapture shall we know
> When round his throne we meet!

> *HP 753. Hymns for Those who Seek*
> *and Those who Have Redemption*
> *in the Blood of Jesus Christ*, 1747

We can visualize an early Methodist class meeting, beginning its informal session:

> Love, like death, hath all destroyed,
> Rendered all distinctions void;

Names and sects and parties fall:
Thou, O Christ, art all in all.

HP 764. *BE* 7, no. 504

Charles Wesley's setting to verse of Dean Brevint's treatise
Christian Sacrament and Sacrifice (1673) has given to the church
some of the richest eucharistic hymns in the language.[32] The
hymns put together in *The Hymns on the Lord's Supper* (1745)
can be taken as an authoritative source of the Wesleys' doctrines
– 'irregular dogmatics' at its finest.

First) the Eucharist is seen as a *memorial of the sufferings and
death of Christ*. It is a dynamic recalling of all that Calvary
meant and can mean in a vital living way. 'O remember Calvary,
And bid us go in peace,' says Charles Wesley addressing God.
This is a remarkable anticipation of the view of the German New
Testament scholar Joachim Jeremias, who sees *anamnesis* as
remembrance before God as well as before humanity.[33]

Second, as a *sign and means of grace*. The Eucharist is not a
'mere memorial' nor a kind of perpetual funeral of Christ but
a communion with a risen, present Lord now. Methodism, in
general, has never thought of 'the real presence' as confined to
the elements in a local sense, nor has any attempt been made to
define the nature of the presence. With the Anglican apologist
Richard Hooker, Wesley would seem to have been content to say
'What the elements are in themselves, it skilleth not, it is enough
for me which take them, they are the body and blood of Christ.
It is Christ who is the host at his supper.' As Queen Elizabeth
may well have said,

> He was the Word that spoke it;
> He took the bread and broke it;
> And what the Word doth make it
> That I believe, and take it.[34]

The Wesleys linked, as did Calvin, the presence of Christ with
the work of the Holy Spirit. Here is a remarkable 'epiclesis' or

invocation of the Holy Spirit, an anticipation of so many modern communion 'anaphoras' or eucharistic prayers.

> Come Holy Ghost, thine influence show
> And realize [i.e. make real] the sign;
> Thy life infuse into the bread,
> Thy power into the wine
> Effectual let the tokens prove
> And made, by heavenly art
> Fit channels to convey thy love
> To every faithful heart.

HP 602. Hymns on the
Lord's Supper, 1745

Here are bound together a spiritual presence, the work of the Holy Spirit and the faithful recipient. This is a view of the presence of Christ in many ways akin to theological insights of John Macquarrie and H. E. W. Turner in the 1970s.[35] They stressed *who* is present not *what*, seeking to move away from a localized presence. Turner asserted that to see the presence as a sign is not a limited view – a flag not only represents but evokes patriotism. A kiss stimulates as well as expressing love. This is a grace–faith relationship, not a mechanical one depending on a 'substance' theology. Macquarrie used the phrase 'transignification' to express the relationship between the signs – bread and wine – and the thing signified, the presence of a personal Lord. It is a great pity that modern Roman Catholic hymn books have not really discovered Charles Wesley.

Third, the Communion is seen as a *foretaste*, a pledge of heaven. It is a 'gospel feast', an anticipation by faith of the 'marriage supper of the Lamb', when Christ and his disciples are finally one. Dr Geoffrey Wainwright[36] has shown how much this idea is to be found in the early church, making clear that here the individual is firmly set in community. Past, present and future are linked together in the Christ who came, who comes and who will come. This is to consider time rather than space as the centre of presence.

Fourth, the Communion implies a *sacrifice*. We plead before
God the sacrifice of Christ made once for all.

> With solemn faith, we offer up,
> And spread before Thy glorious eyes
> That only ground of all our hope
> That precious, bleeding sacrifice
> Which brings thy grace on sinners down
> And perfects all our souls in one.

Hymns on the Lord's Supper, 1745

We must note that there is no suggestion of any repetition of the
sacrifice. This doctrine cannot be said to be typical of later
Methodist thinking, though we may note that no one did more to
show the meaning of the death of Christ as a sacrifice, with its
links with the Eucharist, than the Methodist New Testament
scholar Vincent Taylor (1887–1968).

   This brings us to the fifth major emphasis – *the sacrifice of our
persons*. Taylor states that 'the supper is a means whereby his
disciples may participate in the power of the self-offering . . . theology, therefore, does not build on an uncertain foundation
when it finds in the Eucharist a permanent means whereby, we
may participate in the self-offering of Christ'.[37]

   The last section of the hymns for the Lord's Supper is headed
'After the Sacrament'. We can link this with the Wesleys' conception of the Communion as a 'converting ordinance'. The
Wesleys' mother, Susanna, professed conversion at the Lord's
Table. 'While my son, Hall, was pronouncing the words "The
body of the Lord Jesus Christ which was given for Thee" . . . the
words struck at my heart and I know that God for Christ's sake
had forgiven me and all my sins.'[38]

   The evangelical experience and the sacrament are bound
together. This is an insight that Methodists might hope to
recover and share with other traditions. If preaching is to 'offer
Christ' and offer ourselves to him

'Tis worth living for this
To administer bliss
And salvation in Jesus's Name.

HP 664. BE 7, no. 221

We might add here, as a Methodist note or motif strongly evoked in the Wesley corpus, the stress on communion as fellowship, symbolized by the ways in which communicants go up to the Lord's Table in groups and are dismissed in groups, a custom whose origin is a mystery.

One with the living bread divine
Which now by faith we eat
Our hearts and minds and spirits join,
And all in Jesus meet.

*HP 609. Hymns on the
Lord's Supper, 1745*

Charles Wesley wrote too many hymns. Some are simply 'the mere versification of Evangelical commonplace',[39] but enough rise from the commonplace to become genuine mystical poetry. Hymns were written for every conceivable aspect of human life – there were also many secular poems, too, including one celebrating the victory of his cat over the 'tom' next door.[40] He had hymns for 'taking one's medicine', or 'sending a child to a boarding school', 'for a sick child', 'for a persecuting husband'.
   The Methodist waking in the morning could sing:

Christ whose glory fills the skies
Christ the true, the only light
Sun of righteousness arise
Triumph o'er the shades of night.

*HP 457. Hymns and
Sacred Poems, 1740*

As he set off to the fields, or the mill, he could sing:

> Forth in thy name, O Lord, I go
> My daily labour to pursue
> Thee only thee resolved to know
> In all I think, or speak, or do

> *HP* 381. *BE* 7, no. 315

At night, she can quietly sing:

> But lo, a place he has prepared
> For me, whom watchful angels keep;
> Yea, he himself becomes my guard
> He smooths my bed and gives me sleep.

> *HP* 562. *BE* 7, no. 218

There is an appropriate hymn for a birthday (*HP* 664) and a wedding hymn which had a burst of popularity in Methodist circles recently:

> Thou God of truth and love
> We seek thy perfect way . . .
> Didst thou not make us one,
> That we might one remain . . .

> *HP* 374. *BE* 7, no. 496

John Wesley's life was not without unhappy love affairs. His marriage was most unfortunate, as we have seen. Charles was much more fortunate. His marriage was singularly happy. The 'musical Wesleys'[41] were a notable household, first in Bristol, then in London, even if the boys were a worry to their Uncle John, especially when one of then – Samuel – became a Roman Catholic for a time!

Finally, there are the hymns on the Communion of Saints; some judge the following to be one of the greatest hymns on this theme.

> Come, let us join our friends above
> That have obtained the prize,
> And on the eagle wings of love
> To joys celestial rise:

Let all the saints terrestrial sing
With those to glory gone:
For all the servants of our King,
In earth and heaven, are one.

HP 812. *Funeral Hymns,*
2nd series, 1759

One family we dwell in him.
One church, above, beneath,
Though now divided by the stream
The narrow stream of death.

Wesley's hymns often begin in heaven, descend to earth and ascend again to the heights.

We have tried, at the risk of romanticism, to give a contextual approach to the Wesley corpus. One could seek to place and assess Charles Wesley as poet, as interpreter of the Authorized Version of the Bible – with allusions now often lost on modern congregations. We must not forget John Wesley's translation from the German, his own hymns and his careful editing of his brother's work, which almost produces a corporate Wesley. They can be claimed to be the greatest body of devotional verse in the English language, an extraordinary, probably unique, partnership of brothers. Or as John Wesley put it in 1780, 'When poetry thus keeps its place as the handmaid of piety – it shall attain not a poor perishable wreath but a crown that fadeth not away.'[42]

In the next century, Methodist chapels developed a musical tradition which involved not only congregational singing but amateur choirs and choral societies of distinction, part of the way in which leisure and spirituality blended together remarkably well. The performance of the *Messiah* or Mendelssohn's *Elijah* would be a great date in chapel life, far different from the rather austere approach to music of John Wesley. In the twentieth century the Wesley corpus has become progressively smaller in official hymn books and less used in worship as new musical and devotional styles appeal to a new generation.

4

John Wesley – Folk Theologian: The Religion of the Heart and its Consequences

John Wesley as theologian has been subject to very varied opinions. William Warburton (1689–1779), bishop of Gloucester, a notable contemporary, writer on the relations of church and state, said of him and Ignatius Loyola, 'Where the two talents of Fraud and Fanaticism unite to furnish out the leader of a sect great will be the success of his undertakings.'[1] If a liberal feared 'enthusiasm', a Neo-Calvinist Augustus Montague Toplady (1740–78) – remembered for the hymn 'Rock of Ages' – called him 'a mean and puny tadpole in divinity'. He accused him, not untruthfully, of plagiarism as well as theological and political incompetence.[2] In later Methodism, Wesley did not dominate theologians unduly. Moving into the next generation, the most notable English Methodist theologian, Richard Watson (1781–1833) in his *Theological Institutes* has few direct references to Wesley, though he was in the genuine Arminian tradition. Later William Burt Pope (1822–93) in the important *Compendium of Christian Theology* (2nd edn 1880) analyses Wesley with reference primarily to his doctrine of holiness. His stance can be called evangelical Catholicism.

In the Thirties of the twentieth century, Henry Bett[3] of Handsworth College, Birmingham, following Herbert Workman and George Eayrs, all historians, maintained that in the priority Wesley gave to experience in Christian theology and in Methodist tradition, he carried the Reformation to its logical conclusion. 'The religious contribution of Methodism was the recovery of the evangelical witness and the evangelical experience.' Its theological contribution can be see in its assertion of the offer of grace to all and its doctrine of holiness – limitless grace and limitless love are thus the keys to Methodist theology. Bett clearly saw Wesley as the precursor of Schleiermacher, whose stress on the experiential was very much in vogue in the era of William James's *Varieties of Religious Experience* (1902). This emphasis on an individualist style of self-fulfilment is in vogue again in a post-modernist age, which as easily denigrates the Enlightenment as some Enlightenment thinkers denigrated Wesley as an 'enthusiast'. Certainly personal experience is at the heart of much spirituality as another century begins. 'Theology infused with a personal experience of God's grace – this is Wesleyanism' is a fair summary.

Wesley clearly gave priority to Scripture over experience. But tradition – especially the early church and the Church of England – were also vital factors in Wesley's stance. Scripture is 'the centre of gravity of his thinking' as G. C. Cell put it.[4] Cell was seeking to restore Wesley to the heart of the Reformation tradition. Wesley's theology is illumined by the whole tradition of Christianity, but more especially the Fathers and the Anglican Reformers, often ignored or thought outdated by leading eighteenth-century churchmen. As Jean Orcibal has forcefully argued, the Catholic tradition influenced Wesley in its French manifestations. Pascal was an early influence, with de Renty, Mme Guyon and the Mexican Gregory Lopez, a curious mixture. Tradition is confirmed by the disciplined use of reason and verified in personal experience, which Wesley observed and analysed in his followers. In the 1970s in American scholarship, Wesley was aligned with liberation theology, which was not wholly bizarre when one analyses the anti-slavery campaign. More recently, and trenchantly, by Theodore Runyon, he is linked with human and women's rights, ecumenism, concern for the environment, and passionate concern for the poor.[5] It is natural that this should be so in an attempt to establish a 'Wesleyan' theological tradition, avoiding antiquarianism. The danger is that Wesley is torn out of his context and made into a rather tiresome theological 'icon'. He was not an Augustine, Aquinas or Calvin but rather, as Albert Outler insisted, a folk theologian seeking to offer 'plain truth for plain people'. He was a theologian whose balance and stance could still be relevant while the details must be seen as very much part of the eighteenth-century scene. Despite recent attempts to show a systematic element in Wesley, we need to remember that he had to work out his theology, sometimes literally, on the hoof, and in dialogue by letter and pamphlet with friend and foe. He changed his mind too, and his style. Somewhat ironically Ronald Knox said, 'altogether he is not a good advertisement for reading on horseback'. Much of his written work was also, Knox observed, 'simply condensation' and summarizing, with *The Christian Library*[6] as the supreme example.

The summaries were never without Wesley's particular 'spin'. Rowan Williams[7] has recently written of theology as celebratory, communicative and critical. This can be applied to the Wesley brothers, as can Karl Barth's 'irregular dogmatics', by which he meant a theological style near to the preaching of the gospel. The commentary, the sermon and, in the Methodist case, the hymn are styles of 'irregular dogmatics' and celebratory theology. It is typical of Wesley's pragmatism that *Notes on the New Testament* and a collection of sermons formed the 'standards' of what the first generation of Methodists called, with a touch of sectarianism, 'our doctrines' alongside 'our hymns' and 'our discipline'.

One common, though twentieth-century, way of setting out Wesley's stance has been called the 'Four Alls'. It derives from William B. Fitzgerald in 1903.[8] They provided a useful framework even if there is no specific reference to vital matters like the incarnation, the church, the sacraments and social responsibility. The 'Four Alls', with a fifth added by George Eayrs in 1909, reaffirmed by W. E. Sangster in 1951, are: (1) All need to be saved; (2) All can be saved; (3) All can know they are saved; (4) All can be saved to the uttermost; (5) All must be witnesses to their salvation. It would be more contextual, while keeping the 'All' at the back of our minds, for it was vital to the Wesleys, to follow Gordon Rupp[9] in stating that there were three ways of looking at humanity in the eighteenth century.

First, the *optimism of nature* – the Enlightenment view that humanity was fundamentally good. Given the proper use of reason and education there was nothing humanity could not do. The idea of progress, and utopianism, were made much less attractive in later eras of violence. Second, the *pessimism of grace* – the Calvinist view that humanity was fundamentally evil but God's grace, which was elective and of which preaching was a means, would save some. Third, there is the *optimism of grace*. There is no limit, given the conditions of a fallen world, to what God can do with the human heart. Holiness, happiness and the transformation of the human heart and society are possible. Rupp went on to see Wesley's basic doctrines – justification by faith, the new birth, the witness of the spirit and perfect love – as not so much successive, but more like concentric circles at the heart of which is God – Father, Son and Holy Spirit. The four doctrines are like the instruments of a quartet, the melodies of which support and interpenetrate one another. So we begin with justification by faith in the context of what Wesley saw as God's universal love. This is where Wesley ran full tilt at the Neo-Calvinist doctrine of double predestination. Like Calvin, Wesley was in the mainstream Reformation tradition. He was in no doubt about humankind's sinful state. 'Wherein may we come to the very edge of Calvinism? In denying all natural free will and power antecedent to grace . . . but God will grant that grace to all'[10] (1745).

That last sentence is the essence of the Five Articles of the Dutch Remonstrance of 1610. The Arminians stated that the atonement was intended to be available to all, that people were incapable of saving faith without the Holy Spirit, that divine grace is indispensable for salvation but not irresistible, and that it is not certain that all believers will persevere to the end.[11] Humankind is dependent on grace yet is still free. Wesley imbibed his Arminianism indirectly, not least from his family and local Lincolnshire traditions as well as the Caroline stream of Anglicanism and the Cambridge Platonists. This made him, with others like John Fletcher and the Baptist Dan Taylor, distinctive in the Evangelical Revival. 'A rich man', said Arminius, 'bestows on a poor and famishing beggar alms by which he may be able to maintain himself and his family. Does it cease to be pure gift because the beggar stretches out his hand to receive it?'[12] This maintains the stress on grace, while affirming free will.

Wesley insisted on the total depravity of humanity due to the Fall. The Fall was 'cosmic' before the subsequent fall of Eve and Adam. In the pre-fall cosmos there were, he believed, no earthquakes or volcanoes! This needs some elaboration as it may seem bizarre now. A scientist who is a Christian, Dr Arthur Peacocke, can say, 'There is no sense in which we can talk of a "Fall" from a past perfection. There was no golden age, no perfect past, no original perfect individual "Adam" or "Eve" from whom all human beings have descended and declined. What is true is that humanity manifests aspirations to a perfection not yet attained, a potentiality not yet actualised but no original righteousness. Sin which is real, is about falling short of what God intends us to be and is concomitant with our possession of self-consciousness, freedom and intellectual curiosity. Classical conceptions of the Fall and sin that dominate Christian theologies of redemption urgently need reinterpretation if they are to make any sense to our contemporaries.'[13] It has often been stated that evangelical theology grounded the doctrine of salvation on sin rather than the other way round. F. D. Maurice[14] stated that Wesley made the sinful human being and not the God of all grace the foundation of Christian theology: 'the Fall is commonly regarded as the foundation, the Incarnation and Death of our Lord as provisions against the effect of it'. Maurice would rather begin with Christ than the Fall, a viewpoint picked up by John Scott Lidgett (1854–1953), who clearly began his theology not with the Fall but with the Fatherhood of God. He believed he was in the genuine Wesleyan tradition.

It is clear that Wesley began his picture of humanity not with the fallen Adam but with Adam before the Fall. Wesley pictures Adam in the light of Christ. As D. T. Niles,[15] the Sri Lankan Methodist, has it 'We must know Adam if we are to know the man in Christ Jesus but we can only know Adam when we know Christ.' Adam is made in the image of God naturally (i.e. he has freedom of will), morally (he has perfect love) and politically (he has the right and power to rule the earth). From this happy state Adam falls by misuse of free will, becoming totally corrupt. This corruption affects the whole of human nature. Here Wesley is in the mainstream of not only Reformed but Catholic thinking, going back to Augustine. If we think this is now hopelessly out-moded pre-Darwinian mythology, we can find modern models of alienation.

The historian Sir Herbert Butterfield, writing after the Second World War, could avow that 'What history does is rather to uncover man's universal sin . . . It is essential not to have faith in human nature. Such faith is a recent heresy and a very disastrous one . . . those who do not believe in the doctrine of the Fall hardly deny that human history has always been under the terms and conditions of the Fall.' Alexander Solzhenitsyn[16] in his Nobel Peace Prize speech could say: 'The same old primitive urges rend and plunder our world – greed, envy, licence, malevolence, though now they adopt euphemistic pseudonyms as they go, such as class struggle, racial struggle, the struggle of the masses, the struggle of organised labour and there is the naive confidence of these young people who don't know life – we'll chuck out this crop of cruel venal oppressive rulers and the next lot – that's us – we'll be just and understanding once we've laid aside bombs and guns.' Wesley, Marx, Butterfield, Solzhenitsyn saw humanity as victim as well as responsible being possessing self-consciousness, intellect and freedom. Wesley's dark view is balanced by his view of what humanity could be. Total sin is always seen against a background of total grace.

> Thy undistinguishing regard
> Was cast on Adam's fallen race;
> For all thou has in Christ prepared
> Sufficient, sovereign, saving grace.
>
> *HP* 520

This is the beginning of the healing, the new creation which is salvation. It begins with what Wesley called 'preventing' or prevenient grace operating in all and producing its first fruits – conscience, reason and law. The evangelist in Wesley made clear that his preachers must not neglect to preach the law. Wesley is clearly looking forward and back from his view of humanity as capable of being made whole by grace. He tried to reconcile the Protestant assertion of being declared right with God by faith through grace alone, with the abandonment of the position that God predestines only some to salvation, others to damnation. We have called this 'an optimism of grace'. It is significant that some leading eighteenth-century evangelists like John Newton (1725–1806), who knew the reality of 'Amazing Grace', and Charles Simeon, became very moderate in their statement of a Calvinist position. This is the 'Calvinism of the heart'. All agreed that salvation was by grace through Christ. So Charles Simeon in 1787 said there was far more agreement than difference and 'he must put his dagger away'.[17] Maybe, as Ronald Knox has it, they were trying to 'make a molehill out of a mountain'. In our day, Karl Barth, and more recently, Geoffrey Wainwright[18] have wrestled with the old differences. One can on the other hand recall that the historian Sir Lewis Namier, when moving from Judaism to Christianity, found considerable common sense in Calvin's position.

For a time, after the ambiguous *Minutes* of the Conference of 1770, Wesley's position was grossly misunderstood.[19] His viewpoint infuriated the more extreme Anglo-Calvinists like Rowland Hill and A. M. Toplady.[20] The latter pointed to the Calvinist elements in the Elizabethan version of the Thirty Nine Articles (1571), which Wesley interpreted in an Arminian direction. Toplady, fearing antinomianism, ignored Wesley's stress on the preaching of the law, with tremendous stress in his *Standard Sermons* on the Sermon on the Mount. Why bother about the law at all? Why not be a happy sinner? Unfortunately there were Methodists at whom fingers could be pointed. The Wesleyan stress has always been on the universality of grace.

The morning breaks, the shadows flee
Pure universal love thou art.
Thy nature and thy name is love.

HP 434

Geoffrey Nuttall points to the renewal of Calvinism in Europe in the twentieth century but adds that a revival of Arminianism is difficult to imagine, because, since Wesley, we are Arminians whether we know it or not. Nuttall sees Arminianism as leading naturally and properly to a theology of mission to the unbeliever. The 'Arminianism of the heart' could not be other than christocentric, missionary and evangelical. This could be unfair to the moderate Calvinists like John Newton.

Let us now be clear what justification meant to Wesley. He did not divert from it despite many changes in his theology. Justification is being put right by God and with God on the grounds of grace and on the condition of the gift of faith, freely received. It is forgiveness. It is a change of status before God. We are accepted as we are, not through merit or good works. It is freedom from servile fear, paralleled by change in us which is the beginning of the new creation and the beginning of the anticipation of the final judgement.

It is highly significant that at the beginning of the twenty-first century, the Vatican and the Lutheran churches have agreed on the nature of justification in a way which might have rejoiced Wesley. Hans Küng claimed in an early book that his view of justification was very near to that of Karl Barth, pointing to a recent remarkable synthesis of views. An ecumenical commission representing Roman Catholics and Anglicans agreed on a definition of salvation. 'The will of God, Father, Son and Holy Spirit is to reconcile to himself all that he has created and sustains, to set free the creation from its bondage to decay and to draw all humanity into communion with himself . . . through Christ's life, death and resurrection the mystery of God's love is revealed, we are saved from the powers of evil, sin and death and we receive a share in the life of God. All this is pure, unmerited gift. The Spirit of God is poured into the hearts of believers – the spirit of adoption who makes sons and daughters of God.'[21] What this means in terms of 'political' reality is another matter. In our day, can this 'Arminianism of the heart' withstand the impact not only of the reality of God in other religions and the almost total collapse of belief in hell in the mainstream Christian traditions? The first was over the horizon for Wesley. Had not Dryden written of those who

> With Socrates may see their Maker's face
> While thousand rubric martyrs want a place.

Wesley was not totally unconcerned by other faiths. Fontenelle (1657–1757) was read by him. His *Entretiens sur la Pluralité des Mondes* opened up new worlds in subtle ways. Wesley did not really come to terms with the *philosophes* of the Enlightenment or the view expressed by Lessing (1729–81) in his play *Nathan der Weise* (1779), with its clear assertion of the plurality of religions, all seeking the light. Charles Wesley portrayed Islam and the Turks in an appalling light as late as 1780. Hell, though not over-stressed by Wesley,[22] was clearly part of the apparatus and belief of the folk theologian, but one must not underestimate his doctrine of prevenient grace and use of natural theology. Certainly we can say that the generous side of Wesley's Arminianism has been taken up seriously. The danger now could be an often 'politically correct' universalism, with judgement draining away. The point is made pungently by the historian Michael Watts, who sees in the decline of the preaching of hell one cause of the church's decline in the nineteenth century and afterwards.[23]

The second basic doctrine is the necessity of a personal faith expressed as new birth and assurance. Here is the vision of a young woman in Manchester in 1748.[24] 'I was sitting in the house, while one read the passion hymns . . . on a sudden I saw our Saviour on the cross as plain as if it had been with my bodily eyes and felt it was my sins for which he died. I cried out and had no strength left in me – I could do nothing but weep and mourn day and night. This lasted till Monday in the afternoon.

Then I saw as it were, heaven open and God sitting upon his throne in the midst of the ten thousands of his saints and I saw a large book in which my sins were written and he blotted them out and my heart was filled, with peace and joy and love which I have never lost to this hour.' Like Paul and Luther before him, Wesley put his stress on faith – sure trust in God on the human side, acceptance, pardon, even after a struggle, on God's side, with no merit whatsoever by good deeds, although they must follow. This is what Wesley meant when he said he had exchanged the 'faith of a servant' doing all he could for God for the 'faith of a son' accepting what God had done for him.[25] This is faith as hope but it is also faith as assurance, an assurance that we are pardoned by God. The assurance is not that we hope to be forgiven, but that we *are* forgiven as that woman from Manchester felt. This is an assurance of pardon and of relationship with God the Father, never an assurance that we are worthy. It is the work of the Holy Spirit with the centrality of the eighth chapter of Paul's Letter to the Romans in Wesley's thought and preaching.

Here was a point where there were lurking dangers parallel with the break of Wesley with the Moravians, who could not follow him in a quest for perfection. There is a danger of subjectivism and the self-conscious style of religiosity which can seem arrogant and complacent. Wesley's rather liberal opponents found this alienating. Some early Anglican evangelicals had the same reservations. For some time Wesley and his preachers asserted that unless a person had a conscious assurance of salvation, he or she was simply not pardoned by God at all. He came to see the extravagance of this position, which is possibly why he hardly ever refers directly to the 'experience' of 24 May 1738. Melville Horne (John Fletcher's successor) recalls a conversation later in Wesley's life. ' "When fifty years ago my brother Charles and I in the simplicity of our hearts told the good people of England that unless they knew their sins were forgiven, they were under the wrath and curse of God I marvel, Melville, they did not stone us." The Methodists, I hope, know better now. We preach assurance as we always did as a common privilege of the people of God but we do not enforce it under the pain of damnation.'

Curiously, Wesley, whose memory sometimes played strange tricks, seemed to have forgotten they were stoned quite frequently in the early days![26] The point to stress here is the centrality of being put in right relationship with God by grace through faith. He wrote to John Newton in 1765, 'I think on justification just as I have done at any time these seven and twenty years and just as Calvin does . . . In this respect I do not differ from him an hair's breadth.'[27] Right relationships were the heart of the matter. We need also what Theodore Runyon has called 'orthopraxy', a right way of looking at emotion, saving us from arrogance. Runyon[28] states that true assurance must transcend subjectivism. It is not just emotion but evidence expressing itself in a transformed style of living, in social relationships, in the sacraments, in rational behaviour and always looking to the future, the goal of perfect love.

Experience reflects what is found in Scripture and tradition and is expressed in works that extend to others the grace that has been received. John Fletcher was right when he said, 'I build my faith not on my experience, though this increases, but on the revealed truth of God.' Wesley, himself, in the famous *Letter to a Roman Catholic* of 1749, sums it up, 'I believe the infinite and eternal spirit of God, equal with the Father and the Son to be not only perfectly holy in himself but the immediate cause of all holiness in us, enlightening our understanding, rectifying our wills and affections, renewing our natures, uniting our persons to Christ, assuring us of the adoption of sons, leading us in our actions, purifying and sanctifying our souls and bodies, to a full and eternal enjoyment of God.'[29]

In the twentieth century, after the period when 'experience' in William James's sense was central in liberal Protestant theology, Western Protestants tended to starve the emotions, so that a renewal of the 'religion of the heart' was not surprising in the latter half of the century. The only doctrine of assurance which has any firm basis is one rooted in the work of the Holy Spirit pointing us to what God has done. As Martin Luther, who knew what Winston Churchill called the 'black dog' of depression, put it, 'I have been baptized, God has accepted me.'

Wesley said that salvation was like a house[30] – the porch was repentance, the door faith, the house itself was perfect love. So we come to the fourth of the elements in Wesley's doctrine of grace. Wesley was never static in his thinking about the relationship of people with God. Repeatedly he asserted that Christian perfection, what God does in and with people, is the very emphasis of the Methodists. 'This doctrine is the grand depositum which God has lodged with the people called Methodists and for the sake of propagating this chiefly, he appears to have raised us up.'[31] What did Wesley teach? What happened to his doctrine before and after his death? Has it any significance now? What sort of people did it attract?

First, we can briefly survey the sources of Wesley's teaching, presupposing the Bible as the primary source. The Anglican Reformers and behind them Luther and Calvin gave him the necessary undergirding of justification by faith. The Articles and Homilies of the Church of England were 'patient' of an Arminian interpretation. Wesley may have been as disingenuous as John Henry Newman next century, who believed they were 'patient of a Catholic interpretation'. From the Moravians came his clear assertion of the necessity of new birth and the assurance of faith, a stress which prevented Methodism from ever acceding to a conception of escalator-like progress from womb to tomb. From the Anglicanism of the Caroline tradition, especially Jeremy Taylor and later William Law (and also the earlier Thomas à Kempis), came the stress on the Christian life as utter devotion to Christ. The Cambridge Platonists must not be ignored. John Norris (1657–1711) was clearly influential. It was more than 'an inspiring muddle between learning, philosophy and personal piety'. Then come the Eastern Fathers, especially Gregory of Nyssa (330–99), mediated to Wesley through 'Macarius the Egyptian', whose homilies are now known to be those of a fifth-century Syrian monk. Ephrem Syrus (316–73) – 'the man of a broken heart' – gave a vision of perfection as the goal of the Christian life. As Albert Outler has shown, the conception of perfection of the Eastern Fathers as a process rather than a state gave Wesley a spiritual vision rather different from that envisaged in some Roman Catholic spiritual theology. Likewise the tendency to static quietism and the concept of imputed rather than imparted righteousness of Zinzendorf and his friends seemed inadequate. They never moved on to actual change in the human psyche. Thus the ancient and Eastern tradition of holiness as *disciplined* love became fused in Wesley's mind with his own Anglican position of holiness as *aspiring* love producing a distinctive contribution to Christian thinking.[32]

Wesley was concerned with the goal of Christian life, with 'the faith that works by love'. He saw perfection as a process taking as models not only Eastern Fathers but French Catholics like Jean Baptiste de Renty, who had been a pupil of Bérulle, the Oratorian. Outler summarizes Wesley's view of perfection succinctly. 'It is the conscious certainty, *in a present moment*, of the fullness of one's love for God and neighbour, as this love has been initiated and fulfilled by God's gift of faith, hope and love. This is not a state but a dynamic process: saving faith is its beginning; sanctification is it proper climax. As faith is in order to love, love is in order to goodness – and so also goodness is in order to blessedness. This complex pattern of means and ends is designed to unfold in the life process itself and thus requires some sort of temporal interval for its fulfilment.'[33]

Wesley saw the essence of perfection as perfect love for God and neighbour. This rather than any kind of 'sinlessness' is his main emphasis. It is a gift to be received rather than something to be strained after, though Wesley greatly emphasized the means of grace – the sacraments, prayer and Scripture – as factors assisting the end of perfect love. This was to prevent mere 'enthusiasm'.

For the Reformers, perfection is perfection in faith; to Wesley it was an inherent perfection in love and obedience, not sinless perfection. There are still tempers, infirmities and mistakes, as well as constant temptations. Wesley carefully 'hedges his bets'. 'Perfect love means a restless, passionate, heart breaking consuming concern for other people.'[34] It has an interpersonal reference which saved Wesley from too introverted a view of holiness with which some of his later followers may be charged. 'The

Gospel of Christ knows of no religion but social; no holiness, but social holiness.'[35] We can see here a combination of the Pauline and Johannine elements in the New Testament, each stressing the sovereign will of the Father to give the fruits of the spirit of love to his children. Rightly, Wesley could say that he aspired after what every Anglican prayed for in the Collect for Purity in the Book of Common Prayer – 'Cleanse the thoughts of our hearts by the inspiration of thy Holy Spirit that we may perfectly love Thee and worthily magnify Thy holy name.' Wesley's doctrine is clearly part of his rich teaching on the work of the Holy Spirit. His positive emphasis is to stress love, balancing the Reformed stress on faith alone.

Faith is vital throughout – Wesley never departs from the undergirding of *sola gratia, sola fide* (by grace alone, by faith alone). Faith becomes the handmaid of love, the means of which love is the end. It might be said that if the distinctive word of the Reformers is faith and the distinctive word of Catholic spirituality is love, the distinctive word of Wesley is 'faith working by love', the two inextricably bound together. This is a balanced assertion that given the limitations inherent in existence in a body in an imperfect and alienated world, we dare set no limit to what the generosity of God can do for a person here and now.

So the main assertion is that perfection begins with the new birth. It is a real change in a person. Its characteristic is love for God and neighbour, it is 'to have the mind of Christ' in purity of intention. It is both gradual and sudden. It can be realized in a moment but is never on earth complete. It is always a gift by grace through faith, never an achievement. Those who receive it are conscious of it. It is not only given before death but can happen in this life. It can be lost and recovered. It is not sinless perfection and it is undergirded by love – that is, there is a moral change which can be tested by others. Wesley, who stood a little apart here, never claimed it but claimed it for Fletcher and others, perhaps naively. Is the oft-quoted summary by G. C. Cell viable? 'The Wesleyan reconstruction of the Christian ethic was an original and unique synthesis of the Protestant ethic of grace and the Catholic ethic of holiness.'[36]

What were the difficulties in Wesley's doctrine of perfection? Wesley appeared to operate with a confusing doctrine of sin.[37] Besides his stress on original sin, he defines sin as 'a willful transgression of a known law'. This ignores the unconscious drives of human nature. In our post-Freudian days, we know well enough that the worst sins are likely to be those of which people are unconscious. Sin comes in Wesley's view (and in some of Charles's hymns) to be seen almost like a rotten tooth which can be extracted by a celestial dentist. Sin is surely the self in the wrong relationship with God. Can anyone say that he or she is free from sin? Wesley's stress on consciousness of guilt can cause guilt feeling rather than genuine guilt to assume a dominant role, leading to what E. B. Pusey, the Tractarian, called 'salvation by feeling', accusing Methodists of woeful inadequacy at this point.[38]

It is doubtful whether a view of perfection as instantaneous can be sustained or the notion that the 'sanctified' can be conscious of being sanctified. Cannot this encourage a dangerous type of self-appraisal? Does this not set people not at Christ's feet, but as his equals, as P. T. Forsyth claimed?[39] Vincent Taylor,[40] Methodist New Testament scholar, could find no support in New Testament teaching for a sudden or miraculous sanctification. Since Taylor, the 'Baptism of the Spirit' has come into the centre of charismatic thinking, but Professor James Dunn[41] has convincingly shown that this is not the same as Wesley's Christian perfection.

Wesley stressed 'faith working by love', linking holiness, health and wholeness in a way which can be paralleled with recent thinking on group therapy, not irrelevant to Wesley's stress on development through 'bands' and 'classes'. One can derive from the doctrine of Christian perfection a goal for living, the goal of perfect love. In Wesley's teaching, there is an incentive for living through the work of the Holy Spirit which seeks to foster love at all levels of life. We have to ask of any community, which claims to be Christian, if it is producing whole, healthy people or maimed, stunted people.

One new style of thinking, at which we have already hinted, is germane. This is the concept of what has been called the Second

Journey,[42] which follows on the provisional stability of the 'first journey' in childhood, puberty, adolescence and early adulthood with its frequent high endeavour and motivation. Wesley himself, in his utter devotion to Christ, which he later called 'the faith of a servant', is a good example. The 'breaking' process in Georgia leads to the 'Aldersgate experience', with the subsequent energies and spiritual productivity of the 'Second Journey'. For many bereavement, breakup of marriage or a decision which cannot be put off, or loss or change of job, may be factors in the beginning of a Second Journey. Wesley's doctrine of perfection with its combination of process and crisis could be interpreted in the light of this insight into what can happen to people who need a fresh start, although this can be applied to justification by faith also. Methodists in South America and Africa are striving to develop a new style of holiness which is corporate rather than individualistic, stressing justice as well as freedom and peace. The fact that Methodists in the developing nations wish to explore Wesley more deeply gives some hope that the stream has not dried up.

We return to the eighteenth century and the effect of Wesley's style among early Methodists. Wesley clearly believed that Christian holiness as aspiration and experience was for all, not merely spiritual virtuosi. Professor John Kent,[43] in a trenchant analysis, points to Wesley's dilemma. The eighteenth century saw traditional models of holiness under attack. For example, the Jesuits were under constant threat. Was the monastic style played out in Europe? Wesley's originality was to find a 'monastic' mode for those who had to live in the world, normally marry and make money, even if their standard of living was modest. Could the whole style of ascetic holiness be made applicable to ordinary people? Can one be holy in a market economy? This was the dilemma faced by both Wesley and the Catholic Redemptorists under Alfonso de Liguori (1699–1787) in Italy.

Among Wesley's inspired improvisations, as we have seen, was the use of 'shock troops' of 'extraordinary messengers', a youthful army of preachers, who were pledged to obedience to him as 'sons in the Gospel' and to an effective poverty, living off the Methodist people, then given £12 a year after 1752.[44] If possible they were pledged to a chastity which treated family life almost as marginal – a matter which could not last. Bishop Gore was right to bid his ordinands read the *Lives of the Early Methodist Preachers*, for it is a salutary experience. Here are fascinating descriptions of mystic experience, spiritual agonies and ecstasies. Stonemason John Nelson hears Wesley preach, 'He felt his eyes fixed on him, his heart beats like the pendulum of a clock.' Later an onlooker at a riot said, 'I have heard that a cat has nine lives but I think he has nine score.' Pressed into the army, deluged by a churn of milk, scoffing blackberries with Wesley, when a Methodist society forgot to give them dinner, he preached the first Methodist sermon in Halifax on an upturned barrel on 'the Rocks' near King Cross. There was no great intellectual gulf between these men and their hearers. Without them Wesley's Methodism could not have grown. This was typified by John Bennet and William Darney. These men and their wives are the heroes and heroines of early Methodism, though the 'drop out' rate was very high in the first generation. We can learn as much from their journals as we can from Wesley about the life of the early Methodists. Let us take Christopher Hopper (1722–1802) as representative. Of farming stock, a typical lad who worried cats and stoned frogs, his conversion was classical. 'God, angels, heaven, earth and the whole creation appeared to me in a new light . . . I found love to my God, to his yoke, to his cross, to his saints and to his friends and enemies.' He became a class leader and preacher, prepared for rotten eggs, brickbats, stones and cudgels. He became a teacher, a 'half-itinerant' for a time. Marriage followed after his fiancée was converted. In 1749, he became an itinerant. His money had by now run out – and he was one of the New 'Dominicans'.[45]

Hopper's theology was clear and simple. 'I know whom I have believed. I know God's love. I know it by experience . . . I hate sin as by the grace of God I overcame it. I love holiness, the whole mind that was in Christ and I pursue it by all means . . . that I call Bible religion, genuine Christianity and this religion I call mine.' Hopper chaired the Conference in Wesley's absence in 1780 – 'a

poor helpless worm, Superintendent! President! Great words!'
We can only speculate on what he really thought of Wesley's
insensitive (to us), but not untypical letter of condolence on the
death of his first wife in 1755. 'Consider yourself as now more
than ever married to Christ and his dear people, then even for
this kindly-severe disposition you should proclaim him for ever.'
Wesley's compassion seems curiously selective.[46] Wealthy wives
were sometimes sought out by the preachers!

The wives of these men and the many widows and spinsters in
early Methodism, who enabled the early preachers to do their
work, are a fascinating group of women. Frances Pawson is a
good example. Born in York, she was a highly educated young
woman of fashion. After a brief marriage to a Countess of
Huntingdon minister called Wren, she married John Pawson.
She sold her best silk dresses, attiring herself in a sober, Quakerly
but attractive manner. Her journal (much of it written in French)
described the grim Halifax manse 'under the chapel' which she
took over in 1791. Her spiritual dilemmas are of most interest.[47]
She claimed the experience of 'sanctification' in January 1785,
but when bringing up an apparently mentally handicapped niece,
she realized that aspiration was more important than attainment. This very perceptive journal includes descriptions of a
good deal of spiritual reading and correspondence with other
intelligent women like Elizabeth Ritchie, who became Mrs
Mortimer. Both women were somewhat distressed at the actions
of some of the younger revivalists at the time of the Yorkshire
Revival in the 1790s.

The sociology of the early preachers[48] reveals a solid artisan
strain, with tradesmen, small farmers, clerks, schoolteachers,
soldiers and the almost unique Lincolnshire squire, Robert Carr
Brackenbury, an alumnus of St Catharine's College, Cambridge.
Many, though not all, had some Church of England background.
If we are to find Methodist doctrine in action, we must look at
these men and women. Could they be called Franciscan – as
H. B. Workman affirmed? Maybe Dominican would be a wiser
comparison,[49] because of their stress on preaching as well as their
poverty.

Clearly, some could not cope with the harsh conditions. Not many would tolerate the experience of John Furz, who returned from a preaching tour to find his wife lying naked in her bed, having sold her nightgowns to pay for necessities.[50] Nor were all the wives as Quakerly as Frances Pawson. At the beginning of the next century, it was seen that holiness was not incompatible with normal home life. Kingswood School ensured continuity of education for the sons of itinerant preachers but not normally, as yet, the daughters. The sheer energy and *disponibilité*, or willingness to serve anywhere, of the early Wesleyan missionaries is, to our age, breathtaking. If the Fiji missionaries of the 1830s – David Cargill, John Hunt, James Calvert and their incredibly brave if exploited wives, constantly pregnant – are taken as examples, we find an almost unearthly 'optimism of grace' and a discipline equal to that of any Catholic missionary order.[51] If we want to explore adequately the doctrine and practice of 'entire sanctification', we need to look at the writings of Hunt and Calvert, who, when asked on furlough, 'Were you afraid of being killed?' replied simply, 'No we died before we went.' Dietrich Bonhoeffer, in the 1930s, honoured such men and women when he bowed before their names on the Memorial board at Richmond College in London. Maybe the only remote survival of this style of total availability is the fact that Methodist ordinations are associated with the Conference. Ministers are not ordained to a 'title' as in the Church of England, or in response to a 'call' to a pastorate but to the service of the whole church, a unique feature of British Methodism. This style, for all sorts of complex reasons, is becoming an anachronism in the twenty-first century.

The inherent inconsistencies of Wesley's thinking on holiness became evident in Methodism both in the British Isles and in America. One firm line stressed growth in holiness. This picks up a strand of Wesley's theology – the 'non-Moravian' Catholic stress with some of its roots in Counter-Reformation French spirituality and in the Cappadocian Fathers. As Macarius has it, 'It is not off with one coat and on with another.' Richard Watson's *Institutes* fall into place here as does W. B. Pope's

Compendium a generation later. John Scott Lidgett is next in line, picking up ideas from F. D. Maurice featuring filial consciousness and the life of the Spirit extending holiness to include political and social life, which the Congregationalist R. W. Dale[52] rightly saw as an omission in Wesley, despite his passionate concern for the poor. Philanthropy is not the same as a demand for social change. Hugh Price Hughes (1847–1902) combined a deep search for holiness with a passionate political concern, which was typified in his work at the West London Mission which paralleled Scott Lidgett's long years at the Bermondsey Mission and in London politics and education, including the Vice Chancellorship of the University. Neither Pope nor Scott Lidgett ever claimed any personal attainment of sanctification, nor did their successors, like Newton Flew of Wesley House, Cambridge, or the preacher W. E. Sangster (1900–60), who wrote much on holiness,[53] not least while living in an air raid shelter at Central Hall, Westminster. In various ways here are examples of the central Methodist tradition.

There is another line which emerged in the bitter controversy in the 1760s over George Bell and Thomas Maxfield. Here a particular experience is greatly stressed. Theologically this is found in John Fletcher and Adam Clarke (1760–1832), on any account a fine, if occasionally eccentric, scholar, and in the underrated William Arthur (1819–1901), who picked up and fuelled thinking from the United States. His *Tongue of Fire* (1856) is only one of his formative writings. It is intriguing that Arthur seeks what can only be called 'the baptism of the Spirit' without 'tongues' and 'miracles', possibly a reaction from Edward Irving and the Catholic Apostolic Movement. Phoebe Palmer (1807–72) is typical of the existentialist teaching about entire consecration. In British Methodism, this style was classically expressed by Thomas Cook, Principal of Cliff College, which became a centre of holiness teaching in Wesleyanism. He asserted that 'regeneration is holiness begun . . . Entire sanctification is the finishing of that work . . . It is an eradication, the removal of all roots of bitterness, the seeds of sin's disease.' We grasp by faith the sin-consuming power which sweeps 'the heart clean at a stroke'.

Adam Clarke is brought in to assert, 'Believing now, we are pardoned now; believing now, we are cleansed from all sin now.' Cook makes no mention of the means of grace. 'Instead of frittering away our time in contemplation, let us at once resolutely make up our minds that we will have the blessing now.'[54]

Cook's style was taken up by the more subtle Samuel Chadwick[55] (1860–1932), who, while much more broad and 'Catholic' in his sympathies, appears to equate the baptism of the Spirit with sanctification, a matter disputed by Methodists deeply influenced by the charismatic movement. Can we ask which of these is the genuine tradition or are both the consequences of the deep ambiguities in Wesley's definition of sin and his somewhat simplistic interpretations of the experience of the Methodist people? The divergence produced tensions over worship, liturgy, the authority of the ordained ministry, the polarity of order and ardour which can split Methodist and other communities to this day. There is clearly much continuity from Wesley onwards. But one must not assume that all Methodists were exemplars of Wesley's doctrines. The call of the Methodists in the generation after Wesley was for disciplined, simple lives removed from worldly pleasures, centred on home, chapel and work. The duty of hard work, the evils of luxury, the virtues of foresight, thought and moderation often could seem more significant than the pursuit of perfect love. To the non-Methodist such conscientiousness and earnestness could seem narrowing and self-absorbed. Later in Arnold Bennett's novels of the Five Towns one savours an unfair but not altogether outrageous picture of how religion could appear hypocritical. On the other hand James Hope Moulton (1863–1917), of long Methodist ancestry, Fellow of King's College, Cambridge, later Professor at Manchester, still put the emphasis on conversion and holiness. 'We should be forced to drop the name of Wesley if we were unfaithful to that ideal. The doctrine of experience – that for every man the greatest of all reasons for believing is his own power to say "Once I was blind, but now I see." With it stands the doctrine of holiness – the declaration that nothing less than perfect love to God and man can ever satisfy God's claim upon us

... These were the doctrines that Wesley rediscovered and it is on the strength of our unwavering hold on them that we remain Wesleyans today.'[56]

Almost another century later, Professor Geoffrey Wainwright, a leading Methodist theologian and ecumenist, has summarized Wesley's contribution to Christian theology. 'Allowing for the lapse of two hundred years, there is a close correspondence between the classic ecumenical movement and the profile of John Wesley that informed Methodists and others would recognize. Wesley's vision, program and praxis were marked by the following six principal features. First, he looked to the *Scriptures* as the primary and abiding testimony to the redemptive work of God in Christ, second, he was utterly committed to the ministry of *evangelism* where the Gospel was to be preached to every creature and needed only to be accepted in faith. Third, he valued with respect to the Christian Tradition and the doctrine of the church a *generous orthodoxy*, wherein theological opinions might vary so long as they were consistent with the apostolic tradition. Fourth, he expected *sanctification* to show itself in the moral earnestness and loving deeds of the believers. Fifth, he manifested and encouraged a *social concern* that was directed towards the neediest of neighbours. Sixth, he found in the *Lord's Supper* a sacramental sign of the fellowship graciously bestowed by the Triune God and the responsive sacrifice of praise and thanksgiving on the part of those who will glorify God and enjoy him for ever. Those are the features which must be strengthened in contemporary Methodism, if we are to maintain our historic identity, speak with a significant voice on the ecumenical scene and keep on a recognizable Christian track as the paths diverge.'[57]

Other traditions, of course, also stress the key role of holiness. Here is Cardinal Basil Hume: 'And I set before you today a sincere appeal. Listen to the call of the Holy Spirit. The call today is clear. It is the call to holiness – to be first rate in all we do and not second rate. We are called to be fully human – and dare we say it, more than human, for we are called to share in the very life of God, through the mystery of Christ's redeeming action. Here lies the secret. It is to recognize that God loves each of us and that the strength of his love makes us bigger than we know ourselves to be, makes us Christ-like. It is a call to each of us as Christians. May we respond together in total generosity? That is a sentiment to which Wesley who preached on the *Catholic Spirit* could only say Amen.'[58]

5

The Church of England and John Wesley

How does John Wesley appear from an Anglican perspective? Here is Norman Sykes: 'It is more difficult to place the greatest figure of eighteenth century religion in England, John Wesley, in a history of ecumenical tendencies. For although he touched religious life at many points, both in this country and in the New World, and although it was his proud claim that the world was his parish, yet the principal result of his missionary labours was the foundation of a new Society and the addition thereby of another to the divided members of Christ's Catholic Church . . . in his conviction of the identity of the New Testament bishop and presbyter John Wesley was in accord with a considerable volume of opinion in his own century; but his action in ordaining ministers instead of breaking down the barriers between his Societies and the Established Church served rather to increase their numbers and height. Thus the greatest religious figure of his age contributed more perhaps to the accentuating than to the healing of the divisions of the universal Church.'[1]

This parallels the nineteenth-century Wesleyan, Dr Joseph Beaumont, who saw Wesley like a strong and skilful rower who looked one way while every stroke of his oar took him in the opposite direction.[2] To the end of his ministry Wesley affirmed his affection and allegiance to the church, which never officially repudiated him, an action which might not have been easy since the Convocations were then not meeting. Thus in March 1787, he said: 'I still think when the Methodists leave the Church of

England, God will leave them. Every year more of the clergy are convinced of the truth and grow well attested towards us. It would be contrary to all commonsense as well as good conscience to make a separation now.'[3] To Henry Moore in 1788, he could say: 'I am a Church of England man and as I said fifty years ago, so I say still, in the Church of England, I will live and die unless I am thrust out.'[4] In 1789 he still calls the Church of England 'the most scriptural National Church in the World'.[5] In opposition to those who sought separation, 'I declare once more that I live and die a member of the Church of England and that none who regard my judgment and advice will ever separate from it.' This was the year in which he ordained three men to serve as presbyters in England, a pointer to what Wesley surely saw as an inevitable separation, even if the whole matter was highly ambiguous. He lived and died 'a hearty but inconsistent churchman'.[6]

We must begin by looking at motivation, after what we have called his 'Second Journey'. The letter in which he claimed to look upon all the world as his parish gives a clear statement of principle. 'If by Catholic principles you mean any other than scriptural, they weigh nothing with me. I allow no rule, whether of faith or practice than the Holy Scripture but on scriptural principle I do not think it hard to justify whatever I do. Scripture commands me according to my power to instruct the ignorant, reform the wicked, confirm the virtuous. Man forbids me to do this in another's parish that is in effect not to do it at all; seeing I have no parish of my own, nor probably ever shall.'[7] Wesley's view of church order is here in embryo. It is to be seen in terms of mission, witness and nurture. The interview with Bishop Joseph Butler illustrates the point. Was a theology fundamentally concerned with order compatible with a theology motivated by mission to those with whom the church was not at that time in real contact, like the miners of Kingswood and the North-East?

The mission of Wesley led to the creation of a 'Connexion', a phenomenon of ecclesiastical order, which was neither sect nor denomination. Russell Richey, an American historian, elaborates this point. 'Connexionalism is a distinctive and multi-faceted

ecclesiastical vision including spirituality, unity, mission, gover-
nance and fellowship symbolized most vividly in an itinerant
clergy sent where most needed. It implies a covenantal commitment of faithfulness to God and accountability to the community
of faith, reflected in proportional financial support for shared
ministry. It "connected" the Gospel with need – a practical
experimental style of theology.[8] By 1749 the 'skeleton' of Wesley's
connexion (his was not the only one of course) was already a
factor in English religious life, even if all Richey's points were not
yet in place. Some, like itinerancy, can be romanticized. The
policy of unlimited mission led in the end to the creation of new
fellowships and societies outside the parish system, the erection
or purchase of separate buildings, beginning with the 'Foundery'
in London, the 'New Room' in Bristol, the Orphan House in
Newcastle upon Tyne for worship, the meeting of the societies,
and philanthropy. Inevitably there followed the appointment of
officers in the societies such as stewards, class leaders (men and
women) local preachers and 'exhorters', with the itinerant
preachers rapidly forming a highly mobile order, the regulation
of Methodist preaching places as dissenting places of worship,
the setting up of the legal court of Conference and legal devices
to secure continuity. These were typified by the *Model Deed* of
1763, for property, and the *Deed of Declaration* of 1784, legal-
izing the Conference for the time after Wesley's death. These followed the provision of a church constitution for the Methodists
of the newly created United States of America with the provision
of a revised Prayer Book for America, the colonies and Great
Britain. Ordination of ministers for America, the colonies and
later for Scotland and England followed.

The development of this complex system begins in the relationship of the Methodist societies with the religious societies
which were still extant in the 1740s. One fact of this matter
needs stressing: the relationship between the Methodist societies
and the parish. John Wesley's societies, unlike those of Horneck,
Woodward or Samuel Wesley in earlier days, were never under
episcopal or parochial supervision. Neither the authorities nor
Wesley sought it, so it is not an exaggeration to state that the

principal cause of the schism was the pattern of the 'Wesleyan' societies. In the eighteenth century the society and connexional nature of Wesley's system made the final separation inevitable.

The relationship and correspondence of John Wesley with early evangelicals like Samuel Walker (1714–61) of Truro and Thomas Adam (1701–84) of Wintringham in Cambridgeshire illustrate the dilemma for both the sympathetic local parson and Wesley himself. Walker ran his own evangelical parish society. He begged Wesley several times to abandon extra-parochial itinerancy and societies outside the care of the parish minister, considering them a serious breach of church order. Wesley's position on this never changed.

'At present, I apprehend those and those only, to separate from the church who either renounce her fundamental doctrines or refuse to join in her public worship. As yet we have done neither; nor have we taken one step farther than we were convinced was our bounden duty. It is from a full conviction of this that we have preached abroad, prayed extempore, formed societies and permitted preachers who were not episcopally ordained. And were we pushed on this side, were there no alternative allowed, we should judge it our bounden duty rather wholly to separate from the church than to give up any of these points. Therefore, if we cannot stop a separation without stopping lay preachers, the case is perfectly clear – we cannot separate at all.'[9] Wesley was perfectly aware of the departure from recognized churchmanship – irritating difficulties hindered the work of a wholly parochial Anglican like Charles Simeon at Holy Trinity, Cambridge, until the Act of 1812 (largely engineered by the Wesleyan lawyer Thomas Allan) granted freedom from the 1670 Conventicle Act (22 Car II. c.1) which had haunted Wesley.

Much confusion concerning Wesley's position can be avoided if it is made clear what constituted separation from the Church of England for him. A conference statement of 1760[10] in the usual form of question and answer makes it clear:

Q. Are we dissenters?

A. We are *irregular*.

1 By calling sinners to repentance in all places of God's dominion.
2 By frequently using extempore prayer. Yet we are not dissenters in the only sense which our laws acknowledge, namely persons who believe that it is sinful to attend the service of the church for we do attend it at all opportunities. We will not, dare not, separate from the church for the reasons given several years ago. We are not seceders, nor do we bear any resemblance to them.

At the Conference of 1755 and notably in *The Reasons Against Separation from the Church of England* (1758),[11] Wesley repeated the 'not expedient' argument. To Adam he wrote in October 1755, 'We will not go unless we are thrust out.'[12] He would not stop lay preaching: 'soul damning clergymen lay me under more difficulty than soul saving lay men'.[13] Separation was narrowly averted, when some lay preachers began to preside at Holy Communion, which horrified Charles Wesley and was forbidden by the Conference.

One cannot doubt Wesley's loyalty to the church, but his doctrine of the church needs to be clarified. It is summed up in a letter to Charles Wesley[14] in August 1785. 'What is the Church of England? It is not all the people of England. Papists and dissenters, are no part thereof. Then we should have a glorious church indeed. No, according to our Twentieth Article, a particular church is a congregation of faithful people . . . among whom the word of God is preached and the sacraments duly administered.' Here is a logical definition containing both the essence and the properties of a church, which are faith, evangelism and nurture. Wesley was sure of his loyalty to the 'Catholic Church, the whole body of men endured with faith, working by love, dispersed over the whole earth'.

There was a long tradition – not liked much by Anglicans – of what the Presbyterian Edmund Calamy called 'charity to the church', that is occasional reception of Holy Communion at the parish church. Methodists for a century acted upon it when appropriate, worshipping at the parish church as well as 'chapel'.

There were 90 meeting houses by 1769. It is not difficult to find evidence of large numbers of Methodists attending their parish church well into the nineteenth century in Manchester and Bradford. As late as 1821 the vicar of Bridgwater in Devon said of the Methodists of his parish, 'they all attend church as the House of God, and more regularly than those who have no such meetings'.[15] The first Mayor of Wolverhampton in 1848 attended church in the morning, chapel at night. Frances Knight has recently shown this to be common up to 1870 with mutual benefit. Methodists still celebrated 'rites of passage' in the parish church long after that.

On the other hand, loyalty to the church was often flung in the Methodists' face. Clearly, too, pockets of dissent which were swept into Wesley's connexion cared little for the established church. It is important to remember that the popular style of Methodism was never as 'Wesleyan' as Wesley may have hoped. Wesley himself could be deeply critical of the clergy and would avow, 'What is the end of ecclesiastical order? Is it not to bring souls from the power of Satan to God and to build them up in his fear and love? Order then is so far valuable as it answers these ends, and if it answers them not, it is nothing worth.'[16]

The Church of England has three attitudes to dissent, historically: repression as in the time of Charles II, comprehension attempted in 1688–9, and toleration after 1689, but the toleration implied loyalty. Wesley was plagued by the Caroline legislation all his ministry from the day he asked Bishop Gibson,[17] 'Are the religious societies conventicles?' to correspondence with William Wilberforce and Pretyman-Tomline, Bishop of Lincoln. 'Now sir,' he writes to Wilberforce, 'What are the Methodists to do? They are liable to be ruined by the Conventicle Act and yet they have no relief from the Act of Toleration. If this is not oppressive, what is? . . . If you will speak a word to Pitt upon this matter, you will oblige.' He begs the bishop to remember that Methodists in general are members of the Church of England. 'They hold all her doctrines, attend her services and partake of the sacraments. Do you ask "Who drives them out of the Church?" Your Lordship does . . . they desire a licence to worship

God after their own conscience. Your Lordship refuses it and punishes them for not having a licence. So your Lordship leaves them only this alternative – leave the church or starve . . . O my Lord, for God's sake, for Christ's sake, for pity's sake, suffer the poor people to enjoy their religious as well as civil liberty.'[18]

Wesley himself sought a subtle means of evading this dilemma but his followers had soon to take action to protect their property from mob violence. Only by registering buildings under the Toleration Act could exemption be claimed from the Conventicle Act and the protection of the Riot Act of 1715 be evoked. As far as we know the first occasion on which a request for the registration of a Methodist Meeting House in England occurred was in 1748, when the New Room at Bristol was registered as a Protestant meeting house.[19] In 1759 there was a registration at the Archdeacon's Court at Lincolnshire of a Methodist preaching place as a meeting place for dissenters. The itinerant preacher George Tizard described himself as the minister of a congregation, claiming the full privilege of a dissenting minister.[20] The first known example of a preacher's licence taken out by one of Wesley's preachers is dated 11 January 1758.[21] Action of this kind alarmed Charles Wesley and William Grimshaw, who threatened to sever his links with the connexion. Indeed in 1760 separation was only narrowly averted. Wesley sought to call his buildings plain 'preaching houses' and the preacher was to call himself 'Methodist'. but the magistrates, many of whom were clergymen, were not deceived. The Court of King's Bench in 1766 compelled the Justices of Derby to register the Methodists, but the judgement contained the warning that if the persons using a registered meeting house did not bring themselves under the Toleration Act[22] by taking the necessary oaths, they could not be protected by the law.

An example of what could happen is seen in a letter to Thomas Adam in 1768. Adam implied that the Methodists had become dissenters. Wesley instanced Thomas Adams, who was asked: 'Mr. Adams, are you not of the Church of England? Why then do you desire a licence?' He answered, 'Sir, I am of the Church of England, yet I desire a licence that I may legally defend myself from the illegal violence of oppressive men.'[23] The next year there were still only ninety 'chapels' but by 1784 there were three hundred. Was Methodism to go the way of the Countess of Huntingdon, who reluctantly set up her own connexion after the enforced registration of the Spa Fields Chapel in 1781? It is significant that after Roman Catholics were allowed to maintain meeting houses, they had the same problems over the registration of buildings as the Methodists who needed to appoint trustees fully to legalize the matter.

In 1763 Wesley laid down, as far as he could, the demand, 'Let our Preachers go to church, let all our people go constantly, receive the sacrament at every opportunity, warn against niceness of learning, a great and prevailing evil, warn them likewise against despising the prayers of the church, against calling our society a church or the church, against calling our Preachers ministers, our houses meeting houses, call them plain preaching houses. Do not licence them as such.'[24] By that time, however, Vincent Perronet, a sympathetic Anglican, could write to Charles Wesley, 'It is undoubtedly a trying time for the poor Methodist Church.'[25] In that same year Wesley produced a *Model Deed* for preaching. The Deed instructed the trustees of chapels settled on it 'to permit such persons as shall be appointed at the Year's Conference and no other to have and enjoy the premises provided that they preach no other doctrines than is contained in Wesley's *Notes on the New Testament* and his four *Volumes of Sermons*'. This provision marks off the Methodist preachers as abiding by certain standards which were granted the full recognition of the law. The equipment of the people's preachers were typically a book of exegesis and a book of sermons. It was effectively an act of dissent as was the *Deed of Declaration* of 1784 which gave legal definition to the Conference, setting up the 'Legal Hundred', the 100 preachers who would thereafter ratify the decisions of Conference, establishing a pattern of continuity, including an itinerant ministry.[26]

Dr John Whitehead, Wesley's physician, called 1784 'the grand climacterical year' of Methodism.[27] More recently Dr Frank Baker pointed to that year as the time of irreversible severance from the established church. This climax was the result of the situation in America. In 1782 the Methodist societies there numbered 11,785 members, mainly to be found south of the 'Mason-Dixon' line and especially the Chesapeake, 'the garden of Methodism'. Anglicans were scattered and divided. Many had fled to England. Disputes over episcopacy had been long-term, throwing up surprisingly liberal and pragmatic views such as a book by William White of Philadelphia suggesting that in an emergency presbyters might ordain if necessity demanded it. Cranmer, Hooker, Whitgift, Ussher and Hoadly were cited in support. There is no evidence that Wesley read White's book. He had independently come to the same conclusions.[28] It was not until 1 November 1784 that Samuel Seabury was consecrated by the bishops of the Scottish non-juring Episcopal Church in Aberdeen.

Long before, Wesley began to contemplate emergency action for the Methodists. His views on episcopal government had greatly changed since his Oxford days. In 1746 he read *An Inquiry Into the Constitution, Discipline, Unity and Worship of the Primitive Church* (1691) by Peter King, who eventually became Lord Chancellor, and, later, Edward Stillingfleet's celebrated *Irenicum*, written just before the Restoration. These writings, both by men in their twenties, influenced Wesley even if he misunderstood some of King's argument. He became convinced that the early church did not have monarchical episcopacy and that the episcopal form of government is not laid down in Scripture. 'I still believe the Episcopal form of government to be both scriptural and apostolical I mean well agreeing with the practice and writing of the Apostles. But that it is prescribed in scripture I do not believe.'[29] Further, vital to his future conduct, Wesley accepted King's observation that in the New Testament bishops and presbyters could ordain, though they needed the bishop's permission, a matter Wesley ignored! Wesley drew his own conclusions. 'Read Bishop Stillingfleet's *Irenicon* [*sic*] or any impartial history of the Ancient church and I believe you will think as I do. I verily believe I have as good a right to ordain as to administer the Lord's Supper. But I see abundance of reasons why I should not use that right unless I am turned out of the

Church.' So, long before 1784, Wesley had reached the conclusion summarized in a letter to his brother of 1 August 1785. 'I firmly believe I am a scriptural *episcopos* as much as any man in England or in Europe for the uninterrupted succession I know to be a fable which no man ever did or can prove.'[30] It is fascinating that this is now accepted by biblical scholars writing from Catholic as well as Protestant suppositions.[31]

Wesley's doctrine of the ministry has been obscured by polemical attempts to ensnare him in nineteenth-century conflicts. If we see him in an eighteenth-century setting, we can accept Frank Baker's assertion that his view of the church as a sacramental institution with an evangelical mission was being slowly transformed into that of a missionary society performing sacramental functions, with the Church of England fulfilling the one task and the Methodist societies the other.[32] For Wesley, the gospel and its needs determine church order and there is a clear distinction between the preaching office and presiding at the sacraments. A further principle is that there was a succession in the ministerial office, even if it was not the uninterrupted succession of the apostolic ministry. When Wesley contemplated ordination, it was as a presbyter exercising the inherent right of a New Testament *episcopos*. Wesley was here in line with a liberal Anglican position reaching back to Richard Hooker, who spoke of 'inevitable necessity'[33] in relation to the Protestant Reformed Churches, a view which can be traced through writers like Benjamin Hoadly and contemporaries like Warburton and Paley. Wesley here stands in one Anglican tradition and also the tradition of Richard Baxter and some of the more churchly Puritans.[34]

In very recent ecumenical negotiations, it is significant that in the *Porvoo Agreement* the Church of England has entered into full communion with the Lutheran Churches of Norway, Denmark and the Northern Baltic States which 'lost' the apostolic succession at the time of the Reformation when the Church of Sweden retained it. The presbyters of these churches, if ordained by bishops even if they are not strictly in the succession, are now accepted as presbyters who can preside at the Eucharist in the Church of England. The *Meissen Agreement* between the Church of England and the German Lutheran Churches may be more relevant not only to the concerns of ecumenism in England. It reflects uncannily some of the concerns of John Wesley as in this passage: 'with regard to the continuity, apostolicity and unity of the church, the continuity of the Gospel always takes priority. In both our churches there is unbroken continuity of authorized ordination of ministers. While in the Church of England that continuity of the historic episcopate in terms of the personal succession of bishops served as a focus of unity, uninterrupted by the changes of the Reformation, the continental Reformers found themselves having to choose between the continuity of the Gospel and the existing episcopate and therefore reformed the exercise of *episcopé* in ways which sought to safeguard the priority of the Gospel over any particular form of ministry and *episcopé*. In doing this they referred back to the early patristic model, whereby the *episcopus* was the pastor of the local Christian Community' (para. 67). This sounds strikingly like Wesley's view of the 'scriptural episcopus'. Could contemporary Methodism be accepted in parallel – certainly along the line of *Meissen* if not *Porvoo*?[35]

Wesley's practice, however, was more ambiguous, for he 'set apart' Dr Thomas Coke (1747–1814), already an Anglican priest, as 'Superintendent' for the American Methodists, as well as ordaining Richard Whatcoat and Thomas Vasey as 'presbyters' or 'elders' at Bristol on 2 September 1784. It can be claimed that he was showing his position as an 'Apostolic Man' or 'General Superintendent' of the Methodist people. It was a procedure which infuriated his brother, Charles, who descended to amusing, polemical verse:

> So easily are bishops made
> By man's or woman's whim?
> W. his hands on C. hath laid
> But who laid hands on him?

Of Coke ordaining Asbury in America on Christmas Day 1784, he later wrote:

> A roman Emperor 'tis said
> His favourite horse a consul made;
> But Coke brings greater things to pass
> He makes a bishop of an *ass*.[36]

There followed ordinations for Scotland, which Ronald Knox called 'Gretna Green' ordinations because Wesley said it was proper for Scotland, but the new presbyters were not to preside at the sacraments south of the border.[37] Oddly enough, the Church of England forbade priests ordained in America to cele-brate the sacraments in England![38] Ordinations followed for other parts of the Methodist mission scene and, finally, for England. Some of the Methodist people clearly wished to have the sacraments in their own 'chapels', of which there were three hundred in 1784, from their own preachers who were becoming increasingly ministerial in style. Clearly ordination was tanta-mount to separation, as Lord Chancellor Mansfield made clear to Charles Wesley after the 1784 episodes.[39]

The response of the Church of England was inconsequential. After all, the ordinations and setting apart of Coke as 'Super-intendent' was a somewhat hole-in-the-corner affair, as indeed was the consecration of the Anglican bishop for America in Aberdeen by Scottish Episcopal bishops that same autumn. The whole story might have been very different if Archbishop Secker had not been frustrated in an attempt in 1767 to persuade the government to allow the appointment of bishops in America. In America at Christmas 1784 Coke ordained Asbury with American assistance, on which Asbury insisted. Both Asbury and Coke began to assume episcopal authority and titles, to Wesley's intense displeasure[40] – but if ever a man was an apostolic bishop it was Francis Asbury. The episode illustrates Wesley's concern for the gospel and his pragmatism. The American Methodists needed a church constitution, they needed ministers. They should have both. Having broken their ties with Great Britain, any ties with the established church were broken also, which gave Wesley freedom to manoeuvre without disloyalty, a point often overlooked. Even if Wesley was never to be called bishop by his consent, he had clearly in the Ordinal of 1784 supplied the American Methodists with a style of episcopacy, if not the Anglican style.[41] 'I was determined as little as possible to violate the established order of the National Church to which I belonged. But the case is widely different between England and North America. Here there are bishops who have a legal jurisdiction, in America there are none, neither any parish minister . . . as our American brethren are now totally disentangled from both the state and from the English hierarchy, we dare not entangle them again with the one or the other. They are now at full liberty simply to follow the scriptures and the Primitive Church and we judge it best that they should stand fast in their liberty, wherewith God has so strangely made them free.' Nevertheless, an Anglican bishop, George Horne of Norwich, in 1791 called it a 'spurious episcopacy', rejecting Wesley's pleas of necessity. 'For if a presbyter can consecrate a bishop, we admit that a man may confer a power of which he is not himself possessed as instead of the less being blessed by the greater, the greater is blessed by the less and the order of things is inverted.' William Jones of Nayland, one of the leading 'Catholic' Anglicans, saw here 'Christian godliness without Christian order.' But the ripples on the Anglican sea were not great, for their position was vulnerable also.[42]

Together with providing ordained ministers, Wesley provided the American Methodists with their own Prayer Book. 'I have prepared a liturgy, little differing from that of the Church of England (I think the best constituted National Church in the World).' Wesley's revision of the Prayer Book was certainly another act tending to separation. Whatever may be the doctrinal motives, the practical demands of the American situation are sufficient warrant for many of Wesley's changes, though the omission of the Nicene Creed from the eucharistic rite is strange. The 'man of one book' omits several psalms as 'highly improper for the mouths of a Christian congregation'. It is significant that the rite of confirmation is omitted. Baptism was the rite of admission to Holy Communion, a Wesley concept not without relevance today when confirmation is still a rite searching for a theology and children may receive communion. If the ordinal with its orders of superintendents, elders and deacons seems an ambiguous trimming between episcopacy and presbyterianism, the Americans sailed off in their distinctive way, soon leaving behind much of Wesley's sacramentalism in the new excitement of the Second Evangelical Revival.[43]

The British scene was equally complex. As in America, the desire of the Methodist people for their own sacraments forced Wesley ultimately to ordain men for the ministry in England. Some Methodists, following Wesley's precepts and practice, desired frequent communion presided over by those who preached to them. Wesley urged them to go to their parish church for Holy Communion, but they were sometimes repelled from the Table. Many of them were now a second generation of Methodists, strangers to the parish church, its people, its priest and its worship. The meetings of the 'society' for worship and fellowship were now more than merely supplemental to what happened in the parish church. What Wesley called 'prudential means of grace' were assuming paramount importance. All Methodists did not follow Wesley's 'Catholic' style of sacramentalism.

The root of the problem was the Methodist folk – or many of them – needing to have all the means of grace from their preachers. Throughout their ministry the Wesleys communicated in parish churches when they could. Great crowds at sacramental services, unique at the time, were not infrequent. In Bristol and London from an early period, Holy Communion was celebrated in Methodist preaching houses, when ordained ministers were available. Wesley would not allow lay preachers – even if itinerant – to preside. Methodist services were not officially to be held in 'church hours', making the novelty of evening worship common. The rules could be waived if the minister was a notoriously evil man or if he preached Arian or other pernicious doctrines or when there was no church within two or three miles, a factor in the northern dioceses. Increases in population made the situation difficult, as in Manchester, where at the end of the eighteenth century the parish churches could cater for only 11,000 out of a population of 79,000.

Wesley finally, on 6 August 1788, ordained Alexander Mather as deacon and next day Superintendent. In February 1789 two more itinerants, Thomas Rankin and Henry Moore, were ordained as deacons and elders. Was Mather intended to be a parallel to Asbury? Wesley had failed in his idea of a clerical union of evangelicals of all kinds in 1769. They were 'a rope of sand' – that favourite Wesley phrase. The proposal that John Fletcher should be his successor foundered through Fletcher's premature death, as did the idea of Fletcher and Joseph Benson to establish a 'Methodist Church of England'. Also a possible link with the Moravians was a non-starter.[44] It seems likely that Wesley contemplated a Methodist Superintendency of Coke and Mather to lead Methodism after his death – John Pawson certainly thought so, but the matter is ambiguous.[45] Wesley may well have made incompatible prophecies before his death. Certainly in the end, the British Methodists did not establish any form of episcopacy. The chapels could, after 1795, have sacraments presided over by their itinerant preachers, whose 'reception into full Connexion' became tantamount to ordination. Laying on of hands in ordination was instituted in 1836, but there was no denial of ministerial status to those received before then. Wesley's ordinations were not conceived to have granted any special prerogatives to men like John Pawson, whatever they may have thought to be the case. In 1795 when the *Plan of Pacification* allowed the preachers to preside at sacrament if the society so wished, Methodism was – even if many Anglican corpuscles remained in the bloodstream – an independent community, though the title 'church' was not used for a century. Clearly after Wesley's death there was great tension[46] – some wanting to remain a 'society' within the penumbra of the Church of England, others like Samuel Bradburn wanting downright dissent, others occupying a middle position. Some, like Thomas Coke and John Pawson, wanted an episcopal system, but this was scotched in 1794. A great disadvantage was the continuing rule that Holy Communion should not be held in 'church hours', which pushed Methodist sacramental observance into an evening affair after a preaching service. The use of the Prayer Book or Wesley's abridgement ensured a link with the Cranmerian Communion Office. This was the norm in Wesleyanism and in many Methodist Churches after the union of 1932 until the appearance of the Methodist Service Book of 1975 and the later Methodist Worship Book of 1999.

Much of Wesley's constitution remained, such as the Constitution of the Conference. In 1791, it was laid down that the Presidency should be an annual appointment, like the Moderator of the Church of Scotland. There were to be 'No More Kings in Israel'. The Conference itself, in a slightly pretentious phrase, was thought of as 'the living Wesley'. The fact that it consisted entirely of itinerant preachers made it prone to become a lightning conductor for future conflicts. As early as 1797 the Methodist New Connexion became the first of the schisms in Methodism, which were to mark the history of the next fifty years, until the United Methodist Free Churches of 1857, the last of the fractures in the Connexion which Wesley had created.

Relations with the Church of England were made more difficult by the Tractarian Movement, which 'unchurched' the Wesleyans, and by the conflicts in local areas caused by a resurgent Anglicanism, which clashed politically and socially with a Methodism past the peak of its membership in relation to the population by 1880, if not earlier. Sociological pressures as much as the Oxford Movement exacerbated the old 'church' and 'chapel' cleavage, producing at times open and bitter conflict or sour isolationism before the new initiatives of the twentieth century such as the Edinburgh Conference of 1910 and the Lambeth Conference Appeal of 1920. 'The truth remains', said Archbishop John Habgood in 1985, 'that each needs the other – Methodism a society in search of the church and Anglicanism with its need of warmth, discipline and lay commitment.'[47]

6

John Wesley – His Political and Social Influence

Historians have recently used the phrase 'the long eighteenth century' of the period between the Revolution of 1688–9 and the Parliamentary Acts of 1828–9, when dissenters and Roman Catholics achieved emancipation. England ceased to be a confessional state, even if it still had an established church as did Wales, Ireland and, in a different Presbyterian style, Scotland. The Reform Act of 1832 and the Municipal Corporation Act of 1835 completed the significant series of Acts, but we must not exaggerate new domination by the middle class. The old governing class still had very considerable power. Wesley's political stance, his social thinking and action need to be seen against the background of recent historiography.[1]

We can begin with the analysis of the continuing ideological basis of the Jacobite and non-Jacobite Tories at the beginning of the eighteenth century. The strife between Whig and Tory under Anne is complex – the most dramatic episode was the trial of Henry Sacheverell, which revealed how strong Tory sentiment was. Attempts were made to exclude dissenters from political power by forbidding occasional conformity, i.e. dissenters receiving communion at Anglican churches to gain political office. In 1717 the church lost its 'parliament' when the Convocations were suppressed. The strongest church group at this time, among the hierarchy at least, was probably the 'Latitudinarians', men of tolerance with a hatred of 'enthusiasm', any pretension to extraordinary gifts of the Spirit. The political thinking of Francis Atterbury and of Samuel Wesley was not dissimilar. Following

G. V. Bennett, Professor Linda Colley has revealed the continuing ideological thread of Toryism. She uncovers a continuing
mood of intense patriotism and anti-Catholicism through the
century. Foxe's *Book of Martyrs* and Bunyan's *Pilgrim's
Progress* were still immensely popular. Bunyan was much read in
Pietist circles on the Continent, as were other Puritan writers.
There is no doubt that much of this ethos was part of Wesley's
mind-set. His genuine Toryism was no mere shadow show. Colin
Haydon has shown how the Roman Catholic community – num-
bering about 80,000 – was thought outlandish and unpatriotic.
Wesley's strikingly ambivalent attitude to Catholicism has to be
seen in this context – eirenic to individuals, though he did not
meet many Roman Catholics – as in the *Letter to a Roman
Catholic* (1749). He had a willingness to explore Catholic spirituality with reservations, but later showed a negative attitude to
Catholic emancipation and Catholic rights, which clearly
influenced later Methodism in England and Ireland for a century
or more.

What of politics? Lurking behind contemporary thinking on
'the long eighteenth century' is the figure of Jonathan Clark.
Three of his books are germane. England, claims Clark, was still
an *ancien régime*. The Church of England was still the dominant
ideological force in the localities. There was a semblance of law
and order – the year 1785 saw 500 death sentences and many
transportations. As late as 1753 a woman was burned at the
stake in Gloucester. The interdependence of church, state and
society is typified by the power of the clerical magistrate and
a quarter of justices of the peace were parsons at the end of
the eighteenth century, a factor which greatly impinged on
Methodism.[2] Food riots were intermittent – violence on the
whole was local, if often vicious as in 1757, 1766, 1773–4, 1795
and 1800. A ruling ideology prevailed, which was more traditional than that of Locke and his followers, though this is a
controversial point. The mob disorders against Wesley and his
preachers fit clearly into this claim that England was still regu-
lated by tradition. Clark sees Methodism as a sign of the vitality
of the Church of England, since that church produced it, which

is rather like saying that Martin Luther was a sign of the vitality of the late medieval church, by no means implausible. Clark, too, seeks to show that England was still a confessional state, remaining so until the legislation of 1828–9 ended the political isolation of Roman Catholics as well as dissenters. The Church of England was by then – even if it has never openly acknowledged it – one church among many. Clark's latest book shows indirectly the way in which Wesley reflected Tory opinion on the American Revolution, although, once it had occurred, Wesley pragmatically accepted it since, as W. R. Ward points out, 'Methodism offered a way of affirming their Englishness without being Anglican', the last thing which Clark's model permits.[3] In 1750, 90 per cent of worshippers were Church of England, while in 1850 the proportion was 50 per cent.

A more sober approach is to be found in Paul Langford. He stresses the stability of England in this period compared with the Continent, and the growth in commerce, consumerism and industry, accepting the arguments of McKendrick and Plumb that England was entering a consumer boom which affected much of the population.[4] This is a change of lifestyle remarked on often in Wesley's *Journal* and other writings with his rather obsessive comments on ladies' hats, finery and silk dresses from Macclesfield. He might also have noticed the false bosoms and cork bottoms! Certainly some of the Methodists – largely artisan with more women than men – were becoming increasingly prosperous. This is much more than another 'rising bourgeoisie' theory. It needs, however, to be balanced by the late E. P. Thompson, who appears to consider Langford's account 'patrician', while he is doubtless 'plebeian'. The 'plebeian' living standards were very different from those of the aristocrats and men of commerce. This is the world of food riots, often led by women, of the 'crowd', of wife-selling and 'rough music' and the smugglers, whom Wesley sought to tame, excluding them from the Methodist societies. Thompson was very like William Cobbett, with a dislike of the Industrial Revolution. Allowing for his romanticism, it is impossible to dodge his insights here. Thompson uncovers an England of great economic disparity.

He has one last comment on Methodism: 'The church was profoundly Erastian; had it performed an effective, a psychologically compelling paternalist role, the Methodist movement would have been neither necessary nor possible.' Put that alongside Clark! Roy Porter also shows a dark underside to English society, but also an Enlightenment which greatly influenced Wesley and the Evangelical Revival, even if he did not always realize it.[5]

Porter provides a conclusion to this brief historiographical survey. He depicts starkly the life of the 'labouring classes', a matter on which Wesley's first-hand observations are also given. This is 1753: 'In the afternoon I visited many of the sick, but such scenes who could see unmoved? There are none such to be found in a pagan country. If any of the Indians in Georgia were sick (which indeed, exceedingly rarely happened till they learned gluttony and drunkenness from the Christians) those that were near him gave him whatever he wanted. Oh who will convert the English into honest heathens? . . . I found some in their cells underground, others in their garrets half-starved both with cold and hunger added to weakness and pain. But I found not one of them unemployed who was able to crawl about the room. So wickedly, devilishly false is that common objection – "they are poor because they are idle". If you saw these things with your own eyes could you lay out money in ornaments or superfluities.'[6] This is a constant warning.

Porter, surveying the century, asserts of the lower orders: 'Theirs was not the expropriated, hopeless, begging destitution of parts of the present day third world. The ordinary Georgian working family did not bask in a folksy golden age, but neither did it have one foot outside the refugee camp.' For modern summaries of the economic history of the eighteenth century I would commend the surveys by Edward Royle and John Rule. This is the background which is sometimes lacking in popular attempts to assess Wesley. So we now briefly analyse this paradox, the evangelical who was also a rational conservative and a friend of the poor.

Wesley stands in a long line of Christian conservatives[7] which includes Martin Luther, Richard Hooker, Edmund Burke, William Wilberforce, the Seventh Earl of Shaftesbury and John Henry Newman, whose concern for the liberation of the poor was as real as and often more practical than that of ideological revolutionaries. Christian conservatives stress human imperfection, corporate continuity and tradition, an organic rather than a contractual view of the state and society, a scepticism about any idealization or idolatry of human nature or of politics.[8] Wesley's politics – he more than once eschewed any idea that he was involved in politics,[9] claiming to speak merely as a 'free born Englishman' – were realistic, not utopian, flowing from his genuine Toryism. The Tories were to be seen in opposition to dominant Whig groups, a matter sometimes overlooked, though since Sir Lewis Namier it has not been possible to speak in terms of the modern party system when surveying the Georgian era or the political terminology of the day.

We can identify five areas where Wesley's ideas, practice and long-term influence was significant. First *slavery*. Methodists in a city like Bristol or Liverpool could not ignore the 'triangular trade', then at its height. In Wesley's day cheap goods would be transported from London, Bristol or Liverpool to West Africa and exchanged for slaves, who would then be sold on the other side of the Atlantic, if they survived. Sugar, spices, molasses and cotton would be shipped back to Britain. While it is the case that Africans and Arabs were involved in the trade, it was Europeans who sustained and justified it. In 1746, 46 vessels from London, Bristol and Liverpool were involved in the slave trade, by 1772–5 the average was 161.

Wesley's views and Enlightenment emphasis flow strongly together here. Liberty, benevolence and happiness were the watchwords. The evangelical mind accepted much of the moral philosophy of the day – notably the belief in liberty as a cardinal virtue, in benevolence as a duty of man and woman, and in happiness as a proper goal. If there is the freedom of the sons and daughters of God, does not that freedom include the body? Wesley tapped here not only into William Blackstone, who maintained that slavery is against the law of nature and reason, but the Quaker thinking of Anthony Benezet. *Thoughts upon slavery* (1774)[10] had an immediate impact. Wesley supported the early agitation of Granville Sharp, which reached its climax in 1806–7. Wesley's views were taken up by Methodists in Britain and more ambiguously in America, where, in the end, they split the Methodist Church.

It was to William Wilberforce that Wesley wrote his last letter in early 1791.[11] 'Unless the divine power has raised you up to be as *Athanasius Contra Mundum* [Athanasius Against the World] I see not how you can go through your glorious enterprise opposing that execrable villainy which is the scandal of religion, of England and of human nature. Unless God has raised you up for this very thing, you will be worn out by the opposition of men and devils. But if God be with you, who can be against you? Are any of them together stronger than God? Oh be not weary in well doing! Go on in the Name of God and the power of his might then even American slavery (the vilest that ever saw the sun) shall vanish away before it . . .

'Reading this morning a tract written by a poor African, I was particularly struck by that circumstance that a man who had a black skin being wronged or outraged by a white man can have no redress, it being a law in all our colonies that the oath of a black against a white goes for nothing. What villainy is this!' Did Wesley have a sense of human rights as part of his Arminianism as distinct from, for example, George Whitefield, who kept slaves in Georgia? The later evangelicals, who could not be called Arminian, were to be the leaders in the anti-slavery crusade. There was a notable alliance between evangelicals and Wesleyans in the battle against the English slave trade and slavery itself up to and beyond the crucial legislation of 1833. If Wesleyans were bidden not to preach politics from their pulpits, it did not include moral crusades such as that against slavery.

Second, lest we think Wesley was becoming a political disciple of John Locke in the matter of human rights,[12] conservation of *nationhood* was also part of Wesley's political thought. In Bristol, he could seem a little too conservative even to Edmund

Burke! Yet he could combine eulogies for the king with scepticism about establishment. Of Catherine the Great of Russia he said, 'What a woman is the Czarina, but God is over all,' and of Queen Elizabeth, 'Just and merciful as Nero, and as good a Christian as Mahomet.' For Wesley, power came from God, not from the people[13] in state as well as church. There was little idea of contract in his thinking. He could, as we have seen, behave autocratically but without humbug or *Noblesse Oblige*. He was an opponent of revolution – American or French – though at first he had been sympathetic to some of the American demands. He then appeared, to some, to become a sycophantic court spokesman, which he vehemently denied. He plagiarized a tract written by Samuel Johnson in *A Calm Address to Our American Colonies* (1775), which rapidly sold at least 50,000 copies.[14] The episode infuriated Toplady and other evangelicals. Wesley, however, quickly accepted a fait accompli both for himself and for the future of Methodism in America when the War of Independence ended. Both church and state could be free to develop in their own way. Pragmatism took over at this point, as often was the case.

Wesley was no democrat in the modern sense. He could speak of the human rights of slaves, but the power and the will of the people was a different matter. Opposition to the power of the people in dissenting congregations, the ideas and actions of Wilkes, or the dissenter Richard Price, showed the continuing highly conservative and autocratic side of Wesley.[15]

It is proper to state here his opposition to full Roman Catholic emancipation,[16] or rather the beginning of it in Savile's *Relief Act* of 1778, allowing greater freedom for priests, and at the time of the Gordon Riots of 1780, the worst English riots in the second half of the century. His very concern for human rights led him to see the Church of Rome as a body opposed to freedom, which would not keep faith with heretics, a matter going back, in Wesley's opinion, to the Council of Constance of 1415. Here Wesley was in agreement with John Locke.[17] In 1760 the leading Roman Catholic thinker in England, Richard Challoner (1691–1781), had issued his *Caveat Against the Methodists*. He stated that 'Methodists are not the people of God . . . Nor is their new raised society the true Church of Christ or any part of it.' Pastors were 'ministers of Satan'. Wesley replied at the time, seeing Challoner as attacking all Protestants. The two never met. Wesley professed to be amazed that his preachers were sometimes mistaken for Catholic priests. But 'Peter' and 'Jack', as Eamon Duffy naughtily called Catholics and dissenters, had some similarities, such as itinerant styles and freedom from parochial structures. Indeed in 1766, Bishop Challoner himself could talk of sending six youths to the English seminary in Rome as 'apprentices to learn their trade'. Wesley feared the 'purple power of Rome advancing by hasty strides to overspread the more than happy land'. His stance was not helped by the misrepresentation of Father O'Leary,[18] with whom he later had breakfast! Wesley's position spilled over into nineteenth-century Methodist thought. Jabez Bunting (1779–1858), the outstanding Wesleyan leader of the first half of that century, however, did not oppose Roman Catholic emancipation in 1829. The 'orange tinge' of Methodism continued through the nineteenth century. As late as 1870 the astute William Arthur's *The Pope, the King and the People* gave a Methodist slant on the First Vatican Council of that year. In recent times one of Arthur's notable successors as headmaster of Wesley College, Belfast, Stanley Worrall (1912–91), sought in every way to bring Catholics and Protestants together in Belfast, a matter typified by the work of the Commission appointed by the Vatican and the World Methodist Council.

Wesley's stance here in no way undervalues his view of the need to differentiate between the heart of the faith and *adiaphora* or things indifferent, as in the sermon on the *Catholic Spirit*, but his opinions in 1780 seem very different from the often-quoted eirenic *Letter to a Roman Catholic* of 1749, written after the Cork riots. The linkages in spirituality were very different from concern about the power and intolerance of 'popery'.[19]

Opposition to some forms of democracy did not prevent Wesley from being a genuine friend to the poor, a trait he picked up from his Oxford days. 'I bear the rich, but I love the poor, therefore I spend almost all my time with them.' His position was not far from his Roman Catholic spiritual influences such as de Renty, not to speak of William Law. He would as an old man trudge through the snow in London collecting £200 in a one-man Christian Aid style campaign.[20] He gave away almost all his considerable income from publishing. His style of caring for the London poor at the Foundery is notable, linking with later developments like *The Stranger's Friend Societies*[21], which were an important aspect of the voluntary social welfare work of Methodism in urban areas. Wesley encouraged a number of such projects, particularly in times of distress. In 1785, James Gardner, a member of Wesley's chapel, started a scheme collecting weekly from members for distributing among the poor. Wesley gave a guinea and a promise of three pence a week. A similar society began in Bristol the next year, gifts to go not to Methodists but to 'poor, sick, friendless strangers' irrespective of religion or ethnic background. These are examples of philanthropy rather than any real attempt at an advocacy of social reform, but in one year in Manchester 1,678 families were relieved and 4,271 visits made.[22]

Wellman Warner was probably right when he claimed that Wesley's personal style was too difficult for most of his converts and followers. They might indeed 'make all they could' and 'save all they could', but though generous were not willing to 'give all they can' in the way that Wesley advocated from 1748. He had a horror of capital accumulation. He proposed for a time a Community of Goods,[23] as in the early church, but it was never carried to a practical conclusion. We might recall, too, that when he married it was to a wealthy widow who did not rely on him to maintain her or her family. But Wesley cannot be aligned behind a simplistic Weberian view of the rise of capitalism, as Weber himself shows, though Wesley's followers often could and did move marginally up the social scale by thrift or skill, responsibility and respectability. The 'undeserving' poor got more support from him than the 'idle rich', whom he lambasted as wastrels even if he took their money. Nonconformity is expensive and has always relied on the generosity of the wealthy. The poor gave

Wesley an audience and a welcome on the whole, despite the activities of the mob, the more vulgar stirring up the less. He saw the poor as receptive and humble with hidden talents. It is similar to his attitude to the 'Indians' in Georgia, the 'noble savage'. Methodism was able to awaken and foster some of the poor. John Walsh's statement that in Wesley's hands the denunciatory side of the Protestant work ethic is directed against the rich and not the poor is astute.[24] His economics, as in the *Tract on the Scarcity of Provisions*,[25] when he proposed 'sinking the price of provisions', with distilling prohibited, the supply of horses to be reduced, the number of cattle to be increased and size of farms to be reduced, a matter repeated in the press, may seem naive and pre-Adam Smith. He disclaimed expertise and we cannot take him as a model for today's global economy. The world of pre-industrial, pre-machine-based capitalism cannot be recreated.

In a strange way, he was a man of the Age of Reason, yet in constant touch with the mixture of magic and Christianity which was a feature of popular religion and popular thought among the poor. The popular evangelism of those days filled some of the gaps between 'official' and 'folk' religion that had widened at the Reformation, becoming a chasm in the eighteenth century as an increasingly rational-minded clergy lost touch with the forms of thought of the common people. Methodism did not so much displace the folk beliefs of the common people as translate them into a religious idiom and new forms of society where women especially could feel at home.

Let us see Wesley then as a Tory in an eighteenth-century sense. Yet paradoxically from his system came democratic societies in which 'nobodies' could be come 'somebodies'.[26] What of Methodism and politics after Wesley? It was stated often that Methodism moved from a dominant Toryism to an underlying Liberalism.[27] Now we know from a study of poll books that not a few Methodists, when they obtained the vote in 1832, voted Liberal or Whig, continuing to do so throughout the nineteenth century, though there were always those who voted Tory. The mood of Wesleyanism was certainly conservative in the decade after Wesley's death and up to and beyond the crucial Acts of

1828–9, which saw major concessions to dissenters and Roman Catholics, and the Reform Act, increasing the voting population, although in Halifax with nearly 2,000 Methodist members only 2 per cent of the population had the vote in 1832. Methodism was often suspected of disloyalty and destabilizing the state at the time of the French Revolution and the Napoleonic Wars. This was a time of intense itinerant evangelism by dissenters as well as Methodists. In 1811 a bill sponsored by Lord Sidmouth would have made 'local' and possibly itinerant preaching illegal as the licensing system would insist on preachers being appointed to a congregation. At this time there was a parallel literary campaign against Methodism. William Hazlitt gave a belittling description of a Wesleyan congregation. 'Never was there such a set of scarecrows; Melancholy tailors, consumptive hairdressers, squinting cobblers, women with child or with ague, make up the forlorn hope of the pious cavalcade.' The Wesleyan Committee of Privileges, masterminded by the connexional solicitor Thomas Allan, on opposing Sidmouth's bill was able to present 30,000 signatures to the government supporting the other dissenting groups. This was a portent of things to come – the first stirring of Wesleyan involvement on the nonconformist platform. The subsequent Act of 1812 marked the end of the legislation which had plagued John Wesley. Pluralism of church activity was now an irreversible fact in English life. We shall return to this later.

Jabez Bunting is often depicted as a consistent Tory, but he did not oppose Roman Catholic emancipation in 1829. He opposed Peel's government over the proposal by Sir James Graham in 1843 to establish compulsory education for children in certain industries under the auspices of the Church of England, having in 1838–9 opposed Lord John Russell's proposal for a 'Normal College' for the training of teachers with a more liberal grant system, which appeared to subsidize other denominations including Roman Catholics. There followed opposition to a proposed grant by Peel's government to St Patrick's College, Maynooth, the Roman Catholic seminary in Ireland. It was Ireland which makes it difficult to typecast Wesleyan political involvements, since if Bunting could oppose Tory Peel, later Wesleyans could oppose Liberal Gladstone on Home Rule for Ireland. Bunting is clearly the epitome of 'high Wesleyanism', stressing the connexion, the national and the international, including a major concern for overseas missions illustrating the energy of Wesleyanism at the time. He came to see Wesleyanism as an independent body between church and dissent, clearly influenced by the secession of the Free Kirk of Scotland under Thomas Chalmers in 1843.

The secessions from Wesleyanism were portents of a more liberal, democratic style at local level. 'Low' Wesleyanism was local, lay, prone to revivalism, oriented towards local chapel culture. Alexander Kilham was expelled in 1796, the resulting *Methodist New Connexion*, pioneering the granting of much more power to the laity. His sentiments might be quite different from those of Wesley but were prophetic of what was to come. Methodism is the strange paradox of an organization democratic in local style but autocratic in its superstructure, chiming in with a society slowly moving to partial democracy. This point was seized on by Bernard Semmel in *The Methodist Revolution*.[28] He draws a parallel with demands for democracy typified by the federalists in the American colonies. Methodism, with the much more democratic transatlantic evangelicals, gave an enormous boost to Protestant dissent in England and Wales, which was certainly not Wesley's intention. Later secessions stressed democracy at every level from Conference to local society but were not always necessarily Liberal in politics locally or nationally. The Wesleyans in 1847 began to move to a new direction on education. They not only pushed on with their own school and college programme, but were prepared to accept direct grant from the state and later to accept the full implications of the 1870 Education Act with an eagerness which set them apart from the rest of dissent and secular opinion.

Evangelical pietism has always inclined to a moralistic political stance. It fostered 'crusades' against slavery, or 'Popery', Bulgarian horrors and the Armenian massacres. The 'unspeakable Turk' became a symbol for evil. The moral crusade for total abstinence and prohibition possibly lost Methodism any real impact it had on the 'unrespectable poor', so loved by Wesley, although alcohol today is still a major, and apparently intractable, problem. In the twentieth century, the wholly justified crusade against Apartheid in South Africa had the same style but much more widespread support. There was a consistency below the surface from Wesley's time.

The phrase of the Quaker John Bright, 'What is morally wrong can never by politically right' was used by Hugh Price Hughes at the end of the nineteenth century when he helped to hound the Irish leader Charles Stewart Parnell out of politics because of his involvement in adultery and his divorce. This led to the charge of self-righteousness and humbug. *The Times* coined the phrase 'Nonconformist Conscience', which had three key features: that there should be no strict boundary between religion and politics; an insistence that politicians should be men of the highest character; and a belief that the state should promote the moral welfare of its citizens. The danger, claimed Kitson Clark, is 'the old Puritan vice of imputing base motives to the other side and dividing the world sharply and inaccurately into the godly and ungodly, a habit which even to this day has descended on several who would not recognize its ancestry and have abandoned the creed which originated it'. It could well be that the crusading style of politics only achieves anything – abolition of slavery is a crucial example – when other power groups besides Methodists and nonconformists ally with them. In isolation, Methodism never had the electoral power to push its political aims to a conclusion.[29] It has often underlined, too, Edward Norman's controversial thesis that clerical and lay elites tend to follow intellectual fashion, rarely to create it.[30] Hugh Price Hughes is a good example. He may, on some issues, have seemed radical. Certainly he did so to many Wesleyans. He was a man of his age. Believing the Anglo-Saxons to be a superior race, he carried many Methodists with him in a paternalist concern for the 'inferior races', as when he claimed that the British should 'protect' the Bantu against the Boers, so supporting the Boer War. Earlier, in 1872, the Wesleyan Conference had sent a resolution to W. E. Gladstone affirming that Great Britain should annex the Fiji Islands for their own good.

But we must not underestimate a continuing concern for the poor. Long before the much-publicized *Bitter Cry of Outcast London* in 1883, Thomas Bowman Stephenson (1829–1912) was working among the poor of Bolton, then pioneering in 1869, with London Wesleyan laymen, what became the National Children's Home, still one of the largest charities working among children, although its style has changed dramatically as needs have changed. The researches of William (1890) and Charles Booth (1902) and Joseph Rowntree revealed an 'underclass' of 30 per cent of the population in the large cities. Wesleyanism, as we have already shown, responded with its Central Halls in Manchester, Leeds, London, Birmingham, Bradford and many other cities, seeking to reach the alienated masses with the gospel and the soup ladle hand in hand. They succeeded in some measure, producing radical experiments in women's ministry like the Sisters of the People, under Katherine Price Hughes (1853–1948) in the West London Mission and Samuel Collier (1855–1921) in Manchester. Stephenson followed up the National Children's Home with the Wesley Deaconess Order, which has recently become the Diaconal Order, including men as well as women. The Hospice for the Dying, sponsored by the West London Mission, was pioneering also. The history of the Salvation Army could be considered a style of Methodism, not least in its itinerancy of officers and combination of holiness teaching and social concern.

In 1914 the great alliance between the Whigs, Liberals and nonconformists was breaking up. Many Methodists for a time continued to vote Liberal. An increasing number voted for the new Labour Party, which by 1906 was becoming a force in the House of Commons despite the huge Liberal majority. The ministerial 'intelligentsia' of Methodism tended to a moderate collectivism and non-Marxist socialism, although among the laity a fair number of Wesleyans supported Conservative unionism in the first 35 years of the twentieth century. There were notable Methodists within the Labour movement even if the cliché that the Labour Party is more Methodist than Marxist is a half-truth. Arthur Henderson (1863–1935), Foreign Secretary

1929–31, was a practising Methodist of Wesleyan extraction, certainly one of the creators of the Labour Party. It is interesting that the first two Ministers of Education in Attlee's administration of 1945 – Ellen Wilkinson (1891–1947) and George Tomlinson (1890–1952) were Methodists. Had the Methodists become the conciliators, the moderates in English politics? Certainly, Methodism was a factor in the rise of the great 'helping professions'. 'This is the context of Chapel, a mode of self-control expressed collectively, offering a life of obedience, discipline, duty and noseyness to individuals. In a world where you had only your feet to stand on, there could be no better recipe for stepping heavenwards.'[31] Many served their community well too.

Wesley may have feared for industrialists' souls, but the businessmen who more than 'stood on their own feet' cannot be ignored. Historians are now becoming more perceptive about their contribution to British life. Men like Jesse Boot (1850–1931), Thomas R. Ferens (1847–1930), the Mackintoshes of Halifax (Quality Street indeed), Sir William Hartley (1846–1922), Joseph Rank (1854–1943) of Hovis and his son J. Arthur (1888–1972), the 'man with the gong', make a saga of their own. Their contribution to Methodist building, and concern for secular and religious education and human need, is part of a Methodist culture, even if rather different from Wesley's pre-capitalist economic ethics.[32]

This brief survey of Methodist contribution to politics and concern for the poor which continues into the twenty-first century leads logically to Wesley's concern for education. This begins with the founding of Kingswood School in 1748,[33] which became later the centre for the education of the sons of the itinerant preachers. The school moved to Bath in 1851. At first the regime seems almost incredibly austere by modern standards, but it needs to be judged against the background of almost universal child labour. Wesley had no time for Rousseau – 'he who plays as a boy will play as a man'. Did the Kingswood ethos reveal the influence of John Locke on educational method or was it more that of the Epworth household under Susanna Wesley? The intense phase of religiosity changed into a more public school style. By the beginning of the nineteenth century, John Pawson, the veteran itinerant, was complaining of preachers' wives in posh frocks with their sons at Kingswood School about to climb the social ladder. In the nineteenth century Methodism established a clutch of boarding schools paralleling the Woodard Schools of the Church of England. This clearly expressed the rising prosperity of many Methodists and the influence of a new professional class.

The Methodists could claim that it was a Methodist woman, Miss Hannah Ball (1733–92) of High Wycombe, who pioneered Sunday schools in 1769, before the more celebrated Robert Raikes, whose style became the norm in evangelicalism. In Bolton on Easter Day, 1786, Wesley wrote of 550 children who were taught in Sunday schools there. Two years later he spoke of them 'singing like angels'. By 1800 there were 100,000 children in the various Sunday schools. This was to become in the nine-teenth century a movement involving a large percentage of working-class children. It was very much lay-led, producing a significant 'folk culture' but not large numbers of church members, despite conference concern.[34] A million children were in Methodist Sunday schools in 1900. If class meetings reached their thousands, Sunday schools reached their millions. Here was a bridge between folk culture and domestic piety. Its debacle has not been fully analysed – it was much more than a mere means of social control. After early hesitations, the Wesleyans pioneered their own day schools with as many as 912 of them in the period after the Education Act of 1870, paralleling the Roman Catholics. James H. Rigg (1821–1909), who was principal of Westminster College for the training of teachers from 1868 to 1903, strongly defended the retention of Wesleyan elementary schools against those who wanted them to be placed under the school boards and after 1902 under the new local education authorities. He lost this particular battle, though 28 Methodist primary schools with the same number linked with the Church of England still remain. The 'Dual System' of state and church schools which Rigg supported is still a basic feature of English education. Methodism had its two colleges for training teachers at Westminster (later at Oxford, now part of Oxford Brookes University) and Southlands at Wimbledon, now part of the University of Surrey, Roehampton. If we include the theological colleges which all the Methodist connexions established with close liaison with universities, there is here a considerable contribution to higher education.[35]

Wesley can be seen as a compulsive educator. The Oxford 'don' in him was producing a procession of educational tools from grammars to *The Christian Library* for preachers and the *Arminian Magazine* for ordinary readers. His achievement demolishes the somewhat hostile attitude of Sir John Plumb that Wesley was an irrational 'enthusiast'. His legacy remained in the 'many Methodisms', especially in the contribution of Methodism to education and medicine in America, Africa and Asia.

What of the role of women in early Methodism?[36] Wesley, frankly, cannot be claimed as a champion of women's rights, a concept hardly recognized in his pre-Mary Wollstonecroft days. He did not accept the Quaker view of the equality of the sexes in the society of the church. Yet Wesley, almost unconsciously through his pragmatism and awareness of Providence, became a factor in the liberation of women. He did not take easily to female preaching, in 1761 declaring that 'the Methodists do not allow of women preachers', and as late as 1780 he stated that he was not prepared to allow women to preach, though he had given some support to women whose work resulted in conversions. He could not deny the 'extraordinary Providence of God' in Mary Bosanquet (1739–1815). She was involved in the London revival of 1761–2 with Sarah Crosby (1729–1804) and Sarah Ryan (1724–68). A Christian community was established at Leytonstone, later moving to Cross Hall, Morley, near Leeds. Mary Bosanquet never became an itinerant preacher in the technical sense, nor did any other woman, but she claimed a genuine if extraordinary 'call', trenchantly defending it in a letter to Wesley in 1771. She married John Fletcher in 1781, continuing to preach after his death. Sarah Crosby, in a year, travelled nearly 1,000 miles, conducting 220 public services. Wesley advised her to 'exhort' rather than 'preach from a text', which would have suggested the status of a regular preacher. Mary Barritt (1772–1851), later Mrs Taft, was an effective preacher long after the Wesleyan Conference in 1803 officially forbade women to preach save in a limited sphere to their own sex. Clearly conference statements were not always obeyed, which would be no surprise to Northern Methodists!

Thomas Jackson (1783–1873), one of the leading Wesleyans of the next century, the editor of Wesley's *Works*, was converted under Mary Barritt's preaching. The portrait of a woman preacher in George Eliot's *Adam Bede* is a striking symbol of a continuing tradition, since Dinah Morris was clearly a portrait of Eliot's Wesleyan aunt – Elizabeth Evans (1776–1849). There were about forty women preachers in Wesley's time. Later in the Primitive Methodist and Bible Christian connexions women had an official status as itinerant preachers and there were a considerable number of women local preachers. In Wesleyanism women did not have equal status as local preachers until 1918, and were not admitted to the presbyterial ministry in Methodism until 1972, a generation after the other free churches, although the work of the Wesley Deaconess Order was notable.

The role of women was much wider than preaching. Their place as class leaders and spiritual supporters of the itinerant preachers must not be underestimated. The chapel became a haven for women, a counter-influence to the dominance of the pub. A new form of voluntary culture was developing which was to endure throughout the next century. Not least was the tremendous contribution of women to the support of overseas missions.

Can we summarize Wesley's influence, while avoiding exaggeration? Wesley may not have transformed England – his doctor and biographer John Whitehead said that he may have produced real stability, almost inventing the thesis that Methodism helped to prevent revolution in England. Wesley's aim was 'to spread scriptural holiness through the land'. Clearly he and his connexion, by the renewal of the 'religion of the heart', with the evangelicals and dissenters, were a major factor in making the Great Britain of the nineteenth century deeply religious, and not only an era of increasing secularism especially among the intelligentsia. Wesley, if 'certainly not a self-conscious rebel was far from a comfortable conformist'.[37]

We must press the matter further. What did Methodism achieve?

7

Did Methodism Prevent Revolution?

When the third volume of the *History of the Methodist Church in Great Britain* was published in 1983, the sociologist Professor David Martin, who had once been a Methodist, wrote in a brilliant but naughty review:[1] 'Was Halévy right about Methodism saving England from revolution? Was Morgan Phillips right about the Labour Party owing more to Methodism than to Marx? Did the Liberal party owe more to the provincial chapels than to cosmopolitan exponents of laissez-faire, or to political theorists of social liberalism like Hobhouse or T. H. Green? How could the same religious crucible forge the character of Margaret Thatcher, Prime Minister, the oratory of Michael Foot, the leader of the opposition in 1983, the labour internationalism of Arthur Henderson, Labour Foreign Secretary from 1929–31 who was a Methodist local preacher . . . is it pure accident that three successive Speakers of the House of Commons – Selwyn Lloyd, Horace King and George Thomas – have been Methodists?'

In fact (this is David Hempton) there are *many Methodisms* with quite distinct styles. The bourgeois Methodists of Manchester were very different from the Primitive Methodist pitmen preachers of the Durham coalfield, the tin miners of Cornwall or the agricultural workers of Suffolk during the 'revolt of the field', not to speak of the early Methodists of the Chesapeake or later in new England or south of the 'Mason-Dixon' line, so well described by John H. Wigger and Lynn Lyerly.[2]

We must not forget that Methodism was primarily a religious group developing from a 'society' for promoting the holiness of its members, a 'ginger group' to a wider church, into a large denomination or rather group of denominations. These had all the institutions and paraphernalia which inevitably follow such a development, yet retaining everywhere in an extraordinary manner the 'skeleton' of the system, which John Wesley, that superb pragmatist, devised.

Historians cannot help asking functional questions. The ghosts of Elie Halévy and E. P. Thompson haunt us. We cannot help asking, 'What did Methodism *do* for the people of Britain or of America or of Tonga where the monarch is Methodist?' The Halévy thesis that Methodism and the wider evangelicalism saved England from revolution will not go away. These functional questions were asked a generation ago by Sir John Plumb. He summed up Methodism as being, through Wesley's autocratic style, a religion not *of* the poor but *for* the poor, which may seem simplistic, but is not entirely so. He hazarded the guess that 'By 1760, Methodism was easily the most highly coordinated body of opinion in the country, the most fervent, the most dynamic. Had it been bent on revolution in church and state, nothing could have stopped it.' Gordon Rupp made the riposte that it is 'hard to see how such a body, far removed from the corridors of power could have "saved", still less threatened, the nation. Shopkeepers, tradesmen, skilled artisans and an even higher proportion of young, middle-aged and elderly women could not have stormed any barricades, had they been so minded. There were more Mary Bosanquets (later wife of John Fletcher) than Madelaines and even Mrs Sarah Ryan was no Madame Defarge. Unlike the first Anabaptists, the Methodists of that day were short of female viragos.' Methodists were not revolutionary, even if thought to be so by defenders of the status quo, who linked Methodists with Bonnie Prince Charlie in 1745. This is now shown to be not entirely absurd, at least in the case of Lady Huntingdon, the 'Queen of the Methodists' as Horace Walpole called her. 'Popery', sexual excesses and the break-up of local communities could be added to the list of charges, and later the Jacobinism of revolutionary France. Bishop Horsley – no fool – really did think that the Methodists were dupes of the French and the radicals.[3]

It is interesting that fifteen years after Plumb's book, E. P. Thompson agreed that Wesleyanism was a religion *for* the poor – not very good for them either – but that Primitive Methodism which began in the Potteries in the Napoleonic era, deeply influenced by American revivalism, was indeed a religion *of* the poor founded not by Oxford dons but by a carpenter (Hugh Bourne) and a potter (William Clowes). The Halévy thesis that Methodism and the wider evangelicalism saved England from revolution is still a matter of historical debate.

David Hempton, in the most recent assessment of Methodism, affirms that 'popular evangelicalism did not create the free-born Englishman, nor did it create the capacity for disciplined organization but it did offer a vibrant religious vehicle for both to operate outside the confines of the Established Church without seriously destabilizing the English state'. That final phrase is very important indeed.[4] Hempton calls Methodism a combination of 'passion and piety, zeal and order, faith and works, thrift and charity, Puritanism and decency, individualism and community and verve and vulgarity'.[5] John Walsh[6] has always stressed the 'both . . . and' character of Wesley himself and of Methodism. It offered an intense religious life, with hymn-singing giving a controlled outlet for emotional fervour, but also demanded social virtue. It offered personal religion but fostered it always in small groups. This was Wesley's great strength. It was certainly not just a code of behaviour, but sustained a theology which avoided both predestination and quietism. Faith would result in works including compassion for the poor. It offered indeed emotionalism in religion – sometimes crude in its form to 'men of reason', then and now. It was far more appealing to the adherents of popular 'folk religion' than were the moralistic theologies of a contented worldly generation beginning to enjoy a new affluence, Macclesfield silk frocks and the 'posh' hats Wesley so disliked.

So to the questions that we need to ask:

1 Was there a possibility of revolution in Great Britain? It is difficult to discuss an event which never happened! The notable Marxist historian E. J. Hobsbawm in two pioneering articles

claimed that there were revolutionary situations in 1811–12, 1816–17, 1831–2 and 1847, but asserted as Lenin had argued – a specialist in the subject! – a deterioration of the conditions of life of the masses and an increase in their political activity is not enough to bring about a revolution. There must also be a crisis in the affairs of the ruling order and a body of revolutionaries capable of directing and leading the movement. Both of these were absent. The British ruling class never lost control and the revolutionaries were inexperienced, unclear in their minds and divided. This was true right up to the end of the Chartist agitations in 1850 just after the Year of Revolutions in Europe. There was no revolution. Wesleyan Methodism was hostile to revolution but it does not follow that it was the cause of its non-occurrence. Methodism and radicalism were often running parallel in places of discontent. By 1850, the forces of order were able to deal with ease and humanity with any major disorder.[7]

2 Would 'revolution' have been any advantage to the working class? 'Class' was beginning to be used as a category in determining social status at the turn of the nineteenth century. Is there a hidden agenda here which rejects or accepts revolution before analysing its possibility? Clearly, the French Revolution altered for ever the terms on which religious establishments, the chief device on which the nations of the world had relied for Christianizing the people, must work. England had nonconformist communities in a way which France and German states did not. Monarchies toppled on the continent – churches split in Britain, in Scotland as well as in England.

3 Was stability a continuation of an antiquated status quo or was it something quite new? As we shall see, it could be said to be something new. It did owe an enormous debt to evangelicalism and Methodism. It is interesting that in the 1990s, David Hempton was much more positive on the value of the debate than were Methodist historians like John Kent or Gordon Rupp, who took a swipe at the whole concept: 'Without exaggeration of the number of converted boozers, men and women were turned from disordered characters into

sober, decent people into whose homes there came new stabilities and joys. As with the first Quakers thrift and diligence, the absence of profanity, trustworthiness, put such men on a social escalator which moved.' But he also asserts that to resolve the question why there was no revolution one would have to range over centuries of history culminating in the Civil War, the Glorious Revolution and the growing prosperity and stability of the Hanoverian age.

We can recall from the earlier chapter on Wesley's politics that it was after all Wesleyans who in effect invented the so-called 'Halévy thesis'. When threatened by possibilities of renewed attempts to stamp out unauthorized preaching at local levels they proclaimed at Conference that they were not revolutionaries and had no truck with democracy as defined by the French or, indeed, the Luddites, who were smashing the 'gig mills' in West Yorkshire. The Wesleyans led by Thomas Allan, the almost forgotten connexional solicitor,[8] constantly reiterated the political and constitutional loyalty of Methodism, as did Jabez Bunting (still comparatively young) in Halifax, Thomas Jackson in Sowerby Bridge and Robert Newton in Huddersfield. It was in self-defence that in 1811 Lord Sidmouth, the Home Secretary, sought to eliminate weavers and potters from daring to preach. Allan was also a key figure in the significant Toleration Act of 1812.

Were the Wesleyans diverting the working class from its concerns for amending the poverty in which they lived? On that, the judgement of W. R. Ward[9] has rightly fallen. After the 'Peterloo' massacre in Manchester in 1819, when radicals were cut down in the street, with Wesleyans supporting the magistracy, there was no way in which Wesleyans could become the religion of the working class in the cities. We now know that the alienation of the workers from the churches can be exaggerated. Manchester has been taken as too typical a case, as it was later by Engels. William Cobbett,[10] incidentally, saw the Wesleyans as in league with government. 'They always pray for the *ministry*. I mean the ministry at *Whitehall*. They are most *loyal* souls. "*The Thing*" protects them and they lend aid in upholding *The Thing*.' Cobbett sees the itinerant preachers as 'lazy and impudent fellows who prowl about the country living easy and jovial lives upon the fruit of the labour of other people'. This is a mixture of insight and injustice.

The idea of Methodism preventing revolution appears graphically in the thinking of Frederick Denison Maurice, arguably the greatest Anglican theologian of his day. Maurice's son reports,[11] 'As I have referred to the name of Wesley . . . I will say that I have often heard my father speak of Wesley. It is always in the mode represented by the answer he once gave to the question – "How do you account for the fact that England at the end of the eighteenth century escaped a revolution like that of France?" "Ah," he said at once, "there is not the least doubt as to that. England escaped a political revolution because she had undergone a religious revolution." "You mean that brought about by Wesley and Whitefield?" "Of course." ' That was written before Halévy was born! Ernst Troeltsch, the pioneer sociologist, made the same point. 'Methodism was one of the means by which the English world was rendered proof against the spirit of the French Revolution.' But is revolution to be avoided? Is to prevent it to allow religion to be the 'opium of the people', as Charles Kingsley as well as William Cobbett and Karl Marx feared?[12]

John Lawrence and Barbara Hammond[13] suggested that Methodism produced some democrats, but that by and large it taught the workers submission and made them inhibited and intolerant. The work of Robert F. Wearmouth[14] caused a revision of their harsher judgement. 'So Methodism, if it preached Toryism in its official declarations and a pietism that thought only of the next world in many of its chapels, it was in fact an admirable school of democrats equipping working men for popular leadership.' Perhaps the working men were not as naive as some historians appear to think. The key figure in the last century was the French historian Elie Halévy. In 1906, in an essay, he referred to Methodism as a preventive of riotous[15] behaviour around Bristol in mining settlements in 1740. He saw it as a rebirth of Puritan melancholia. Certainly there was social discontent in 1740, but the Methodist societies in their infancy were hardly strong enough to be a normative influence in a whole area, however much they affected the life of the few.

It was in the later *History of the English People*[16] – still notable as a survey – that he propounded what came to be called the 'Halévy thesis'. 'In the vast work of social organization which is one of the dominant characteristics of nineteenth century England, it would be difficult to overestimate the part played by the Wesleyan revival . . . we shall witness Methodism bringing under its influence first the dissenting sects, then the Establishment and finally secular opinion. We shall attempt to find here the key to the problem that has hitherto escaped us . . . we shall explore by this movement the extraordinary stability which English society was destined to enjoy throughout a period of revolution and crises which we can truly term the miracle of modern England, anarchist but orderly, practical and business-like, religious and even pietist.' We must note that Halévy does not claim that Methodism did it all alone, but that it was a key to understanding Victorian stability, by influencing all the other groups, a claim which depends on a particular view of the Evangelical Revival which has been shown by recent historians to be not the case.[17] We have shown that evangelicalism did not originate with Methodism, but was parallel to it and even rather patronized it. Anglican evangelicals have never really accepted Methodism.[18]

That does not dispose of the thesis. Even if the various groups in the revival were quite independent of Methodism the result could be the same stability which Halévy claimed, with powerful evidence, to typify English society. This is a point maintained consistently by David Hempton, who sees Methodism adapting itself, or being adopted by society, in England, Ireland, Wales and the USA alike. How was it that Wesleyan Arminianism, itin-erant preaching, lay leadership, 'class' systems, love feasts and hymn-singing came successfully to be exported to many different social contexts in different parts of the world from 1750 to 1850? Once established, Methodism provided a means by which there could be a combination of social stability and, in England, the erosion of the confessional state. The Methodist quarterly membership ticket was as much a symbol of the demise of the English confessional state as the Toleration Act of 1812 or the constitutional revolution of 1828 to 1832. The point is that stability remained, while the confessional state was eclipsed. The role of His or Her Majesty's loyal religious opposition is crucial.[19]

The thesis of Methodism preventing revolution was taken a step further by Maldwyn Edwards, who, while sceptical about Wesley preventing an English version of the French Revolution, suggests that 'the greatest single reason why so many workers were so little disturbed by the prevailing discontents of 1848 was that they were under the influence of the Methodist church'. The failure of England to produce a revolution in 1848 – the Year of Revolutions – has been successively attributed by Methodists to Methodism, by historians of Christian socialism to F. D. Maurice, J. M. Ludlow and their friends, and by Sir Philip Magnus to the Anti-Corn Law League. A Roman Catholic writer concludes that 'the coherence and strength of the Catholic church in England has been shown in the elimination of any anti-religious character from the trade union movement'. This is to steal Methodism's thunder with a vengeance. Such arguments appear to have little foundation in fact – even though the 'Hungry Forties' saw a million Irish die of starvation. The year 1848 saw the beginning of a notable economic boom which gave the death blow to many radical movements like Chartism for a decade or so, until the cotton famine. Methodism was, however, torn apart in the years after 1849, showing that, although its schisms were internal, it was also a 'lightning conductor' for conflicts still endemic in early industrial England.[20]

Halévy's thesis was really stood on its head by our modern Cobbett, E. P. Thompson, in *The Making of the English Working Class*, which stands like a colossal boulder across the path of every subsequent historian and is without peer in its capacity to ask the relevant questions, including exploring what Methodist experience was really like, although his avowed object was clearly stated: 'I am seeking to rescue the poor stockinger, the Luddite cropper, the obsolete hand-loom weaver, the "Utopian" artisan and even the deluded followers of Joanna Southcott from the enormous condescension of posterity.'[21] It is, as Hempton[22] puts it, 'an immensely enjoyable read and such a dangerous piece of social history', even more enjoyable when *Customs in Common* (1991) and *William Blake and the Moral Law* (1993) are added.[23] Every history student likes to quote the passage in which he calls Methodism 'a psychic ordeal in which the character-structure of the rebellious pre-industrial labourer or artisan was violently recast into that of the submissive industrial worker'. Energies in the week could go into work which was made easier by the 'Sabbath orgasms of feeling'. It was a 'ritualized form of psychic masturbation'. Methodism was the 'chiliasm of the defeated and the hopeless'. 'The box-like blackening chapels stood in the industrial districts like great traps for the human psyche . . . ' Thompson forgets how many *rural* Methodists like my harness-maker grandfather kept 'Saint Monday' after their 'orgasms'. 'The idea of a passionate Methodist lover in those days is ludicrous.' The other side of that last crack is the story of Samuel Bradburn, who had an alcohol problem also!,[24] and other itinerant preachers with their frequent pastoral calls to remote farmhouses where there were attractive daughters. Their love affairs slightly undermine Thompson's critique, as do Dr Peter Gay's[25] fascinating explorations of Victorian sexuality. Even Jabez Bunting (despite his adding up a series of reasons for asking for the hand of his lady friend or for ending the relationship) hoped for a cold night on a coach ride, writing to Miss Maclardie, 'We shall be obliged to squeeze as close to each other as we can.'[26] Incidentally, Jabez Bunting, when at Halifax, made pejorative comments on revivalism and the antics which Thompson also mocked! In 1813, he wrote to George Marsden in the wake of the Luddite executions, 'However solicitous to make the best of this, it is after all an awful fact; and confirms me in my fixed opinions that the progress of Methodism in the West Riding of Yorkshire has been *more swift than solid; more extensive than deep*; more an increase in numbers than in the diffusion of that kind of piety which shines so brightly and operates so visibly at home, as in the Prayer Meeting and the crowded Lovefeast.'[27] It is not always clear why Thompson thinks anyone wanted to be a Methodist. But we can be grateful that 'lapsed' Methodists like Thompson and Christopher Hill have written such lively history!

Was Thompson accurate? Dr John Kent – a stern critic of Thompson in some ways – followed Professor Pollard[28] in showing that the factory owners had many grim means of discipline besides Methodism and that 'chiliasm' or millenarianism was never characteristic of Methodism; but that was not quite Thompson's point in this context. His 'oscillation' theory that distress leads to religion is dubious, though by no means wholly inaccurate as Black Country cholera outbreaks later show. But to be fair to Thompson we need to note the somewhat repressive antics of the mill owners Ackroyd in Halifax and the brothers John and James Shutt at the Shaw Mills in Nidderdale. Earlier, Robert Peel (Senior) at Bury boasted that he left his mills in the hands of Methodists and they served him 'excellently well'. Wesley feared for his soul! These men found the Methodist virtues of honesty, sobriety and discipline doubly rewarding in themselves. They made for success in business, and in the workers they helped to create an orderly labour force which would accept the discipline of the factory.[29]

This supports Thompson, and much of his evidence is from the West Riding of Yorkshire, where lapsed Methodists might be Luddites but few, if any, members of Methodist societies. What of the scenario in Manchester in 1821? James Stephens, Superintendent Minister (father of the radical Joseph Rayner Stephens), writes to Bunting: 'The objects we have kept in view are: 1st to give the sound part of the society a decided ascendancy; 2. so to put down the opposition as to disable them from doing mischief; 3. to cure those of them that are worth saving; 4. to take the rest one by one and crush them when they notoriously commit themselves . . . they are growing tired of radicalism and as that dies religion will revive. Our congregations are good. Methodism stands high among the respectable people.' Parallel with Stephens were the local preachers of Burnley, who in December

1818 were asked, 'What is the opinion of the meeting respecting local preachers abetting the cause of combination and encouraging revolutionary measures?' The answer given is, 'We are unanimous in our opinion that as preachers of righteousness and followers of Christ whose Kingdom is not of this world we ought to respect every ordinance of man for the Lord's sake whether of the King as Supreme Governor of the Realm or of magistrates acting under authority.' This is precisely Cobbett's point and Thompson's also![30]

Any contrary view might bring swift retribution.[31] William Stephenson, a local preacher of North Shields, protested at Newcastle up on Tyne about 'Peterloo'. Robert Pilter, the superintendent, advised Stephenson to hold his tongue. The Conservative Edmund Grindrod and Jabez Bunting became involved, as did the 'Committee of Privileges'. Stephenson lost his job as a teacher in a colliery school and was expelled from Wesleyanism, and as a consequence fourteen Independent Methodist Societies were founded in the Newcastle area. The price of protection under the law was silence on politics – or rather on *radical* politics. This was true at conference level in all the Methodist connexions, though we need to remember that Methodism has always had those who sat loose to conference resolutions. This is certainly the case in Yorkshire! Incidentally, Thompson makes the ironic comment that the Labour Party Conference had many features of the Methodist Conference, caucuses and all![32] There are indeed 'many Methodisms'.

What can we say forty years after Thompson's critique of Methodism and ninety years after Halévy? Methodism clearly became a religion of the 'labour aristocracy' and the groups just below them.[33] Dissent flourished among those groups in society which could be somewhat independent of paternal squirearchy or its urban equivalents. It was the middling groups of society which could afford the luxury of dissent. When 'dependency' in the parishes began to break down, dissent could be a possibility much lower in the social scale. It almost became historical orthodoxy that Methodism filled gaps in the parish system, particularly as new industries often grew in villages as well as large towns.[34] Areas like Calderdale around Halifax, Rossendale between Burnley and Bury, the Isle of Wight and Cornwall are classic instances. The southern counties, except for the South-West and Middlesex, where parishes were smaller and more 'closed', continued to be a 'Methodist desert' well into the nineteenth century.

Does John Walsh's summary still hold up?[35] Methodism was able to enlarge and articulate existing cells of godliness, and weave into a connexional system all sorts of little marginal outgroups and expatriates. Converts often had a traditional religious background. The ideal conditions for a new society would be that it be sited in a large freehold parish well stocked with artisans or industrial workers or small freeholders with a number of leaderless disgruntled nonconformists ready to be woven into the connexional system in a parish with no resident clergyman. In 1743 out of 837 parishes in the diocese of York, 393 had non-resident incumbents and 315 were held by pluralists or immoral clergymen. Societies of Methodists could grow near to good roads, close to other settlements not far from the avuncular protection of a town society with an eloquent assistant preacher. Yet even with these circumstances a society might not thrive or might be bedevilled by divisions – Methodism flourished under the shadow of the Minster at York, as Dr Royle has shown, and in parishes in Lincolnshire, where there were more ancient parishes than anywhere save Norfolk. Generalizations are dangerous. There are 'many Methodisms'.

What is clear beyond a doubt is that the *male* constituency was largely artisan[36] – masons, shoemakers, cordwainers, harness-makers, saddlers, carpenters, potters, croppers, stockingers, and the like, out of proportion to their numbers in the population. This was also true in America for the first generation or so. Thompson's thesis that Methodism acted as a repressive element in creating a new non-revolutionary working-class consciousness does not apply to eighteenth-century Methodism. Here was a society or 'connexion' developing into a denomination which enabled artisans to express their sense of belonging outside what Professor Harold Perkin calls 'the dependency system'. The early preachers came from the same constituency. So it could be argued, as it was by Alan Gilbert,[37] that 'Evangelical Nonconformity echoed the aspirations rather than the despair of the working class.' In the next generation, it stimulated aspiration and improvement, and later the symbols of that aspiration – the vitally important Sunday schools; for self-improving and education were much more working-class than meets the eye, as Lacqueur[38] convincingly showed. There were *friendly societies* to keep people out of the workhouse, like the later *Local Preachers' Mutual Aid Association*;[39] and later, there were the *trade unions*, in which Methodists, especially Primitive Methodists in the North-East, played a key role – the treasurers were often trusted Methodists! Later there was a role of conciliation rather than strident protest, although Methodists in Seaton Delaval in 1844[40] prayed for the death of 'blacklegs' and strikebreakers. Some Methodists were Chartists, like William Thornton of Halifax, who in 1839 prayed at a great Chartist rally. Feargus O'Connor, the radical leader, clapped him on the shoulder. 'Well done Thornton, when we get the Charter, I'll see you are made Archbishop of York.' Thornton forthwith emigrated![41]

Wesleyan Methodism might still be said to be *for* the poor rather than *of* the poor. In the early nineteenth century 62 per cent of male Wesleyans were artisans, 9.5 per cent were labourers and 7.6 per cent were colliers, compared with 47 per cent of Primitive Methodists being artisans, 16 per cent labourers and 12 per cent colliers. While some artisans could be poor, the Primitives were more representative of the labouring poor. But let us not forget that about 60 per cent of members were women, many of them domestic servants.[42] Many had their modes of self-respect, the 'poor man's masonry' of friendly societies which at least assured money from 'the box' when you were ill and a ham tea at your funeral. In 1872 there were 4 million men in friendly societies. Temperance or *total abstinence* was firstly a working-class movement, part of aspiration and self-fulfilment. 'The pledge' became almost a kind of substitute for evangelical conversion, a badge of self-esteem and respectability which gave some working wives a freedom from the worst of gross poverty, but also drove a wedge between the 'respectable' and the 'unrespectable' poor, whose centre was the pub. Friendly societies split on this issue. The Methodist chapel in Blakenhall, Wolverhampton, was opposite the appropriately named Fighting Cocks! In Durham Edward Welbourne[43] wrote of the Methodists 'taking away from the pitman his dog, his fighting cock and his gun. Prayer meetings would replace pay night frolics.' Roman Catholic priests got on better with the unrespectable poor.

It all seems like a secularization of scriptural holiness[44] – a mode of life for the 'sparrows' rather than the 'eagles'. Idleness, irresponsibility, indiscipline became the enemy. Giving to the poor became Christian stewardship. Methodism became the religion of lower-middle-class self-respect, though if we could tell the whole story it would be a tale of intense responsibility for society also, often enough expressed in civic and political and charitable behaviour and earnestness. The Municipal Corporation Act of 1835 was vitally important. Not for nothing was Salem Methodist New Connexion Chapel, Halifax, called the 'mayor's nest' so many town mayors came from that particular chapel. Under the clock at Darlington Street Chapel, Wolverhampton, in 1848 sat the first mayor, ironmaster G. B. Thorneycroft, John Hartley (1813–84), head of the enterprise, and H. H. Fowler (1830–1911), later Lord Wolverhampton, the first Methodist to sit in the Cabinet. Occasionally ironmaster Baldwin might appear from Bewdley. A new liberal Methodist bourgeoisie was becoming important in the provinces.

The 1960s saw another thesis – that of Professor Harold Perkin.[45] He argued that religion in Victorian England was a *midwife* of class consciousness – the midwife not the mother or the child! Many went through Methodism into the wider world of politics. This is still so. Ask David Blunkett,[46] Home Secretary in 2002, where he learned the art of public speaking. It was as a Methodist local preacher! Likewise Sir David Frost, the TV guru. Margaret Thatcher gave her first public addresses as a member of the John Wesley Society at Oxford, leading worship in country chapels with her 'team'.[47]

Perkin saw religion as having three roles in the Industrial

Revolution. It gave expression to emancipation from the dependency system before it hardened into overt class antagonism. Emancipation from pastoral and religious disciplines went hand in hand with urbanization. Here is the sharpest paradox of the nineteenth century, the emergence, in the midst of the greatest revival of religious faith since the Middle Ages, of the agnosticism and indifference which was to be the dominant spiritual position of modern society. Both were part of the emancipation from the old paternal society. The existence of competing groups, which was characteristic of England compared with the continent, provides a series of stepping stones by which the emancipated industrial worker could make his way from the church to any position of Christian belief, or in the end into unbelief. I think that when one looks at the conditions of work before 1875, there is a little romanticism here. Perkin exaggerates the role of some of the smaller Methodist groups here, building too much on the memoirs of Thomas Cooper or Joseph Barker – lapsed Methodists both – but the basic point is certainly arguable.

Some modern research has shown that more working men – and more particularly working *women* – were linked with churches and chapels than previously thought. Thompson wrote his book when living at Siddal, a somewhat run-down part of Halifax. Dr Simon Green has recently shown a great deal of working-class involvement in the chapels there.[48] The same is true of Oldham[49] and Bolton, and later the small railway town of Horwich, where I live. In 1880 Horwich had 3,000 inhabitants, with bleaching as the main industry. In 1900 there were 14,000, due to the railway works providing a sudden boom. In moved the Irish 'diaspora'; Catholic churches and schools were built, including a now notable comprehensive school. The Welsh 'diaspora' patronized the Wesleyans, who built two chapels. The United Methodists matched the Wesleyans' 'Victoria' with their 'Brunswick'! The Independent Methodists built a large chapel. Numbers in Sunday schools were very large indeed, with all the rapid development of the 'institutional church'. Even today, a century later, I would hazard the observation that church attendance is higher than in many places. In Methodism the predominance of artisans and engineers has been displaced by an extraordinary number of people at every level of the education system. Horwich is an interesting paradigm of Methodist development in the generation after that which concerned Thompson.

Methodism in the nineteenth century provided the means or, at least, the modes of class organization, the moral earnestness, the sense of calling, the tight-knit organization which spilled over into secular groups. Trained in oratory, initiative and discipline, lay preachers naturally gravitated to leadership in any movement they joined. The Methodists and lapsed Methodists – Lovett (who taught the Methodist twentieth-century radical S. E. Keeble), Cooper and others, from whatever 'connexion' – brought considerable powers of charismatic leadership to the political societies and trade unions. The legacy was the training and organization, the instinct for and style of non-violent conflict through negotiation and discussion which, paradoxically, the English working class was to teach their employers and rulers. That last point needs to be put alongside Patrick Joyce's[50] recent analysis of towns like Bolton in *Visions of the People* and David Cannadine's *Class in Britain*. Can it be claimed that there developed what Perkin called a 'viable class society' moving away from the appalling work discipline which Thompson rightly abominated, a kind of camaraderie across class boundaries in the mills and other industries towards the end of the nineteenth century, though Saltaire in Bradford is much earlier, followed later by Akroyden in Halifax and Port Sunlight?

Perkin's third point follows. Not so much by positive teaching and patience but by active example of the non-violent tactics, there was administered 'an analgesic against the pains of labour'. If we compare Robert Colls's[51] picture of the Durham miners, we move from those who prayed for the death of blacklegs to the more conciliatory style portrayed by Robert Moore in his *Pitmen, Preachers and Politics*, a style which owed so much to Primitive Methodism, and which had passed away by the time of the General Strike of 1926. We can go there now and spend a day at Beamish, a living museum of a way of life including a chapel in which a lecture is given on former days with musical illustrations. It is a world, including the closed pits, which is now as far away as Thompson's croppers.

Perhaps Harold Perkin is a latter day Halévy telling us that Methodism – and dissent – saved England from the Russian Revolution, a by no means foolish concept.

Here are four vignettes of what I have called the 'many Methodisms'.

First Jack Lawson[52] – Lord Lawson of Attlee's government of 1945. He is in the pit. 'As we went "out by" my pony trotting before, we would talk books while we walked bent double in the dark roadway. I remember well when this elderly man first "struck" Nietzsche. That was a find – and I also remember how the man turned me upside down mentally, which was all to my good. This man read the New Testament in Greek! Methodism took the nobodies and made the most humble and hopeless somebody. They set aside the things that are not good for a man. They had some little pride in their dress, they made their homes to be things of beauty and aspired and worked to give their children a better life and opportunity than themselves.'

Down in Suffolk and Norfolk there was the 'Revolt of the Field'. Sir George Edwards[53] began as an illiterate crow scarer. In Primitive Methodism he found a purpose, a wife and call to preach which led to social concern. 'With my study of theology, I soon began to realize that the social conditions of the people were not as God intended they should be. The gross injustice meted out to my parents and the terrible suffering I had undergone in my boyhood burned themselves into my soul like a hot iron. Many a time did I vow that I would do something to better the conditions of my class.'

A little later, we move to the Wesleyans, in Tysoe in Warwickshire about 1900. 'It was when Arthur was nine that the new vicar arrived. One day he came into school shortly before midday and talked to the children on the subject of manners. He spoke of his father, the General, and the order of ranks in the army. The children were omitting to curtsy to his wife and daughter and their governess. Girls should not say "Good morning" but they should silently curtsy. Boys should not raise their caps but should touch them only. God divinely appointed us our places in society and we should learn the appropriate manners. Arthur enlivened the dinner table with a spirited account of this talk and was surprised to see his father rise in terrible anger and go off there and then to the vicarage. He would not have his children taught ridiculous manners. The vicar must confine himself to Scripture periods and he and his friends would withdraw their children under the *Cowper Temple* clause.' There is that 'consciousness of effortless superiority', once ascribed to the members of Balliol College, Oxford, which even now can still occur in relationships between Anglicans and Free Church people. The result is a quite proper dissent. Methodism was now part of the Nonconformist Conscience.[54]

Lastly we go to Cumbria. The poet and writer, the late Norman Nicholson, describes Wesleyanism in the 1920s in *Wednesday Early Closing*. 'If my father had married five or ten years later I would have missed some of the voices and much of the fervour but in 1922, though the high tornado of the Evangelical Revival had been dying away for at least half a century, there was still a following wind that blew through these services. Conversion, the changed life, "the heart strangely warmed" were still at the centre of Methodist theology even if for many they were now something of a formality. Indeed, few of the congregation were converts to Wesley's sense – they were children of converts or grandchildren or more likely great grandchildren. In the church they had a "mission" each year. "It's the same crowd that gets saved every blessed time" my father would say in an aggrieved voice. "You'd wonder how they ever found time to get lost."

'But there are men and women walking about Millom today whose upbringing would have been quite different if their fathers or grandfathers had not suddenly given up drinking or gambling or knocking his wife about and turning on the snap of a response into a sober, hard working, hard serving, hard praying chapel man.

'It came to me as complete surprise in my teenage years to find that Methodists were considered to be killjoys who got little pleasure out of life. For at least up to the age of thirteen, the chapel seemed to me one of the happiest places in the town.'[55]

What of the twentieth century? I have attempted to summarize English Methodism's recent history in *Modern Methodism in England 1932–1998* and will not repeat it. Dr John Habgood, former Archbishop of York,[56] pointed recently to a European story of the inverse relationship between religious adherence and crime. In very broad terms the rise and fall of Protestant church adherence in Britain over the last 150 years clearly parallels the rise in the number of indictable crimes. Habgood cites Geoffrey Gorer from 1950. 'In public life the English are certainly among the most peaceful, gentle, courteous and orderly populations that the civilized world has ever seen . . . the control of aggression has gone to such remarkable lengths that you hardly ever see a fight in a bar, when football crowds are as orderly as church meetings . . . the orderliness and gentleness, the absence of overt aggression calls for explanation.' In 2001 the picture seems almost ludicrous and incredible. Was it the case? I began to go to league football matches in 1944. Even in very large crowds I was never scared – not until the 1970s. But now? We might ask the French police at the World Cup in 1998. Could what Gorer and Richard Hoggart[57] and Norman Nicholson talk about be explained at all in terms of organized religion or even more 'folk' and 'popular' religion passed on by bodies like Sunday schools, and youth and uniformed organizations, up to the Second World War and beyond? Methodism still had a million youngsters on its premises in 1950. The role of the day school must not be underestimated either.

There was no revolution in the 1930s in England, with no Nazi-style party of great strength despite Sir Oswald Mosley – although one needs to remember that in an industrial town like Wolverhampton as late as 1910 'Catholic' and 'Wesleyan' boys from their respective denominational schools would hurl insults and even bricks at one another on St Patrick's Day! Is Gorer's picture merely romantic? Will a historian resurrect Halévy's thesis to show the role of the churches and chapels and the almost total lack of that role in recent years?

Very recently Dr Callum Brown in *The Death of Christian Britain*[58] has almost resurrected the Halévy thesis by claiming to show the predominance of evangelicalism in Victorian Britain, including its much greater influence on the working class. He seeks to show that British religiosity became highly feminized with the woman the 'angel' and indeed the mistress in the home. He then claims that a great change came after 1960, not only 'believing but not belonging' but a total change in discourse from a Christian style paralleling changes in femininity. On Brown's clash with the secularization theories, which see a much more long-term change, we cannot here comment, but it fits some of the earlier arguments of this chapter. His claim is that it fails to realize that Christian discourse dominates the mind-set of women and that popular religiosity was much stronger than the sociologists have realized. If he is right, that is part of the influence and impact of Methodism. Halévy lives still.

8

Church of the People: Primitive Methodism

As we have seen, J. H. Plumb's statement that Methodism was not a religion *of* the poor but *for* the poor was elaborated upon by E. P. Thompson, who added the rider that 'the poor man's dissent of Bunyan, of Dan Taylor and later of the Primitive Methodists *was* a religion of the poor'. Robert Colls, more recently, describing the Primitive Methodists of the Durham coalfield in the 1840s, writes: 'On the one hand they were blamed for their zeal. Proclaiming a particular kind of working class confidence; on the other hand they were praised for their order, producing a kind of control which other agencies could not achieve. Both judgements are essentially correct – an apparent paradox which has confused historians ever since.' He goes on, 'the men trickled into trade unionism and politics as a working class vanguard. The women ran the home and taught the family to overcome poverty and illness and filth which engulfed them. Chapel was their ground of being, life was where it was practised. What we see in Primitive Methodism is a politics of religion, the production of men and women who are Christians and can be Christians in society. In the coalfields, the Methodist contribution to trade unionism, Liberalism and the Labour Party was not so much a contribution of ideology as a direct giving of persons of a new kind. It lasted a hundred years.'[1]

Primitive Methodism is a paradigm of the development of an evangelistic sect into a full-blown denomination, but it is the case that such judgement needs developing now in the light of new approaches to folk traditions and folk religion. Primitive

Methodism became an independent group of evangelical Arminians from the Wesleyans, even if, clearly, it sprang from Wesleyanism. There were 'many Methodisms'. Its founders were a carpenter and a potter, not Oxford dons! It was more of the Age of Romanticism than of the Age of Reason. It can be seen – this is Colls's paradox – as a folk tradition both opposing aspects of the life of labouring people and blending with some of it, then becoming an instrument of working-class organizations and consciousness well before the more middle-class styles of Victorian self-help, with which they should not be confused and which were outlined in the previous chapter.[2]

Primitive Methodism was a religion of the poor in the first generation. If the early Primitive Methodists can be seen at least in name as the remote descendants of the 'Ranters' of an earlier age – 'Christ against culture', to use Richard Niebuhr's still valid categorization – the later Primitive Methodists take on almost unconsciously the role of 'Christ the transformer of culture'. Both continued Wesley's claim to 'spread scriptural holiness', prefiguring the Labour Party in politics and the liberalization of theology in the free churches, which helped the churches to come to terms with Darwin, Freud and Marx.[3] Is there a link between the pitmen of Seaton Delaval in 1844, led by three Primitive Methodist local preachers, who, when on strike, prayed for the success of the strike – they even prayed that 'blacklegs' brought in from a distance might be injured or killed, cheering when it happened – and the conciliatory style of Peter Lee (1864–1935)? Of him it was said, 'In the chapels of County Durham from one end to the other, Sunday by Sunday, he preached the gospel, coal-hewer, checkweighman, miners' agent, County Councillor and Alderman, magistrate and MP.' Here was a typical Primitive Methodist politician, a fine illustration of the paradox, which baffles the historian. Let us seek to unravel the puzzle.[4]

The Second Revival

We begin in the 1790s after Wesley's death. A new style of evangelism and revivalism is spreading across the Atlantic. The

'Frontier Tradition' is very different from the style of the Wesleys, who were nearer the heart of the Enlightenment, with Scripture, tradition, reason and experience subtly balanced, even if, for Wesley, Scripture was the primary authority. If the Evangelical Revival was a broad stream, the confluence of many tributaries, so was the Second Great Awakening[5] spilling over into Great Britain with the itinerancy of Lorenzo Dow, linking with the Yorkshire Revival in the 1790s[6] and sparking revival in the Potteries. Revivalistic evangelism of an undenominational style was common in the 1790s and was a transatlantic phenomenon, as was the first awakening. Bishops like Pretyman-Tomline of Lincoln feared a return to the days of Oliver Cromwell. The style was lay, more exuberant, perhaps lacking in order but not in ardour, personified in eccentric 'Crazy Dow', hair down to his waist, with flashing eyes, harsh voice and crude gestures, asthmatic and epileptic. He was so bizarre that Thomas Coke[7] thought him a spy, reporting him to the government, a matter not forgotten when he appeared again at camp meetings, religious 'pop festivals', tame compared with the days' long American variety, which enabled the revivalists to develop feasts and fasts in deliberate rivalry to the wakes and statute fairs.

The first tributary is clearly the work of Francis Asbury (1745–1816),[8] the first bishop of the American Methodist Church. Now here really was the horse rider! Ralph Waldo Emerson said, 'America is Europe up to the Appalachians, beyond that is real America.' Asbury, even if centred near the Chesapeake, crossed those mountains many times taking the faith to 'the Frontier'. For forty-five years he journeyed. 'From Maine to Virginia, through the Carolinas, wading through swamps, swimming the rivers that flow from the eastern slopes of the Alleghenies to the Atlantic, or down to Georgia, back to North Carolina, through the mountains to Tennessee, three hundred miles and back through the unbroken wilderness of Kentucky, back again to New York, to New England, then from the Atlantic to the Hudson, over a rough road, mountainous and difficult on to Ohio.' Asbury – an artisan apprentice from the Black Country, of the type so crucial in Methodism – inherited that strange combination of autocracy and democracy which was early English Methodism. His message from 1771 onwards was free grace, conversion and holiness. In 1783 there were 4,000 members, in 1816 there were 217,000 members, more than in England. With Asbury church orders and liturgy were subordinate to mission, but the class meeting remained always the means of preventing revival from becoming hysterical chaos. The Quarterly Meetings of the preachers and leaders – a fairly sedate affair in England except at times of protest at autocracy – became a means of prayer and renewal, which in the end was the spark for the camp meetings which the Presbyterians began in 1801, which were hijacked by the Methodists. They lasted several days, with preaching, praying, singing. 'This is fishing with a large net,' said Asbury in 1802. The faith was offered in a way that people could understand and 'own'. Churches were 'planted', as we would say today. It was, indeed, a religion of the poor. In subtle ways Primitive Methodism in England was a 'frontier' faith, too, even if the more concentrated population of industrial England was very different from that across the Appalachians and Alleghenies. As Russell Richey puts it, the Methodists of Asbury's style were 'at war with war, at war with slavery, at war with the genteel world with its elaborate rituals of fashion, display, gambling and combat, at war with the "old" Anglicanism that embraced the world'.[9] Women were affirmed, a bi-racial society was on the horizon, although, alas, ante-bellum America saw the churches split on slavery.[10] It was Nathan Söderblom, the Swedish ecumenist, who said, 'Methodism has become the most characteristic form of religion in the New World – Luther's evangelical certainty of faith translated into soul suffering intensity and Anglo-Saxon capability of action.'[11]

The Potteries Revival

We return to the Cheshire Plain and the Potteries.[12] The Second Revival found a ready soil here, where the parish system was weak in the huge Chester diocese. There were pockets of undenominational revivalism, which crystallized out in the Quaker or

Independent Methodists of Warrington and Macclesfield, the 'Band Room' Methodists of Manchester, the revivalists of Leeds – 'the Kirkgate Screamers' led by James Sigston, who emerges again in the 1820s when the trustees of Brunswick Chapel wanted their famous organ against the desire of the circuit, provoking schism. Then there were the 'Magic Methodists' of Delamere Forest, who specialized in trance-like states, led by James Crawfoot, the 'old man of the forest'. Revivalism shades off into all sorts of pre-millenarian groups, like the followers of Joanna Southcott and 'Mother Lee', whose Shakers had Manchester origins.[13] The links here are with Quakerism and left-wing relics of Puritanism, much of which was picked up by the Primitive Methodists, when their revival moved swiftly down the Trent Valley in the Great Midlands Revival after the end of the Napoleonic Wars – one of the most rapid revivals in British church history from 200 members in 1811 to 33,507 by 1824. In fact one may almost speak of what the Americans called a 'burned over District',[14] though the 'burnings' were of longer duration and at wider intervals. Here were the heartlands of Lollardy and radical Puritanism – John Wycliffe, George Fox, a continuing 'secret multitude of true professors' perhaps – weavers and outworkers, leaders of radicalism and revival for centuries. Primitive Methodism was in some way a revivalistic form of Quakerism,[15] so that it was not for nothing that they were christened 'Ranters' in Belper.

Working-class life was harsh and wild, with noisy 'wakes' and popular magic. If there was a thin line between the female saint and the 'wise woman', there was a similar thin line between James Crawfoot (who was the first paid itinerant of Primitive Methodism), the Magic Methodists of Delamere Forest and belief in witches, boggarts, the actions of the devil and special providence. We must not exaggerate. There has always been a Puritan-like thirst for knowledge in a self-taught man like Hugh Bourne, who was converted through books. Hugh Bourne (1772–1852) belongs to the revivalist ethos, as did William Clowes (1780–1851), a converted dancer, revivalist potter, whose story is a miracle of grace.

Primitive Methodists' 'mythology' is more plebeian than its Wesleyan counterpart – no Fellows of Lincoln College and their attractive lady friends; a shy carpenter (there's precedent there!), Hugh Bourne, wondering whether to go Quaker or Methodist, converting his cousin Shubotham by 'conversation preaching', gossiping the gospel, building his chapel at Harriseahead, preaching with semi-authority from the Burslem Wesleyans, gathering converts, being promised by Shubotham 'a day's praying on Mow' one day. Mow Cop is that outcrop of the Pennines dominating the Cheshire Plain. In this area itinerant preachers were common, and Lorenzo Dow came here for the second time. He worked among the Methodist New Connexion, then in what Richard Carwardine has called 'third division' revivalism[16], groups like those led by Peter Phillips, a friend of Bourne, who later led the Independent Methodists.[17] Bourne, for all his Wesleyanism, belongs to this ethos, as later does William Clowes. When Clowes follows Bourne, expelled from Wesleyanism for 'not attending class' – which clearly meant attending or 'setting up other forms of worship' or in Bourne's case taking out a preacher's licence without permission – the two groups of Camp Meeting Methodists, led by Bourne, and the 'Clowesites' coalesce using the phrase 'Primitive Methodist'. This had been used by John Pawson and by the eccentric James Crawfoot in 1807, when expelled from Wesleyanism. This, in 1812, was an attempt to recall revivalist roots in contrast to the staid, more urban, increasingly bourgeois style of Wesleyanism, which repelled them.

The camp meetings were sober compared with the American style. The famous occasions at Mow and the Norton meeting in 1807 were all Sunday affairs – preaching, praying – always of paramount importance to Bourne and Clowes – singing, gathering converts in contradiction to the hiring and firing of labourers at 'wakes'. The Wesleyan Conference dissociated itself in 1807 from camp meetings in England. From the standpoint of the Wesleyan itinerants, this was a dangerous time. The war against Napoleon was being waged. Invasion scares or fears of Jacobinism were still rife. Governmental action might be taken against the Methodists. Toleration had only survived by a whisker in

1800.[18] The Home Secretary, Lord Sidmouth, in 1811,[19] with at first some support from Thomas Coke and even Adam Clarke, tried to pilot his infamous bill through the House of Lords. Magistrate Sparrow had written to Sidmouth from Stafford stating that fifteen potters had asked for licences as Methodist preachers – Bourne certainly had a licence to go ahead with the Mow Cop meetings. Sidmouth disliked what he called 'blacksmiths, cobblers, tailors, peddlers, chimney sweepers and what not' being granted licences. The bill to demand that preachers should have settled congregations would have pole-axed local preaching, as we have seen.

Wesleyanism, as well as revivalism across dissent, was involved in Sidmouth's policy. Their fears were not without cause – the Kilhamite schism was not long in the past and prone to revivalism which sent shivers down the spines of young ministers like Jabez Bunting, rapidly rising to leadership, who forgot their own radical origins.[20] The whole matter is the perennial tension between 'order' and 'ardour'. Ironically, within a very short time some of the revivalists were complaining of what they called the 'Tunstall non-mission law' – a demand by Bourne for a time of consolidation and discipline before the revival spread again. More than once Bourne had to apply his 'chopper' to those who seemed to him to be precisely what he had seemed to the Wesleyans. So the early style was of cottage meetings, camp meetings and class groups – a kind of exuberant Quakerism with no trace of clericalism. As yet this was local and small-scale – in 1811 there were 200 members. At the first assembly – a Quaker phrase – or conference of 1820 there were 7,842 members, eight circuits with 48 'travelling preachers'.

The Midlands Revival 1814-25 and Its Consequences

The 'Non-Mission Law' was swept aside by John Benton, who, armed with Dow's hymn book, missioned the Derbyshire villages. Into the picture comes Miss Sarah Kirkland,[21] the first of the remarkable group of women itinerants which ended as late as 1890 with the death of the formidable Miss Elizabeth Bultitude, who had 'travelled' for thirty years and lived in retirement for almost as long. This is a remarkable chapter in the movement for women's freedom for, like the Quakers, Primitive Methodism allowed a measure of sexual equality, although none of the female itinerants became superintendents. They were expected to be 'models of plainness in their dress', another Quakerly trait. Miss Bultitude later emphasized that her stipend did not permit her to buy the fashionable dresses which some members of her congregation might have preferred.

Lorenzo Dow comes into the picture again in the Midlands Revival, which can be dated from camp meetings at Mercaston in Derbyshire in June 1816 and in Nottingham Forest on Whit Sunday of the same year. Sarah Kirkland 'opened', to use the contemporary phrase, Nottingham. The 'work' advanced into Lincolnshire and Leicestershire, with Loughborough becoming a centre in 1818. The Primitives offered the old gospel – the three 'R's of ruin, repentance and redemption – to those apparently outside the reach of parish church and Wesleyan chapel alike – such as farm labourers, miners, fisher folk and later the nailers of the Black Country. The small industrial village and the extracting industries became, as well as country areas, the heartlands of Primitive Methodism. Their congregations had a higher proportion of labourers than did the Wesleyans, who had more artisans, although in the next generation a town Primitive Methodist society could be higher in the social scale than some Wesleyan chapels in villages. Often the leading lay person in a society would be a shopkeeper. A trustees' minute book from Motcombe in Dorset as late as 1892 shows that five trustees were labourers, two farmers, two blacksmiths, and there was the village grocer. He was, not surprisingly, treasurer. The little chapel at Horwich Moor in Lancashire, as recently as 1950, had as its list of trustees, two warehousemen, a plumber, a fitter, a joiner, an electrical fitter, a female shop assistant, a housewife, a crane driver, a sub-postmaster and an accountant – the typical Primitive Methodist scenario surviving well after Methodist Union, with clear evidence of some rise in the social scale from labourer to 'labour aristocracy'.[22]

From the Midlands Revival the Nottingham circuit threw out a 'branch' into Hull,[23] from which town Clowes began his remarkable revivalist work in the East Riding and further to the North-West, breaking up new ground as far as Cumberland. The journeyings and sheer energy of the men and women who were full-time itinerants is quite extraordinary. Clowes was a practical mystic. 'When I have to preach I dare not leave my room till God has given me the congregation, and then I go up the pulpit stairs with majesty.' But the pulpit stairs might just as likely be a bench or a chair or a wheelbarrow.[24] Villages could be missioned by zealous preachers with a Franciscan optimism – praying, preaching, singing with equal fervour, with a gospel of forgiveness which could reach men and women on the margins of society. These were the heroic days of circuit initiative when Hull opened up 'missions' in Kent, and when Bolton missioned the Isle of Man. In 1829 the Hull and Tunstall circuits combined in sending four missionaries – one a woman – to the United States, following the tracks of emigrants whose numbers were growing. Their 'equipment' included a supply of hand bills which were to make known to the inhabitants of America the reason for their arrival.

It is tempting to seek economic and social roots and causes for the success of revival. Indeed there is no doubt that Primitive Methodism was particularly sensitive to cyclical fluctuations and periods of unemployment. The historian of Primitive Methodism, H. B. Kendall, at the beginning of the twentieth century, explained fluctuations in membership figures primarily in economic terms.[25] It is interesting that a fall in Wesleyan numbers coincided with the Midlands Revival at its height. Clearly Primitive Methodism was appealing to a different stratum of the population. The year of the so-called 'Peterloo' massacre in Manchester – 1819 – marked a large increase. Have we here what E. P. Thompson called 'the chiliasm of the despairing and defeated'? 1824–5, years of economic depression and gross unemployment, saw the great crisis of Primitive Methodism when Bourne and Clowes were forced to prune the ranks of the travelling preachers of undesirable time-servers – 'runners out of circuits', Bourne called them. They were men seeking employment as preachers rather than semi-starvation 'on the parish'. Certainly the astute Marxist historian Eric Hobsbawm in *Primitive Rebels*[26] is right to point out the way in which Primitive Methodism could quickly establish societies in villages or semi-village areas, places where industry was relatively underdeveloped, a pattern of living which tended to disappear as the modern pattern of urbanization and factory industry grew. W. R. Ward has pointed to the effects of 'enclosures', battles over tithes, the unpopularity of the clergy who formed a quarter of the bench of magistrates in 1830. Labourers seeking an end to dependency could easily become followers of 'Ned Ludd', or later in 1830 'Captain Swing', and remain within Primitive Methodism, even if Hugh Bourne did throw a man he called a 'speeching radical' out of an early conference. 'If ever a movement was created on a shoestring, it was Primitive Methodism and the years of business upturn which followed the slumps of 1819, 1832 and 1848 were golden ones for the revivalists. On the other hand, the denomination was threatened with collapse during the downturn from the business peak of 1825, and had only one really good year (as business was picking up from the slump of 1842) in the unhappy period between 1837 and 1848.'[27] The figures of membership show a remarkable pattern as from 1819 to 1824 the membership rose from 7,842 to 33,507. It was the harvest of the Midlands Revival and Clowes's work from Hull. Tunstall circuit had opened up work in Manchester and in what Hobsbawm calls the 'miserable zone of petty and archaic industries in the West Midlands'. Black Country villages with social homogeneity were a Primitive Methodist seedbed. East Anglia had 9,000 members by 1842. Somewhat earlier, Wiltshire, Hampshire and Berkshire saw much persecution by squire and parson, who equated 'ranters' with rickburners. In the Conference of 1842, connexional membership had risen to 85,565, much swifter increases than the primary growth of Wesley's Methodism, though we need to remember it was a booming population. It is sociologically significant that William Clowes could never achieve much in London – the rural and industrial village was the typical centre of a Primitive Methodist Society.

What changes did it bring to people? Methodism did not so much displace folk beliefs as translate them into a religious idiom.[28] The general direction of Methodist culture in all its forms was towards living a temperate, thrifty, hard-working life. Among the Durham miners the Methodists fought drunkenness, gambling and improvidence, even if by no means all turned from pay night frolics to prayer meetings.[29] If the miner was less picturesque, he could be less squalid. He could learn to read and speak in chapel. Here is more than meets the eye. This was for some, especially the women needing a quieter style of fellowship, a substitution of one type of folk activity for another. Sometimes it was the deliberate creation of a new sub-culture. We have already noted the coincidence of camp meetings and 'wakes'. Methodism sought to change the style of recreation of their converts and community. It is significant that rural local preachers would often meet on a Monday morning – a curious example of the custom of 'Saint Monday' among artisans which oral history reveals as continuing into the late nineteenth century.

Traditional sports were replaced by more sedentary hobbies; out went the fighting cocks! 'Athletic exercises of quoits, wrestling, football (in the street with a pig's bladder) "prison-bars", shooting with the longbow' were becoming obsolete in Lancashire in 1821, cites E. P. Thompson, reflecting on Wesleyanism.[30] They are now pigeon fanciers, canary breeders and tulip growers. This was still so in inner-city Darnall in Sheffield in the 1960s, although football had long made its comeback! Methodism, especially Primitive Methodism, seemed to link up with folk custom and folk religion, remoulding them to some extent, although Wesley Perrins, the Birmingham MP in the 1970s, told of his Primitive Methodist nailer grandfather, who made sure that his whippets were well fed![31]

Much of this can be traced right through the century to the North-East, and into the twentieth century. Here is Ernest Armstrong (1915–96), Labour politician and Vice President of the Methodist Conference in 1974. 'I grew up in a West Durham village that still exerts considerable influence on my life. The chapel was my social centre as well as a training ground and a place of worship . . . The Methodist church was the forum for discussion and men who were denied recognition at work found dignity, self-respect and confidence . . . This was the working man's church an effective force carrying the Gospel into daily life . . . Methodists were not given permission to take part in politics, they were expected to do so.'[32] It is not without significance that Armstrong, like Lord Lawson, was Wesleyan. Here was an appeal to labourers and artisans and their wives giving them a sense of belonging, purpose, self-help and responsibility.

Another positive point in the change from 'Christ against culture' to transformation of society is that the Primitive Methodist chapel was a safe zone for women. Deborah Valenze[33] and Dorothy Graham have recently stressed the appeal of early Primitive Methodism to working-class women, relating the work of the female itinerants to their concern for strengthening the family at a time when it was under heavy strain. A Chatham woman, converted by the very similar Bible Christians testifies that the house was previously 'a little hell', but now was transformed. Cottage meetings in the early days fit into this pattern.[34]

The quite early espousal of total abstinence slots into this scenario. The Temperance Movement[35] was a radical working-class matter in its early days, supported by Chartists like Lovett. Primitive Methodism almost insisted on it as a mark of true conversion. Robert Colls, on the Durham miners, comments, 'Conversion resulted in the convert transforming his self-image and therefore his habits.' He quotes the Primitive Methodist John Wilson, leader of the Durham Miners Association in the late nineteenth century, to the effect that his conversion led him to give up drinking and gambling and made him see life in new terms, 'a gift and something to be stewarded'. That last word is significant. Robert Moore, referring to the Deerness Valley,[36] tells of the convert joked at about Jesus turning water into wine – 'Well if Jesus can turn beer into clothes for my children and furniture for the house would he not be able to turn water into wine?' The negative side of this is a division of working men into 'pub' or 'chapel', respectable or unrespectable working class. The positive side is that working men trusted the Primitive

Methodists with office in the union or with the money in the friendly society. The Methodists were trusted and the children of many families attended Sunday school. They might laugh at them at the pub, but trusted them so long as they did not prove to be pious humbugs. But we are running into late Victorian days. Let us pull back a little.

The Period of District Autonomy

The third period of Primitive Methodism is that of district auton-omy. A 'way in' is to look at the variety of church activity this threw up. The Midlands Revival quickly pushed into Lincoln-shire. It is significant that a village like Scotter in Lincolnshire became not only the heart of a circuit but the venue for an early conference, which Kendall called a 'gerousia', a court of the elderly. This was a period when farm labourers were degraded into abject helots, forelock-pulling charity receivers. When the preachers arrived, very quickly they and the people developed their own feasts and fasts. This was sometimes in open opposi-tion to the church calendar, a matter about which social anthro-pologists like Mary Douglas, with stress on new 'feasts and fasts' as necessary to sects, are more perceptive than some liturgists. The revival style is now highlighted by liturgical scholars of the calibre of James White. There were 'preaching services', 'prayer meetings', 'protracted meetings', lasting on and off for several evenings, love feasts, which were often more common than Holy Communion. Later in the era of consolidation, after 1840, there were the Sunday school anniversary processions – begging for villagers' pence as well as their souls. Then there was the chapel anniversary when the poor tried valiantly to pay off the chapel debt.[37]

Revival could overreach itself. John Stamp gives an account of three years at Louth, where he was stationed from 1836. 'We have built 16 chapels, enlarged one, bought another and fitted up a large room and have had an increase of 25 local preachers and 416 members. Our last quarter's income was £65 more than the first ... I have walked more than 10,000 miles and have preached upwards of 1500 sermons and visited near 6000 families.' Stamp was a disastrous incompetent, and 'discontinued' as a travelling preacher soon afterwards! He was paid £62 12s. a year – little more than a skilled artisan. The 'Junior Itinerant' got £36, about as much as a labourer.[38]

The quarterly meetings exercised salty discipline. One preacher at Alford was asked to study brevity in his pulpit exercises . . . when he and brother Dawson are out together and both speak at the same time, resolved that they do not exceed ten minutes each, or they 'sink on the plan', that is they are demoted as preachers! Hugh Bourne once advised that a sharp poke in the foot from an umbrella after twenty minutes was necessary to prevent a bore from continuing at a camp meeting.

Worship among the Primitive Methodists was charismatic, lively and often entertaining, although in some areas, such as the Welsh border around Cym and Kingstone, it was Quakerlike. As late as the 1970s there were here former Primitive Methodist chapels for whom the Holy Communion was a recent innovation. More typical is this statement from the Brandon, Lincolnshire, circuit plan in 1854.

'Beloved brethren, never disappoint a congregation if you can possibly attend. Go to your important work in the spirit of prayer, choose the plainest text that you can. If your discourse aims at the glory of God, the conversion of sinners, do not allow as some of you formerly have, slight bodily indisposition a long journey dark night or inclement weather deter you from your important duties. The soul! The soul! That is your province, the mysterious essence, which never can decay but shall stand forth unchanged and unscathed at the resurrection fire. Resolve, by divine aid any time you preach, to be instrumental in the salvation of undying spirits . . . exhibit the cross prominently. Our stake is for the higher throne of glory or a deeper hell . . . Up to your master's work till the hand of death shall strike off your armour.' In that circuit a brother was expelled for pub-crawling, another for wife beating! In the end Primitive Methodism produced the hard-working, thrifty farm labourer or labour aristocrat who could or would fight for his place in the sun – with a tough wife counting the pence – but who later would tend to be a conciliator rather than a revolutionary who might later be as opposed to the working-class scapegoats as to the hardline Marxists. Primitive Methodism created a religious counter-culture, which offered an alternative to the parish church, to village culture and to some aspects of working-class culture while all the time interacting with it. 'It appeared', as James Obelkevich put it, 'at a critical moment as the traditional culture was passing away but before the subsequent working class culture had developed to replace it.'[39]

Within the chapel, there was a sense of community, a sense of belonging at a time of social unease. A high proportion of members held some office. Women and the poor had scope. A 'no politics' rule was observed in the pulpit, but there was no ban on participation in unions. The skill in organization or speech learned in chapel might be taken into union politics. If we move to Oxford,[40] research shows that all the chief officers of the Oxford branch of the Agricultural Union were Methodists, mainly Primitives. Joseph Arch, champion hedge cutter, founded the Agricultural Workers Union in 1872. He was a Primitive Methodist local preacher – early in life the class divisions that made his mother subservient to the squire's lady at Holy Communion alienated him from his parish church. Antagonism at this time between 'church' and 'chapel' had social as well as theological roots. In 1872 the bishop of Oxford, John Fielden Mackarness,[41] devoted his first 'charge' to attacking noncon-formity. He denied to their ministers and preachers the validity of their call and went on to accuse them of filching promising sons from the church. He taunted the ministers with 'desiring a social equality with the parish clergy which nothing, not even a revolution would give them'. Arch – incidentally – became an Anglican, patronized by the radical Countess of Warwick.

Later in Norfolk,[42] we find the unions using Primitive Methodist methods – camp meetings and love feasts – which heightened tension between 'church' and 'chapel'. In Lincolnshire, Norfolk and Suffolk, Primitive Methodism played an important part in the 'Revolt of the Field' between 1872 and

1896. We have already featured Sir George Edwards, converted to Primitive Methodism in 1869, taught to read by his wife so that he could preach, moving from crow scaring to Parliament.[43] Edwards had many precursors and successors, who found their ability to speak and think and debate in chapel. They combined their theology often enough with radical politics.

Moving back to the Midlands, there was much Methodist and especially Primitive Methodist leadership in the Nottingham and Derbyshire coalfields in the period from 1840 to 1890 and indeed up and beyond Methodist Union in 1932. One South Derbyshire magistrate, Thomas Beaumont, informed the Home Office of the danger of the 'Ranters' – groups very different from the docile Methodists E. P. Thompson claims to have analysed in Yorkshire and Lancashire. In 'radical Leicester' we find the handloom weavers and stockingers in pitiful economic plight with wages as low as 4s. 6d. a week in 1841. Joseph Markham, a shoemaker and auctioneer, had been a local preacher among the Primitives until he was expelled. John Skevington, snubbed by Bourne, avowed that 'a man could not be a Christian who was not a Chartist save through ignorance'.[44] He attempted to rejoin, but Bourne was as averse to some of the radicals as were some Wesleyans. Primitive Methodism, like Wesleyanism ironically, was both producing men who revolted against the established order and disowning them if their activities seemed to imperil the religious societies' existence.[45]

In Cheshire, we find links with Chartism. Joseph Capper,[46] who had been converted at the Mow Cop camp meeting, was a Chartist. He was arrested in 1842, standing trial for sedition, conspiracy and rioting. He was in prison for two years. It was said of Capper that his tongue was like the sledgehammer he used in his blacksmith's shop. Certainly the Chartists used Methodist-style methods. At Barnsley on 1 May 1842, 'there was a grand teetotal and anti-tobacco camp meeting on the bare-bones. The preacher span a long yarn about "the great principles of the Charter" and as was expected all Hull, Hell and Halifax was there'. The nature of the meeting suggests Primitive influence if not participation. As we have seen, teetotalism was a sign of radicalism and later mild collectivism as well as Primitive Methodism. Rough-hewn Yorkshire figures like the Halifax 'Prim' Ben Wilson recalled the famous occasion at Peep Green near Liversedge on Whit Monday 1839 when Feargus O'Connor spoke and another Halifax Primitive Methodist William Thornton offered prayers.[47]

In Lancashire, it is possible to find ways in which religion could unite in community both owners and workers in a paternalistic system, as Patrick Joyce has recently shown.[48] This opens up a newer way of looking at industry rather different from the constant stress on struggle and conflict of earlier Marxist historians. Robert Moore hinted at some of the same patterns in the North-East, though the dynamics of a cotton mill and a coalmine are quite different.

Before we leave the Durham miners let us briefly look at worship. Primitive Methodist worship was in origin a curious amalgam of the Quaker and the charismatic, though we need to recall that Quakerism in George Fox's time was charismatic. In the North-East the participation was noisy and congregational style intense. Parallels can be drawn with Pentecostalism and the black churches of twentieth-century America. Hymn styles reflected a kind of theology of liberation, which could switch from

> My heart is fixed eternal God
> Fixed on Thee
> And my immortal choice is made
> Christ for me

to the rewriting of the Chartist freedom song, 'The lion of freedom is come from his den'

> For the Lion of Judah shall break every chain
> And give us the victory again and again.[49]

The change from the old revivalist 'small' hymn book and Bourne's 'large' book to the more sober Flesher's Book of 1853 was too much for some 'Prims' in Hampshire, who formed the 'Old Hymn Bookers', paralleling those in Belper who broke away when ministers' stipends went up from sixteen to eighteen shillings a week! Here is a description of a Durham Society at worship.[50]

'It is to the chapel we are going . . . It is a plain unpretentious building . . . In the pulpit is a tall spare man with a face in which mysticism and intelligence are strangely blended. We learn that he is a miner for a neighbouring colliery. Never shall I forget the singing of that service. There was a little scraping and twanging of fiddle strings before all the stringed instruments, of which there were a dozen, were brought into accord with the organ, but then such a glorious outburst of music as could not fail to help the spirit of devotion . . . Forgotten in the ecstatic bliss of mystic communion with Heaven was the bare unsightly walls, the hard seats, the dreary pit . . . forgotten the hardship, the dull, aching monotony and the familiar threat of death. After the hymn came the prayer. Prayer is not for criticism. When a man is talking with his Maker he should be safe from the attacks of fault finders. But there are men who have what the old Methodists called the gift of prayer and the preacher had that gift . . . The preacher carried his congregation away on the strong pinions of his own faith, until a low rumbling of murmured responses broke forth in loud "amens". Suddenly one man sprang to his feet, and with a loud shout of "Praise the Lord" jumped into the air . . . The reading of the scriptures was interspersed with a few remarks here and there more or less appropriate – generally less . . . But the sermon, who shall describe it? It was a sermon to be heard, not to be reported. What a mixture of humour, passionate appeal, thrilling exhortations and apposite illustrations it was . . . Laughter and tears this preacher commanded at will, and when he closed with heart searching appeals to the unconverted to fly to the Cross for pardon, one almost wondered that men and women did not spring to their feet and rush somewhere, anywhere, exclaiming with Bunyan's Pilgrim – Life, Life, eternal life'! The writer of the description will not forget 'this rugged Elijah of the coalpit, a hewer of coal for six days in the deep, dark mine, and a very flame of fire on the seventh'.

We see a different mood in Sunderland, centre of a powerful district, one of the large towns like Hull where the Primitives were strong.[51] The districts often had their distinctive emphases. The training of the ministry became a concern here. In 1844 the first call from Sunderland came for a college, but there was preference for training itinerant preachers on the job, although Elmfield House School was used both for training preachers as well as a boys' school. The Sunderland College opened in 1869 to be absorbed into the Manchester College in 1881. One reason for a breakaway of some Sunderland Primitives was fear of ministerial domination and a stifling of revivalism – an argument to be taken seriously. They feared that Primitive Methodism would cease to be the people's church, with a ministry which would lose touch with the common man and woman. This was no foolish fear. However, many of the children of the chapel families moved into higher education and were challenged by new thinking about the origins of life associated with Darwin on the one hand and modern biblical criticism on the other. The ministry needed to be able to preach meaningfully to them.

We end our analysis of the districts by visiting Lye, Brierley Hill and Cradley Heath in the West Midlands – the home of the nailers and glass blowers. In a fascinating recent oral interview, Wesley Perrins, a former Labour MP born in nail-making Lye in 1905, tells how his grandfather was the only nailer among his mates who could read. Knowledge was power. He would bring a daily paper to read to the men. He was a Primitive Methodist local preacher. It all has the whiff of what in South America they call 'basic communities'. Bible, education and action go together.[52] Jump a generation or two and we are in the world of Perrins's youth, when he learned to speak articulately and pray in the Christian Endeavour movement. He got pushed into local preaching with the style of training that went back to Wesley's day, learning the craft from another. Dr Alan Wilkinson, son of J. T. Wilkinson, later principal of Hartley Victoria College, gives a fine later picture of Grainger's Lane Primitive Methodist Church (they call it 'church' not 'chapel' now!) in the 1920s. It was all very different from the 'ranters' of the Lorenzo Dow era.

It was a development more complex than a 'routinization of charisma', to use Max Weber's term. The whole church buzzed with educational and communal activity. The worship was highly intellectual compared with that of 'the Elijah of the coal pit'. Scholarly ministers like J. T. Wilkinson, Herbert Marsh (a scholar of St Catharine's College, Cambridge) and Walter Chrimes had long and distinguished ministries. The emphasis in the Sunday school of 600 was 'mind-expanding and character-building'. The chapel had moved from nailer's shop to Tudor gothic, side pulpit, gowned choir. Sons and daughters of the congregation began to go to university with the Methodist Church beginning its fine work among university and college students. Was this the assimilation of dissent? Were the free churches junior partners of the establishment? The changes typified here illustrate the change from sect to denomination very clearly.[53]

Primitive Methodism up to Methodist Union

The turn of the century saw an increasing church consciousness in Primitive Methodism. The Thanksgiving Fund of 1892, and the Church Aid and Church Extension Fund (1900), enabled new building schemes to be carried out. The title 'Church' rather than 'Connexion' appeared on class tickets in 1902.[54] In 1912 the Hymnal of 1886 was given a supplement, a collection which catches the somewhat exuberant and even romantic atmosphere of Edwardian England. Primitive Methodism had its Forward Movement, though inevitably on a small scale compared with Wesleyanism with its Central Halls and National Children's Home. Thomas Jackson's Whitechapel Mission and the work of James Flanagan in Southwark, including the establishment of a Sisters' Settlement and Training Home, were notable. A fitting headquarters for the denomination was acquired in Holborn Hall in 1912.

The debt of a church, which was never affluent, to the paternal benevolence of Sir William P. Hartley (1846–1922)[55] was great. Hartley – an astute and theologically aware jam manufacturer – saw the need for proper education of the ordained ministry. He was largely responsible for the Manchester College, renamed Hartley College in 1906, which boasted that it was the largest denominational training college in Europe! Without doubt, Hartley's most significant move was to bring the Oxford-trained Arthur Samuel Peake (1865–1929) to Manchester in 1892.[56] It was Peake, 27 when he came to Manchester, who moulded the theological outlook of a whole generation of ministers, many of whom went into the unified Methodist Church of 1932. Peake felt a divine compulsion to be a theological middleman between scholarship, pulpit and pew, leading the Anglican lay scholar F. C. Burkitt to claim that Peake greatly helped to prevent a modernist–fundamentalist clash in Britain. Certainly, he combined consummate and accurate scholarship, clarity in communication and a vigorous use of historical method with a loyalty to the subjective style of the evangelical faith, which enabled many who otherwise might have drifted into the irrational fundamentalism which sometimes accompanies rapid social change to remain in the church. Not all Primitive Methodists agreed! Dr Ian Sellers recalled going, as a schoolboy, to a camp meeting. He heard a preacher cry 'Burn the college, burn the college', because of Peake's famous *Commentary* of 1919, which Hartley made available to Primitive Methodist preachers. Peake can now be thought too optimistic in his claims for the historical-critical method.

Peake, himself, summed up his aims. 'People have often disappointed me by putting the emphasis of my work where I should never have dreamed of putting it myself. It is something, no doubt, to be grateful for, that we have come through the difficulties raised by biblical criticism so well. But criticism for me has never been more than a means to an end. It is not merely that critical problems attract me much less than some other biblical problems but that I regard them as less than fundamental . . . If I am remembered for anything . . . I hope it will not be as a student of biblical criticism but as an interpreter of the great personalities of scripture and their contribution to religious thought.'

Primitive Methodism was not without its heresy trials – as were the Wesleyans later with the claims against George Jackson.

John Day Thompson[57] showed the tension between the liberal and revivalist approaches. Thompson shared the fight against 'Toryism, tyranny and beer' but agreed with Peake that 'our people have failed to keep pace with the advance of the nation in education and general culture'. Thompson was arraigned for heresy, while in Australia. The veteran James Macpherson claimed that Thompson was in contravention of Methodist doctrine. The tide was, however, turning in a liberal direction, and Macpherson lost that battle. Thompson returned to England, becoming Hartley's minister. He became Secretary of the Conference and President in 1915. It was Thompson, before Peake, who sought the liberalization of Primitive Methodist doctrinal standards. 'The living Christ is more to us than the dead Wesley.' He had Peake's support in this, for Peake pointed out that still to demand some conformity to Wesley's *Notes on the New Testament* was to give too much attention to 'an outmoded exegete'. We have already made clear that the exegete was Bengel, the Pietist. Peake failed later to eliminate reference to the *Notes* and the *Forty Four Sermons* in the Deed of Union of 1932, the doctrinal clauses of which were drafted by him and John Scott Lidgett before Peake's death in 1929. Clearly he was responsible for the clause about 'the divine revelation recorded in the Holy scriptures'. The Methodist Church acknowledges this revelation as 'the supreme rule of faith and practice'. This is both critical orthodoxy *and* an acknowledgement of a revelation prior to Scripture, which is the product of a believing community. Argue how you will, A. S. Peake's approach still allows conservative evangelicals and more liberal evangelicals to live together in the same church.

Primitive Methodism brought much to the union of Methodism. Institutionally, it was not as strong as the Wesleyans, or the United Methodists who had come together in 1907. Elmfield House, York, from 1865 was the Connexional Boys' School, and from 1895 Bourne College, Birmingham, was another small private school.[58] In social thinking, the Primitives paralleled Wesleyanism but with more enthusiasm for teetotalism and an Anti-Cigarette League which was prophetic. For youth work the

Young Peoples' Society of Christian Endeavour had a full-time
secretary from 1898. Here young folk could learn to set their
thoughts in order, pray, debate and often find their marriage
partners. Although, as we have seen, individual Primitive
Methodists were active in politics, the official statements of the
church tended to be rather pietistic, stemming back to Hugh
Bourne and his dislike of 'speeching radicals'. In 1908 the
Primitive Methodist Social Service Union was recognized by
Conference, paralleling similar groups in Anglicanism and
Wesleyanism. In 1924, to take a typical year, there were conference resolutions on housing, unemployment, education,
gambling, rodeo exhibitions, royalty and the turf, and one
supporting the COPEC resolutions with a typical rider that 'all
social conditions, economic or industrial, national or international relations are widely acknowledged to be dependent
primarily upon a change of heart in the individual'.

What features were notable in the early twentieth century, when
there was a mixture of optimism, and a slow and inexorable
decline in numbers relative to population, which has dogged
Methodism throughout the twentieth century?[59]

First, Primitive Methodism kept a close kinship with non-
Methodist Free Churches, especially in armed forces chaplaincy
and in support for Free Church federation. Second, the principle
of circuit and district autonomy remained, especially in the
unique (for Methodism) prolonged district meetings, which
could include the ordination of the itinerant ministry. Wider
Methodism missed an opportunity here, as the present-day
synod is a boring waste of a Saturday morning, compared with
the combination of debate, worship and fellowship which could
mark the Primitive District Meeting. Third, the travelling
preachers were seen as partners with lay people in ministry.
Ordination did not demand or confer any gift not available to
other preachers, who could on occasion preside at the Lord's
Table. At connexional level a layman could be President of
Conference, as was the case with Sir William Hartley in 1909.
No doubt there was an anti-clerical strain here, even if Peake
vehemently repudiated a 'low' view of the ministry. But the

positive element of lay leadership is a matter all churches are now seeking to regain. Fourth, the Primitives testified to the value of free worship which can exist alongside and assist more 'liturgical' styles. Participation can take many different forms, a matter commonplace now right across the churches. Fifth, influenced by Hartley, long-term investments were avoided. This had the effect of producing burdensome chapel debts. Chapel Aid was set up to help here, a body which now serves the wider church.[60] It also had its merit in a time of inflation, but it gave the air of poverty to a still largely working-class community. Sixth, the 'Peake tradition' of scholarship produced in the last generation of Primitive Methodism a notable team of scholars – ministerial and lay – such as Atkinson Lee, A. L. Humphries, W. L. Wardle, H. G. Meacham, Edward Rogers, N. H. Snaith, Victor Murray and J. T. Wilkinson, all of whom played their part in reunited Methodism and outside it. Seventh, the Primitive Methodists were positive about Methodist union – more so than some Wesleyans!

There was an early move to unite with the Bible Christians, with whom they had similar revivalist origins. This failed for economic and sociological reasons. From the end of the First World War, led by Peake, the mood for fuller union was maintained. At a time when federation was supported by some Free Churchmen like P. T. Forsyth and J. H. Moulton, Peake urged reunion, not just of Methodism, but of Christendom, on the grounds that social change had eroded great differences between churches, that Methodism was one at its heart, that the world saw a divided church as inimicable to its teaching and that evangelism could be better pursued in a united Methodism. It was optimistic forecasting. In any case union fitted in with the world of industrial mergers and the League of Nations! Peake certainly deserved the eulogy of Wesleyans for playing a vital part in the union negotiations as also for his positive approach to the Lambeth Appeal for Christian unity in 1920, typified in Peake's address to the Free Church Council in 1928.[61]

The older forms of Primitive Methodism could not survive long into a new century. There was clearly a shift from a close-knit to a more broadly based style of church life.

Here lies an important paradox. Working-class people, both inside and outside the churches, are more prone to be 'locals', more prone to parochialism and sectarianism.[62] Because of its class structure, Primitive Methodism retained a 'localist' outlook rather longer than Wesleyanism, where there was more spatial and cognitive mobility through education, work or marriage. Certainly there was some 'leakage' of membership through migration from areas of traditional strength, despite church building in London, the South-East, the Thames Valley and the South Midlands. Quite new forms of mission among the working classes were needed in inner-city areas, where denominational barriers were entirely irrelevant.

We have come a long way from 'a day's praying on Mow Hill' in 1807, yet the story of this fascinating community has a unity. This is the priority of the will of Christ in the individual and the community. In the last analysis, there is an 'optimism of grace' about the Arminian style of evangelicalism. It is quite remarkable that Methodism in all its divisions and schisms has never divided since Whitefield and Wesley on this issue. Salvation must be for all. If Primitive Methodism began as 'Christ against culture', it was never a negative retreat from the world. It was always 'conversionist' as is much contemporary Pentecostalism. It never despised learning, so long as it was not Olympian in its remoteness from the life of the people. The nailers of Lye saw knowledge as power. They would have given short shrift to preachers who did not stimulate the imagination of their congregation.

When churches unite, they bring together not so much doctrines and liturgies as people. Primitive Methodism brought into the united church of 1932 men and women who combined a genuine piety of a single style, a concern for social righteousness and social justice. We have already referred to Peter Lee, after whom a new town was named after the Second World War. His progress from miner to Parliament did not mean any diminution of his social concern or Christian faith. Very similar was Jim Simmons, a member of the Labour administration of 1945.

It must be admitted, however, that a deep fissure had opened up between politics and religion, particularly at the time of the

General Strike of 1926. There was an alienation between church and labour politics which has widened since, although Tony Blair has, since 1997, underlined once more the links. Methodists like Hilary Armstrong and Paul Boateng are in the government. Primitive Methodism, even if it seems an interim faith, played a role as a midwife in the painful birth of English socialism out of all proportion to its numerical size. To the Methodist Church of 1932 Primitive Methodism was able to bring 220,021 members. This compared with 517,551 members of the Wesleyan Methodist Church and 179,527 from the United Methodists.

But this is Great Britain. If John Wesley was the 'founder' of Methodism, his foundation is now a worldwide church, one of the largest Protestant communions. It is very strong in the United States. If there is a 'special relationship' between Britain and the USA, Methodism is a significant part of it and indeed one cause of it. President George W. Bush is a United Methodist member. Methodism is small but vigorous in South America, strong in parts of West, South and East Africa, strong in the Pacific Islands like Tonga, small but not entirely overshadowed by the Lutheran and Reformed traditions in Europe, including the former Soviet Union, and it is united, though not in its American style, with other Communions in North and South India, Pakistan, Canada, Australia and France. In Great Britain there are at the beginning of the twenty-first century about 350,000 members. In England Methodism has prepared twice for unity or ultimate union with other churches, with a goal of 'one church renewed for mission'. Possibilities are again on the horizon in a world very different from that in which Wesley rode his horse.

Notes

1 The Evangelical Revival: An Overview

1 D. W. Bebbington, *Evangelicalism in Modern Britain: A History from the 1730s to 1980s* (Unwin Hyman, 1989), p. 3. M. A. Noll, D. W. Bebbington and G. A. Rawlyk (eds), *Evangelicalism: Comparative Studies of Popular Protestantism in North America, the British Isles and Beyond, 1700–1990* (Oxford University Press, 1994). For the European background: W. R. Ward, *The Protestant Evangelical Awakening* (Cambridge University Press, 1992); *Faith and Faction* (Epworth Press, 1993); *Christianity under the Ancien Regime 1648–1789* (Cambridge University Press, 1999).

2 *Lives* 6, p. 150; *Lives* 1, p. 274; 4, pp. 122, 286; 5, pp. 11, 114.

3 Cited in Bebbington, *Evangelicalism*, p. 12.

4 Cited in Bebbington, *Evangelicalism*, p. 14.

5 B. Hilton, *The Age of Atonement: The Influence of Evangelicalism on Social and Economic Thought 1786–1865* (Oxford University Press, 1988).

6 J. Scott Lidgett, *The Spiritual Principle of the Atonement* (C. H. Kelly, 1897). W. F. Lofthouse, *Ethics and Atonement* (Methuen, 1906).

7 Cf. S. J. Jones, *John Wesley's Conception and Use of Scripture* (Abingdon Press, 1995).

8 Cited in W. R. Ward, 'The Protestant Frame of Mind', *History Today* 40 (September 1990), p. 19.

9 P. Hazard, *The European Mind 1680–1715* (Penguin, 1964).

10 G. Rupp, *Worldmanship and Churchmanship* (Epworth Press, 1958), pp. 7ff.; *Religion in England*, pp. 207ff.

11 H. Butterfield, *The Origins of Modern Science 1700–1800* (Bell, 1949), p. viii.

12 G. R. Cragg, *The Church and the Age of Reason* (Penguin, 1960), pp. 13, 96ff. P. K. Monod, *The Power of Kings: Monarchy and Religion in Europe 1589–1715* (Yale University Press, 1999), p. 288.

13 Rupp, pp. 218ff. J. Boehme, *Mysterious Magnum: The Principles of the Divine Essence*, tr. J. Sparrow (Kessinger, 1997).

14 Cf. G. S. Wakefield (ed.), *A Dictionary of Christian Spirituality* (SCM Press, 1983), pp. 300–1. A. L. Drummond, *German Protestantism Since Luther* (Epworth Press, 1951), pp. 52ff. Ward, *The Protestant Evangelical Awakening*, pp. 54ff.

15 J. T. Wilkinson, *Arthur Samuel Peake* (Epworth Press, 1971), p. 167. *Primitive Methodist Leader*, 19 February 1920. But cf. F. Hildebrandt, *Christianity According to the Wesleys* (Epworth Press, 1956).

16 A. J. Lewis, *Zinzendorf the Ecumenical Pioneer* (SCM Press, 1962). E. E. Stoeffler, *The Rise of Evangelical Pietism* (Brill, 1971).

17 Heitzenrater, *Wesley*, p. 82. Ward, *The Protestant Evangelical Awakening*, p. 312.

18 *Journal* 2, pp. 488ff. BE 19, pp. 211ff. R. Niebuhr, *The Nature and Destiny of Man*, vol. 2 (Nisbet, 1943), pp. 180ff.

19 C. J. Podmore, *The Moravian Church in England 1728–1760* (Oxford University Press, 1998). N. Sykes, *Daniel Ernst Jablonski and the Church of England* (SPCK, 1950).

20 R. E. Davies, *Methodism* (Epworth Press, 1976), pp. 11–12, 21.

21 T. A. Campbell, *The Religion of the Heart* (University of South Carolina Press, 1991), ch. 2.

22 O. Chadwick, *The Popes and European Revolution* (Oxford University Press, 1981), pp. 159–61.

23 G. V. Bennett and J. D. Walsh (eds), *Essays in Modern English Church History* (A. and C. Black, 1966), p. 157.

24 R. H. Bainton, *The Penguin History of Christianity*, vol. 2 (Penguin, 1967), p. 217.

25 Bainton, *History*, vol. 2, pp. 223ff.

26 M. A. Noll, *A History of Christianity in the USA and Canada* (Eerdmans/SPCK, 1992), pp. 85ff. J. H. S. Kent, 'Christian Theology in the Eighteenth to the Twentieth Century', in H. Cunliffe-Jones (ed.), *A History of Christian Doctrine* (T. and T. Clark, 1978), p. 467. Jonathan Edwards, *Basic Writings*, ed. O. E. Winslow (Signet Classics, 1966), pp. 84ff., 150ff. Cf. J. E. Smith, *Jonathan Edwards* (Geoffrey Chapman, 1993). S. R. Holmes, *God of Grace and God of Glory* (T. and T. Clark, 2000). C. Goodwin, 'John Wesley's Indebtedness to Jonathan Edwards', *Epworth Review* 25.2, pp. 89ff.

27 A. Fawcett, *The Cambuslang Revival* (Banner of Truth Trust, 1971). Noll et al., *Evangelicalism*, pp. 58ff.

28 *Letters* 6, p. 151, 19 May 1775; 7, p. 182, 13 July 1783; 7, p. 352, 26 November 1786.

29 J. D. Walsh, *John Wesley: A Bicentennial Tribute* (Dr Williams's Trust, 1993), p. 6; 'Methodism and the Origins of English Speaking Evangelicalism', in Noll et al., *Evangelicalism*, pp. 33–4.

30 M. Watts, *The Dissenters*, vol. 1 (Oxford University Press, 1978), pp. 401, 406ff. *The Report of the Methodist Church on the Toronto*

Blessing, 1996, in *Statements and Reports of the Methodist Church on Faith and Order* (Methodist Publishing House, 2000) vol. 2, Part 2, pp. 618ff.

31 W. Sargent, *Battle for the Mind* (Pan Books, 1959). O. Brandon, *The Battle for the Soul* (Hodder and Stoughton, 1960). Watts, *The Dissenters*, pp. 409ff.

32 D. Pyke, 'The Religious Societies 1678–1738', *PWHS* 35.1–2 (March and June 1965). H. D. Rack, 'Religious Societies and the Origins of Methodism', *Journal of Ecclesiastical History* (October 1987), pp. 582–95. J. D. Walsh, 'Religious Societies, Methodist and Evangelical 1738–1800', *Studies in Church History* 23 (Blackwell, 1986), pp. 279–302. S. R. Valentine, *John Bennett and the Origins of Methodism* (Scarecrow Press, 1997), chs 1–5. G. F. Nuttall, 'George Whitefield's Curate: Gloucestershire Dissent and the Revival', *JEH* 27 (October 1976). Cf. *Journal of the United Reformed Church History Society* 2.8 (1981).

33 J. D. Walsh et al., *The Church of England 1688–1833* (Cambridge University Press, 1993), ch. 5, ch. 7. D. W. R. Bahlman, *The Moral Revolution of 1688* (Yale University Press, 1957). G. V. Portus, *Caritas Anglicana* (Mowbray, 1912). J. Spurr, *The Restoration Church of England 1646–1689* (Yale University Press, 1981). D. O'Connor et al., *Three Centuries of Mission: The USPG 1701–2000* (Continuum, 2000).

34 Ward, *The Protestant Evangelical Awakening*, p. 319. M. G. Jones, *The Charity School Movement* (Cambridge University Press, 1938), pp. 302–9.

35 Joseph Butler, *The Analogy of Religion* (J. M. Dent, 1906), p. 1. Bishops Berkeley and Secker made similar comments.

36 Noll et al., *Evangelicalism*, pp. 58ff. H. S. Stout, *The Divine Dramatist George Whitefield and the Rise of Modern Evangelicalism* (Eerdmans, 1991). A. R. Dallimore, *George Whitefield*, 2 vols (Banner of Truth Trust, 1970, 1980).

37 Cragg, *The Church and the Age of Reason*, p. 145.

38 D. Llwyd Morgan, *The Great Awakening in Wales* (Epworth Press, 1988). G. Tudur, *Howell Harris, From Conversion to Separation 1735–1750* (University of Wales, 2000). G. F. Nuttall, *Howell Harris 1714–1773* (University of Wales Press, 1965). Ward, *The Protestant Evangelical Awakening*, pp. 316–17. Cited in text.

39 B. S. Schlenther, *Queen of the Methodists: The Countess of Huntingdon and the Eighteenth Century Crisis of Faith and Society* (Durham Academic Press, 1997). E. Welch, *Spiritual Pilgrim: A Reassessment of the Life of the Countess of Huntingdon* (University of Wales Press, 1995); 'John Fletcher and the Trevecka College Revival', *PWHS* 51.2 (May 1997).

40 Cited in A. S. Wood, *The Inextinguishable Blaze* (Paternoster, 1960), p. 197.

41 G. C. B. Davies, *The Early Cornish Evangelicals* (SPCK, 1951). K. Hylson-Smith, *Evangelicals in the Church of England 1734–1984* (T. and T. Clark, 1988), pp. 1–60. C. Smyth, *Simeon and Church Order* (Cambridge University Press, 1940).

42 Watts, *The Dissenters*, vol. 1, pp. 394ff.

43 J. D. C. Clark, *English Society 1688–1832* (Oxford University Press, 1985).

44 D. Lovegrove, *Established Church and Sectarian People: Itinerancy and the Transformation of English Dissent 1780–1830* (Cambridge University Press, 1988).

45 Watts, *The Dissenters*, vol. 2 (Oxford University Press, 1995) has a store of statistics on the growth of Dissent between 1789 and 1851 with an analysis of Dissent in every county in 1851.

2   *John Wesley – Eighteenth-Century Man*

1 J. A. Newton, *Susanna Wesley and the Puritan Tradition in Methodism* (Epworth Press, 1968), pp. 87ff. Cf. C. Wallace (ed.), *Susanna Wesley: Complete Writings* (Oxford University Press, 1997).

2 G. S. Wakefield, 'John Wesley' (Methodist Publishing House, 1990), p. 6. Cf. D. Butler, *Epworth Review* (October 1998), pp. 50ff. R. Williams, *Open to Judgement* (Darton, Longman and Todd, 1994), pp. 202ff.

3 *Works* 7, Sermon 194. *BE* 3, p. 478; 19, p. 265. Baker, pp. 59, 359. L. W. Barnard, *John Potter* (Arthur H. Stockwell, 1988), p. 100.

4 L. Stone, *The Family, Sex and Marriage in England 1500–1800* (Penguin, 1985), pp. 207ff. Rupp, p. 349.

5 Rupp, p. 345. Cf. R. P. Heitzenrater, *Mirror and Memory* (Abingdon Press, 1986), chs 1, 4, 5. F. Baker, *Charles Wesley as Revealed in His Letters* (Epworth Press, 1948), p. 14. *HMGB* 4, pp. 7ff.

6 Heitzenrater, *The Elusive Mr Wesley*, vol. 2, pp. 28ff.

7 P. Nockles, *The Oxford Movement in Context* (Cambridge University Press, 1994); 'Church Parties in the Pre-Tractarian Church of England 1750–1833', in J. Walsh et al., *The Church of England 1685–1833* (Oxford University Press, 1993), pp. 334ff.

8 L. F. Church, *Oglethorpe* (Epworth Press, 1932).

9 *Journal* 1, p. 151, 8 February 1736. *BE* 18, pp. 145–6.

10 For the Georgia period, cf. Rack, pp. 107–36.

11 G. O. Collins, *The Second Journey* (Paulist Press, 1987), pp. 21ff.

12 *Journal* 1, pp. 440–2, 2 February 1738. *BE* 18, p. 226. J. W. Fowler, 'John Wesley's Development in Faith', in M. D. Meeks (ed.), *The Future of Methodist Theological Traditions* (Abingdon Press, 1985), pp. 172ff.

13 Schmidt, vol. 1, p. 237.

14 *Journal* 1, pp. 458ff, 1 May 1738. *BE* 18, p. 236. Rupp, p. 316.

15 *Journal* 1, p. 472, 24 May 1738. *BE* 18, pp. 550ff. P. E. More and F. L. Cross, *Anglicanism* (SPCK, 1957), pp. 222ff.

16 H. Bett, *The Spirit of Methodism* (Epworth Press, 1937), pp. 27ff. P. S. Watson, *The Message of the Wesleys* (Epworth Press, 1965), pp. 7ff. *Works of Martin Luther* (Philadelphia, 1932), vol. 6, pp. 449ff.

17 Heitzenrater, *Wesley*, pp. 261, 302. *Works* 7, Sermons 106, 110. *BE* 4, pp. 28ff., 187ff.

18 *The Journal of Charles Wesley*, vol. 1: *The Early Journal* (Culley, 1909), pp. 36–9. *HMGB* 4, pp. 11ff. B. Holland, 'The Conversions of John and Charles Wesley and their Place in Methodist Tradition', *PWHS* 38.2–3 (August and December 1971).

19 *Journal* 2, p. 121, 1 January 1739. *BE* 19, p. 616.

20 Newton, *Susanna Wesley*, pp. 144ff., 165. Rack, pp. 465ff.

21 *Works* 7, Sermon 128 'Free Grace' (1740). *BE* 3, p. 542; 19, p. 332. A. Brown-Lawson, *John Wesley and the Anglican Evangelicals of the Eighteenth Century* (Pentland Press, 1994), pp. 161ff. *HMGB* 4, pp. 35ff.

22 2 August 1745. Cf. A. C. Outler, *John Wesley* (Oxford University Press, 1994), p. 152. *Letters* 4, pp. 297–300, 14 May 1765.

23 A. P. Sell, *The Great Debate: Calvinism, Arminianism and Salvation* (H. E. Walter, 1982). G. Wainwright, *On Wesley and Calvin* (Melbourne, 1987). G. F. Nuttall, *The Puritan Spirit* (Epworth Press, 1967), ch. 8. D. M. Baillie, *Out of Nazareth* (St Andrew Press, 1958), p. 11.

24 *Journal* 2, pp. 216ff, 11 June 1739. *BE* 25, pp. 614–17, 693; 19, pp. 66–7. A. Outler, 'Did Methodists Have a Doctrine of the Church?', in D. Kirkpatrick (ed.), *The Doctrine of the Church* (Epworth Press, 1964), pp. 11–28.

25 G. Whitefield, *Works* 1 (Dilly, 1771), p. 105, 10 November 1739.

26 *Journal* 2, pp. 172–3, 12 April 1739. *BE* 19, p. 46.

27 J. A. Hargreaves, *Halifax* (Edinburgh University Press, 1999), p. 48. *BE* 19, p. 271.

28 J. D. Walsh, 'Elie Halévy and the Birth of Methodism', *Transactions of the Royal Historical Society* 25 (1975), pp. 1–20. E. Halévy, *The Birth of Methodism in England*, ed. B. Semmel (Chicago, 1971).

29 *BE* 19, pp. 471ff. *HMGB* 4, pp. 29f. F. Baker, 'John Wesley and Bishop Butler', *PWHS* (May 1980), pp. 93–9.

30 *BE* 9, pp. 67ff., 77ff. *HMGB* 4, pp. 23ff., 71ff.

31 H. Bett, 'A French Marquis and the Class Meeting', *PWHS* (1931), pp. 4ff. D. L. Watson, *The Early Methodist Class Meeting* (Abingdon Press, 1985).

32 P. Clark, *British Clubs and Societies 1650–1800* (Oxford University

Press, 2000). *BE* 9, p. 259. W. L. Doughty, *John Wesley – Preacher* (Epworth Press, 1953), p. 57.

33 *HMGB* 1, ch. 7, 'Polity', F. Baker. *HMGB* 4, pp. 67ff., 76ff., 86ff.

34 Schmidt, vol. 2, Part 1, p. 227. *BE* 11, Replies to Gibson, Lavington, Warburton, etc.

35 J. D. Walsh, 'Methodism and the Mob', *Studies in Church History* 8 (Cambridge University Press, 1972), pp. 213ff.

36 J. L. Waddy, *The Bitter Sacred Cup: The Wednesbury Riots 1743–4* (World Methodist History Society, 1976).

37 *Journal* 2, pp. 211ff. *BE* 19, p. 64, June 1739. Cf. *Journal* 8, p. 13, 19 September 1789.

38 W. S. Gunter, *The Limits of Divine Love* (Abingdon Press, 1989). Rack, pp. 338ff.

39 F. Baker, *William Grimshaw 1708–63* (Epworth Press, 1963). F. Cook, *William Grimshaw of Haworth* (Banner of Truth Trust, 1997). P. Streiff, *Reluctant Saint* (Epworth Press, 2001).

40 Heitzenrater, *Wesley*, pp. 109ff. *BE* 19, p. 61.

41 *Letters* 2, p. 94, 25 March 1747. *BE* 26, pp. 129ff.

42 A. Outler, *John Wesley's Sermons: An Introduction* (Abingdon Press, 1991). R. P. Heitzenrater, 'John Wesley's Principles and Practices of Preaching', in R. Sykes (ed.), *Beyond the Boundaries* (Westminster College, Oxford, 1998), pp. 12–40. *HMGB* 4, pp. 81ff., 159ff. *Works* 8 (1856), p. 304. *Letters* 3, p. 78, 20 December 1751. *BE* 26, p. 486 (1856 edn).

43 J. Hampson, *Memoirs of the Late John Wesley*, vol. 3 (J. Graham, Sunderland, 1791), pp. 190f.

44 R. P. Heitzenrater, *The Elusive Mr Wesley*, vol. 1, pp. 134ff.; vol. 2, pp. 128ff. G. Gadsby and F. Dewhurst, 'John Wesley's Contribution to the Evolution of Alternatives and Holistic Healing', *Epworth Review* 26.1 (January 1999), pp. 93ff.

45 S. R. Valentine, *John Bennet and the Origins of Methodism and the Evangelical Revival in England*,(Scarecrow Press, 1997), pp. 193ff.

46 Green, p. 104.

47 K. J. Collins, 'John Wesley's Relationship with his Wife as Revealed in his Correspondence', *Methodist History* 32.1 (October 1993), pp. 14–18. B. W. Coe, *John Wesley's Marriage*, (Associated London University Presses, 1996).

48 Stone, *The Family, Sex and Marriage*, pp. 217ff. H. D. Rack, 'But, Lord, Let it be Betsy: Love and Marriage in Early Methodism', *PWHS* 53 (February 2001), pp. 1–13.

49 *Journal* 5, pp. 395–400, 23 January 1771. *BE* 22, p. 262.

50 *BE* 26, 12 May 1755, pp. 587ff. Cf. *BE* 26, 17 May 1742. To Martha Hall.

51 *Journal* 8, p. 3, 18 August 1789.

52 Cf. Heitzenrater, *The Elusive Mr Wesley*, vol. 2, pp. 150ff.

53 R. Ollard, *A. L. Rowse: Man of Contradictions* (Allen Lane, 1999), p. 270.

54 *The Letters of John Pawson*, vol. 1, ed. J. C. Bowmer and J. A. Vickers (Methodist Publishing House, 1994), pp. 96–7. H. Rack, 'Wesley Observed', *PWHS* 49.1 (February 1993), pp. 11ff.

55 J. C. Bowmer, *The Sacrament of the Lord's Supper in Early Methodism* (Black, 1951).

56 Baker, pp. 159, 251.

57 Green, p. 141.

3   *John Wesley's Strategy, Spirituality and Charles Wesley's Hymns*

1 R. A. Knox, *Enthusiasm* (Oxford University Press, 1950), p. 457. *BE* 26, p. 55, 21 April 1741.

2 B. L. Manning, *The Making of Modern English Religion* (Independent Press, 1967), p. 96.

3 *BE* 9, pp. 77ff. *HMGB* 4, pp. 23ff.

4 G. Wakefield, *John Wesley* (Methodist Publishing House, 1990), p. 27.

5 *HMGB* 3, pp. 159ff. Rack. J. M. Turner, *Modern Methodism in England 1932–1998* (Epworth Press, 1998), pp. 76ff. P. F. Hardt, 'The Soul of Methodism: The Class Meeting', in *Early New York Methodism* (University Press of America, 2000).

6 J. H. Lenton, *My Sons in the Gospel*, Wesley Historical Society Lecture, 2000. G. Milburn and M. Batty (eds), *Workaday Preachers* (Methodist Publishing House, 1993).

7 *HMGB* 1, ch. 8, 'The Means of Grace', A. R. George.

8 A. Warne, *Church and Society in Eighteenth Century Devon* (David and Charles, 1969), p. 109.

9 N. Wallwork, 'Wesley's Legacy in Worship', in J. Stacey (ed.), *John Wesley in Contemporary Perspectives* (Epworth Press, 1988), pp. 83ff. *BE* 9, p. 528, 'Worship at the Foundery'.

10 O. Chadwick, *A History of Christianity* (Weidenfeld and Nicolson, 1995), p. 241.

11 *Minutes of Conference 1766* (1862), 1st edn, p. 59. *Works* 13, 4 August 1786, 'Thoughts Upon Methodism'.

12 Cf. J. F. White, *Protestant Worship* (John Knox Press, 1989), pp. 171ff. C. G. Finney, *Lecture on Revivals of Religion* (Harvard University Press, 1960), p. 273.

13 F. Baker, *Methodism and the Love Feast* (Epworth Press, 1957). *BE* 19, p. 258 'Watchnight'.

14 D. Tripp, *The Renewal of the Covenant in the Methodist Tradition*

(Epworth Press, 1969), pp. 81–2.

15 C. Longley, *The Times*, 29 February 1988.

16 *BE* 7: *A Collection of the Hymns for the Use of the People called Methodists* (1780), ed. F. Hildebrandt and O. A. Beckerlegge. *The Poetical Works of John and Charles Wesley*, 13 vols, ed. G. Osborn (Wesleyan Conference, 1868–72). *Hymns and Psalms: A Methodist and Ecumenical Hymn Book* (Methodist Publishing House, 1983). F. Baker, *Representative Verse of Charles Wesley* (Epworth Press, 1962). I. Rivers, *Reason, Grace and Sentiment: Whichcote to Wesley* (Cambridge University Press, 1981). D. Davie, *A Gathered Church* (Routledge and Kegan Paul, 1978); *Dissentient Voice* (Notre Dame, 1982); *The Eighteenth Century Hymn in England* (Cambridge University Press, 1993). R. Watson, *The English Hymn* (Oxford University Press, 1997). S. T. Kimbrough (ed.), *Charles Wesley: Poet and Theologian* (Abingdon Press, 1992); *A Heart to Praise My God: Wesley's Hymns for Today* (Abingdon Press, 1996).

17 D. Martin, *A Sociology of English Religion* (Heinemann, 1967), p. 88.

18 B. L. Manning, *The Hymns of Wesley and Watts* (Epworth Press, 1942/1988), p. 14. E. Routley, 'Charles Wesley and His Vigorous Future', *Epworth Review* (January 1981). A. Dunstan, 'The Use of Wesley's Hymns in Contemporary Worship', *Epworth Review* (May 1988).

19 *BE* 7, pp. 73–5, 77ff. Contents. Cf. Streiff, *Reluctant Saint*, pp. 149ff.

20 B. Hindmarsh, *John Newton and English Evangelical Religion* (Oxford University Press, 1996), p. 271. G. Wakefield, *An Outline of Christian Worship* (T. and T. Clark, 1998), pp. 1, 38f.

21 J. E. Rattenbury, *The Evangelical Doctrines of Charles Wesley's Hymns* (Epworth Press, 1941), pp. 28ff.

22 *HMGB* 1, ch. 4, W. F. Lofthouse, p. 135.

23 F. Baker, *Charles Wesley as Revealed by His Letters* (Epworth Press, 1948). *HMGB* 1, ch. 4. F. C. Gill, *Charles Wesley* (Lutterworth Press, 1964). G. Wakefield, 'John and Charles Wesley: A Tale of Two Brothers', in G. Rowell (ed.), *The English Religious Tradition and the Genius of Anglicanism* (Ikon, 1992), pp. 165ff. *The Early Journal of Charles Wesley 1736–9* (Culley, 1909).

24 J. Scott Lidgett, *The Idea of God and Social Ideals* (Epworth Press, 1938), p. 83.

25 *Works* 7, section 7, 'Large Minutes'.

26 H. Bett, *The Hymns of Methodism* (Epworth Press, 1945), p. 110.

27 D. Davie, *The Eighteenth Century Hymn*, ch. 5, 'The Carnality of Charles Wesley'.

28 *HMGB* 1, ch. 4, pp. 142ff.

29 Manning, *Hymns*, p. 28.

30 G. Wainwright, *Doxology* (Epworth Press, 1980), p. 205.

31 F. Young, *Face to Face* (Epworth Press, 1985), p. 58.

32 J. E. Rattenbury, *The Eucharistic Hymns of John and Charles Wesley* (Epworth Press, 1948), pp. 176ff. G. Wakefield, *Methodist Spirituality* (Epworth Press, 1999), ch. 4.

33 J. Jeremias, *The Eucharistic Words of Jesus* (Blackwell, 1955), p. 159.

34 R. Hooker, *Laws of Ecclesiastical Polity*, vol. 2 (Dent, 1911), p. 331. Cf. Queen Elizabeth I, cited by A. M. Ramsey, *The Anglican Spirit* (SPCK, 1991), p. 17.

35 H. E. W. Turner, 'The Eucharistic Presence', in I. T. Ramsey (ed.), *Thinking About the Eucharist* (SCM Press, 1972), pp. 99ff. J. MacQuarrie, *Paths in Spirituality* (SCM Press, 1972), pp. 82–4.

36 G. Wainwright, *Eucharist and Eschatology* (Epworth Press, 1968), pp. 197–8.

37 V. Taylor, *Jesus and His Sacrifice* (Macmillan, 1937), pp. 312–14.

38 J. A. Newton, *Susanna Wesley* (Epworth Press, 1968), pp. 197–8.

39 Bett, *Hymns*, p. 10.

40 S. J. Kimbrough and O. H. Beckerlegge, *The Unpublished Poetry of Charles Wesley*, 3 vols (Abingdon Press, 1990).

41 E. Routley, *The Musical Wesleys* (Herbert Seakins, 1968).

42 Bett, *Hymns*, p. 169. Cf. also H. A. Hodges and A. M. Allchin, *A Rapture of Praise* (Hodder and Stoughton, 1966). B. E. Beck, 'Rattenbury Revisited: The Theology of Charles Wesley's Hymns', *Epworth Review* (April 1999). T. Berger, *Theology in Hymns?* (Abingdon Press, 1995).

4 John Wesley – Folk Theologian: The Religion of the Heart and Its Consequences

1 R. Maddox, *Responsible Grace: John Wesley's Practical Theology* (Abingdon Press, 1994). W. Warburton, *Works* 8 (1811), p. 380.

2 Cf. Heitzenrater, *The Elusive Mr Wesley*, vol. 2, ch. 10.

3 H. Bett, *The Spirit of Methodism* (Epworth Press, 1937), pp. 127, 144, 165. H. B. Workman, *The Place of Methodism in the Catholic Church* (Epworth Press, 1921). G. Eayrs, *John Wesley, Christian Philosopher and Church Founder* (Epworth Press, 1926), pp. 15–198. T. A. Langford, *Methodist Theology* (Epworth Press, 1998).

4 S. T. Jones, *John Wesley's Conception and Use of Scripture* (Abingdon Press, 1995). Cf. G. Wainwright, *Methodist in Dialog* (Abingdon Press, 1994), pp. 101, 176, 263.

5 T. Runyon, *The New Creation: John Wesley's Theology Today* (Abingdon Press, 1998), pp. 168ff. also T. Runyon (ed.), *Sanctification and Liberation* (Abingdon Press, 1981).

6 R. A. Knox, *Enthusiasm* (Oxford University Press, 1950), pp. 447–8.

7 R. Williams, *On Christian Theology* (Blackwell, 2000), p. xiii.

8 W. B. Fitzgerald, *The Roots of Methodism*, 2nd edn (Epworth Press, 1930), p. 173. *Proceedings of the Eighth Ecumenical Methodist Conference 1951* (Epworth Press, 1952), p. 73.

9 G. Rupp, *Principalities and Powers* (Epworth Press, 1952), ch. 5; *Religion in England*, pp. 416ff. *Works* 8, Second Conference, 1745.

10 Outler, *John Wesley*, p. 152. *Letters* 4, pp. 144, 298, 14 May 1765.

11 H. Bettenson, *Documents of the Christian Church* (Oxford University Press, 1967), pp. 268–9.

12 Cited in Bett, *The Spirit of Methodism*, p. 153.

13 A. R. Peacocke, *Theology for a Scientific Age* (SCM Press, 1993), pp. 222ff.; cf. *Paths from Science Towards God* (One World, 2001), pp. 78–9.

14 F. D. Maurice, *Theological Essays* (London, 1853), p. xvi. Cf. A. R. Vidler, *The Theology of F. D. Maurice* (SCM Press, 1948), p. 37.

15 Cf. D. T. Niles, *The Power at Work Among Us* (Epworth Press, 1968), pp. 122ff.

16 *The Listener*, 14 September 1972. H. Butterfield, *Christianity and History* (Bell, 1949), pp. 26, 45–7, 106.

17 A. Brown-Lawson, *John Wesley and the Anglican Evangelicals of the Eighteenth Century* (Pentland Press, 1994), pp. 301ff. Streiff, *Reluctant Saint*, pp. 149ff.

18 G. Wainwright, *On Wesley and Calvin* (Melbourne, 1987).

19 Outler, *John Wesley*, pp. 425ff. Brown-Lawson, *John Wesley and the Anglican Evangelicals*, pp. 301ff. *Minutes*, 1762. *Works* 8. *HMGB* 4, pp. 164f.

20 G. Lawton, *Within the Rock of Ages: Life and Work of A. M. Toplady* (Clarke, 1983), pp. 195ff. B. Semmel, *The Methodist Revolution* (Heinemann, 1974).

21 A. McGrath, *Iustitia Dei: A History of the Christian Doctrine of Justification*, 2nd edn (Cambridge University Press, 1998). M. E. Brinkman, 'Justification', in N. Lossky et al. (eds), *Dictionary of the Ecumenical Movement* (World Council of Churches, 1991), pp. 560ff. H. Küng, *Justification* (Burns and Oates, 1981). ARCIC II, *Salvation and the Church*. J. M. Turner, 'Salvation and Church History', in D. English (ed.), *Windows on Salvation* (Darton, Longman and Todd, 1994), pp. 56ff. G. F. Nuttall, *The Puritan Spirit* (Epworth Press, 1967), ch. 8. *Joint Declaration of the Doctrine of Justification Between the Lutheran World Federation and the Roman Catholic Church*, Augsburg, 31 October 1999.

22 H. McGonigle, 'John Wesley's Eschatology', in Meadows, *Windows on Wesley*, pp. 153ff.

23 M. Watts, *Why Did the English Stop Going to Church?* (Dr Williams's Trust, 1995), p. 10.

24 H. Rack, *Church Times*, 18 February 2000.

25 Heitzenrater, *Wesley*, p. 261. Cf. *Sermons* 1, pp. 60–1, 'The Almost Christian'. *Works* 7, Sermon 106. *BE* 1, p. 131; 4, pp. 29ff., 187ff.

26 Melville Horne, *An Investigation of the Definition of Justifying Faith* (Longmans, 1809), pp. 1–4, 7–10, 12, 14.

27 *Letters* 4, p. 298, 14 May 1765.

28 Runyon, *The New Creation*, pp. 146ff.

29 D. Butler, *John Wesley and the Catholic Church in the Eighteenth Century* (Darton, Longman and Todd, 1995), pp. 211ff. L. Tyerman, *Wesley's Designated Successor* (Hodder and Stoughton, 1982), p. 412.

30 *Letters* 2, p. 268. *BE* 9, p. 227, 1746.

31 *Letters* 8, p. 238, 15 September 1790. Cf. *A Plain Account of Christian Perfection* (Epworth Press, 1952).

32 Outler, *John Wesley*, pp. 9–10. Cf. H. Lindström, *John Wesley and Sanctification* (Epworth Press, 1950).

33 Outler, *John Wesley*, p. 31. Cf. A. Outler, Preface to F. Whaling, *John and Charles Wesley* (SPCK, 1981), p. xv.

34 W. R. Cannon, *London Quarterly and Holborn Review* (July 1959), p. 217.

35 Preface to *Hymns and Sacred Poems* (1739), p. 22. *Poetical Works*, vol. 1.

36 G. C. Cell, *The Rediscovery of John Wesley* (Holt, 1935), p. 347.

37 Cf R. N. Flew, *The Idea of Perfection in Christian Theology* (Oxford University Press, 1934), pp. 322ff. F. Greeves, *The Meaning of Sin* (Epworth Press, 1957), pp. 167ff.

38 E. B. Pusey, *Letter to the Archbishop of Canterbury*, 3rd edn, Parker, 1842.

39 P. T. Forsyth, *God the Holy Father* (Independent Press, 1957), pp. 102–17.

40 V. Taylor, *Forgiveness and Reconciliation* (Macmillan, 1941), p. 154.

41 J. D. G. Dunn, *Baptism in the Holy Spirit* (SCM Press, 1970); *Jesus and the Spirit* (SCM Press, 1975).

42 G. O'Collins, *The Second Journey* (Paulist Press, 1978).

43 J. H. S. Kent, in H. Cunliffe Jones and B. Drewery (eds), *A History of Christian Doctrine* (T. and T. Clark, 1978), pp. 472ff.

44 A. K. Lloyd, *The Labourers Hire* (Wesley Historical Society, 1968). J. H. Lenton, *My Sons in the Gospel* (Wesley Historical Society, 2000).

45 *Lives* 1, pp. 179ff. S. R. Valentine, *John Bennet and the Origins of Methodism and the Evangelical Revival in England* (Scarecrow Press, 1997).

46 *Letters* 3, p. 141, 12 September 1755. *BE* 26, p. 587. *Works* 11, 'Thoughts on a Single Life', 'A Thought Upon Marriage'. Lenton, *My Sons in the Gospel*, p. 23.

47 *Journal of Frances Pawson*, John Rylands Library, Manchester. Cf.

G. Malmgreen, 'Women and the Family in East Cheshire Methodism 1750–1830', in J. Obelkevich et al., *Disciplines of Faith* (Routledge and Kegan Paul, 1997), pp. 55–70.

48 H. Bett, *The Early Methodist Preachers* (Epworth Press, 1935), p. 33. T. R. Albin, 'An Empirical Study of Early Methodist Spirituality', in R. E. Richey (ed.), *Rethinking Methodist History* (Abingdon Press, 1985), pp. 1–56.

49 H. B. Workman, *The Place of Methodism in the Catholic Church* (Epworth Press, 1921), p. 65.

50 *Lives* 5, p. 132.

51 A. Birtwhistle, *In his Armour: John Hunt of Fiji* (Cargate Press, 1954). M. Dixon, *The Inseparable Grief. Margaret Cargill of Fiji* (Epworth Press, 1978). J. A. Newton, 'Methodism and Obedience', *Epworth Review* (September 1980), pp. 55–61.

52 R. W. Dale, *The Evangelical Revival* (Hodder and Stoughton, 1880), pp. 1–40.

53 R. E. Davies (ed.), *John Scott Lidgett* (Epworth Press, 1957).

54 N. W. Taggart, *William Arthur* (Epworth Press, 1993). D. W. Bebbington, 'Holiness in Nineteenth Century British Methodism', in W. A. Jacob and N. Yates (eds), *Crown and Mitre* (Boydell Press, 1993), pp. 161–74. T. Cook, *New Testament Holiness* (Epworth Press, 1902), pp. 33ff., 133.

55 D. H. Howarth, *Samuel Chadwick: Fifty Years On* (Cliff College, 1993).

56 J. H. Moulton, *A Neglected Sacrament* (Epworth Press, 1919), pp. 20–1.

57 G. Wainwright, *Methodists in Dialog* (Abingdon Press, 1995), pp. 283–4.

58 Cardinal Basil Hume, at Westminster Cathedral, 25 March 1976.

5 The Church of England and John Wesley

1 N. Sykes, in R. Rouse and S. Neil (eds), *A History of the Ecumenical Movement 1517–1948* (SPCK, 1967), pp. 164–5.

2 B. Gregory, *Sidelights on the Conflict of Methodism* (London, 1898), p. 161.

3 *Letters* 7, p. 324, 6 April 1786; p. 326, 18 April 1786; p. 377, 25 March 1787.

4 *Letters* 8, p. 58, 11 May 1788.

5 11 December 1789, *Arminian Magazine* (April 1790). Cf. Baker, pp. 320–2.

6 L. Tyerman, *Life and Times of John Wesley*, vol. 3 (Hodder and Stoughton, 1871), p. 636. C. W. Williams, *John Wesley's Theology*

Today (Epworth Press, 1960), pp. 207–22. John Kent, *PWHS* 35, pp. 10–14.

7 *Journal* 2, pp. 216ff. *BE* 25, pp. 614–17, 693; 19, pp. 66ff., 11 June 1739.

8 R. E. Richey, *The Methodist Conference in America* (Abingdon Press, 1996). B. E. Beck, 'Some Reflections on Connexionalism', *Epworth Review* (May and September 1991; also October 2000). F. Baker, *John Wesley and the Church of England* (Epworth Press, 1970, 2000), ch. 5.

9 *Letters* 3, p. 146, to Walker, 24 September 1755. *BE* 26, pp. 592ff.

10 *Minutes of Conference* 1, 1766, p. 58. Tyerman, *Life and Times of John Wesley*, vol. 11, p. 576. *HMGB* 4, pp. 128ff.

11 *Minutes* 1, 1755, p. 46. *Works* 13, section 11, pp. 213ff. (1856 edn). *Works* 8, pp. 308ff. (1856 edn).

12 *Letters* 3, pp. 149ff, to Adam, 30 October 1755. *BE* 26, pp. 603–11.

13 *Letters* 3, p. 151, to Adam. *BE* 26, p. 610.

14 *Letters* 7, pp. 284–5, 18 August 1785. Cf. *Minutes*, 1744. *BE* 11, p. 77. Williams, *John Wesley's Theology Today*, pp. 141ff.

15 N. Sykes, *From Sheldon to Secker* (Cambridge University Press, 1959), p. 96. A. Warne, *Church and Society in Eighteenth Century Devon*, ch. 8. Cf. F. Knight, *The Nineteenth Century Church and English Society* (Cambridge University Press, 1998), pp. 24ff.

16 Baker, *John Wesley*, p. 161. *Letters* 2, pp. 71–8, 25 June 1746. *BE* 26, pp. 197–207. Rupp, pp. 379ff. B. Hill, 'Occasional Conformity', in R. Knox (ed.), *Reformation, Conformity and Dissent* (Epworth Press, 1977), pp. 199–220. P. Collinson, 'The English Conventicle', in W. J. Sheils (ed.), *Studies in Church History* 23 (1986), pp. 223–59.

17 N. Sykes, *Edward Gibson* (Oxford University Press, 1926), pp. 301ff. D. Hempton, *The Religion of the People 1750–1960* (Routledge, 1996), p. 147. *BE* 11, pp. 336ff.

18 *Letters* 8, pp. 224–5, 26 June 1790; p. 230, July 1790.

19 J. S. Simon, *John Wesley and the Advance of Methodism* (Epworth Press, 1925), pp. 56ff., 179–80. Cf. Baker, Who stresses the use of Huguenot Chapel in West Street after 1743.

20 F. Baker, *The Story of Cleethorpes Methodist Church* (Epworth Press, 1953), pp. 24–9.

21 Baker, pp. 176–7.

22 J. S. Simon, *John Wesley, the Master-Builder* (Epworth Press, 1927), pp. 75ff., 117, 142, 196ff.

23 *Letters* 5, pp. 97–9, to Adam, 19 July 1768. Baker, pp. 195–6.

24 'or *chapels*' was added in 1780 to the phrase 'plain preaching houses'. *Minutes*, 1763. *HMGB* 4, pp. 148ff.

25 T. Jackson, *Charles Wesley*, vol. 2 (Mason, 1841), pp. 148ff.

26 A. R. George, *Expository Times* (1990), pp. 260–4. Text of Deed of Declaration in *A New History of Methodism*, ed. W. J. Townsend et al.

(Hodder & Stoughton, 1909), vol. 2, Appendix B. *HMGB* 4, pp. 195ff. *Journal* 8, pp. 335ff.

27 J. Whitehead, *Life of Wesley*, vol. 2 (London, 1796), p. 404. Baker, p. 218. Hempton, *Religion of the People*, p. 148.

28 F. Baker, *From Wesley to Asbury* (Duke University Press, 1976). F. V. Mills, *Bishops by Ballot: The Eighteenth Century Ecclesiastical Revolution* (Oxford University Press, 1978).

29 *Letters* 3, p. 182, 3 July 1756.

30 *Letters* 7, p. 21, June 1780; p. 284, 19 August 1785.

31 *Eucharistic Presidency: A Theological Statement by the House of Bishops of the General Synod* (Church House, 1997).

32 Baker, pp. 159, 251.

33 N. Sykes, *The Church of England and Non-Episcopal Churches in the Sixteenth and Seventeenth Centuries* (SPCK, 1948); *Old Priest and New Presbyter* (Cambridge University Press, 1956), chs 2, 6.

34 R. C. Monk, *John Wesley: His Puritan Heritage* (Epworth Press, 1966).

35 *The Porvoo Common Statement*, Council for Christian Unity, General Synod, 1993. *The Porvoo Declaration*, ibid., 1994. *The Meissen Agreement*, Council for Christian Unity Occasional Paper No. 2 (1993). But cf. *Episcopé and Episcopacy*, Methodist Conference Statement, 2000. *Over to You* (Methodist Publishing House, 2000), pp. 32ff. Cf. G. Wainwright, 'Is Episcopal Succession a Matter of Dogma for Anglicans?', in C. Podmore (ed.), *Community, Unity, Communion* (Church House, 1988), pp. 164ff.

36 *HMGB* 2, ch. 4. Baker, pp. 256ff. Rack, pp. 506ff. J. Vickers, *Thomas Coke* (Epworth Press, 1969), pp. 100ff.

37 R. A. Knox, *Enthusiasm* (Oxford University Press, 1960), p. 511.

38 26 George III, c.84.

39 Baker, pp. 273ff. Tyerman, *Life and Times of John Wesley*, vol. 3, p. 439.

40 Sykes, *From Sheldon to Secker*, p. 210. Vickers, *Thomas Coke*, pp. 114ff. Baker, p. 271.

41 *Letters* 7, pp. 237–9, 10 September 1984; p. 262, March 1785.

42 A. J. Mason, *The Church of England and Episcopacy* (Cambridge University Press, 1914), cited from G. Horne, *Works* 11, p. 570.

43 *Letters* 7, pp. 237–9. Baker, pp. 234–55. *HMGB* 1, pp. 259–77, A. R. George.

44 Baker, pp. 180–96. C. W. Towlson, *Moravian and Methodist* (Epworth Press, 1957), pp. 118ff. *Journal* 8, Appendix, pp. 328ff.

45 A. B. Lawson, *John Wesley and the Christian Ministry* (SPCK, 1963), pp. 130ff. J. C. Bowmer and J. Vickers (eds), *The Letters of John Pawson* (Methodist Publishing House, 1994), vol. 1, p. 104, May 1791; pp. 121ff., 15 June 1792; pp. 156–7, 7 December 1793; pp. 161, 166–7, January and April, 1794.

46 *HMGB* 1, ch. 9, John Walsh. J. M. Turner, *Conflict and Reconciliation* (Epworth Press, 1985), ch. 5.

47 Turner, *Conflict and Reconciliation*, Foreword by J. S Habgood.

6 *John Wesley – His Political and Social Influence*

1 Cf. F. O'Gorman, *The Long Eighteenth Century* (Arnold, 1997). E. Royle, *Modern Britain: A Social History*, 2nd edn (Arnold, 1998). J. G. Rule, *Albion's People: English Society 1714–1815* (Longmans, 1992); *The Vital Century: England's Developing Economy* (Longmans, 1993). R. Porter, *English Society in the Eighteenth Century* (Penguin, 1982); *Enlightenment Britain and the Creation of the Modern World* (Penguin, 2000). G. V. Bennett, *The Tory Crisis in Church and State 1688–1730* (Oxford University Press, 1976). L. Colley, *In Defiance of Oligarchy: The Tory Party 1714–60* (Oxford University Press, 1983). L. Colley, *Britons: Forging the Nation* (Yale University Press, 1992). J. Clark, *English Society, Ideology, Social Structure and Political Practice During the Ancien Regime* (Cambridge University Press, 1985); *Revolution and Rebellion, State and Society in England in the Seventeenth and Eighteenth Centuries* (Oxford University Press, 1986); *The Language of Liberty: Political Discussion and Social Dynamic in the Anglo-American World* (Cambridge University Press, 1994). C. Haydon, *Anti-Catholicism in Eighteenth Century England* (Manchester University Press, 1993).

2 R. Wearmouth, *Methodism and the Common People of the Eighteenth Century* (Epworth Press, 1945), pp. 97, 105. Cf. I. Gilmour, *Riot, Risings and Revolution* (Hutchinson, 1992). p. Virgin, *The Church in the Age of Negligence* (Clarke, 1988). I. Christie, *Stress and Stability in the Eighteenth Century* (Oxford University Press, 1984).

3 W. R. Ward, in S. Gilley and W. J. Sheils (eds), *A History of Religion in Britain* (Blackwell, 1994), p. 268.

4 P. Langford, *A Polite and Commercial People: England 1727–1783* (Oxford University Press, 1992).

5 E. P. Thompson, *Customs in Common* (Merlin Press, 1991), p. 18 (on Langford), p. 49 (Methodism); *Whigs and Hunters* (Penguin, 1977). D. Hey (ed.), *Albion's Fatal Tree* (Allen Lane, 1975). *Works* 11, Part 19, *A Word to a Smuggler* (1767).

6 *Journal* 4, p. 52, 8 February 1753. *BE* 20, p. 445. Porter, *English Society*, p. 160.

7 J. M. Turner, 'John Wesley Theologian for the People', *Journal of the United Reformed Church History Society* (May 1988), pp. 320ff.

8 A. Quinton, *The Politics of Imperfection* (Faber and Faber, 1978).

9 *Works* 11, Part 2, *Free Thoughts on the Present State of Public Affairs* (1768).

10 R. Anstey, *The Atlantic Slave Trade and British Abolition 1760–1810* (Macmillan, 1975). H. Thomas, *The Slave Trade: A History of the Atlantic Slave Trade 1440–1870* (Picador, 1997). Rule, *The Vital Century*, p. 268. *Works* 11, Part 6, *Thoughts Upon Slavery* (1774).

11 *Letters* 8, 11 October 1787, p. 16; 24 February 1781, p. 265.

12 D. Hempton, *The Religion of the People* (Routledge, 1996), chs 4, 8; *Methodism and Politics in British Society 1750–1850* (Hutchinson, 1985), pp. 11–54.

13 *Journal* 5, 29 April 1768, p. 257. *BE* 22, p. 128. *Letters* 8, 13 January 1790, p. 196. *Journal* 8, 20 September 1790, p. 97.

14 *Works* 11, Part 7, *A Calm Address to Our American Colonies* (1775).

15 *Works* 11, Parts 4, 5, 7, 10, 11, writings of the 1770s.

16 E. Duffy, 'Primitive Christianity Revived', *Studies in Church History* 14 (1972), pp. 287ff. E. Duffy (ed.), *Challoner and his Church* (Darton, Longman and Todd, 1981), ch. 5. E. Duffy, *Peter and Jack* (Dr Williams's Trust, 1982); 'John Wesley and the Counter Reformation', in J. Garnett (ed.), *Revival and Religion Since 1700* (London, 1993), pp. 1–19. D. Butler, *Methodists and Papists* (Darton, Longman and Todd, 1995). Turner, *Conflict and Reconciliation*, ch. 3.

17 J. W. Gough (ed.), *The Second Treatise of Civil Government and a Letter Concerning Toleration: John Locke* (Blackwell, 1948), p. 155. Cf. *Works* 10, Parts 2, 3, 6, 7, 8.

18 Butler, *Methodists and Papists*, pp. 161f.

19 Butler, *Methodists and Papists*, pp. 211–16. *Sermons* 2, pp. 126ff. *BE* 2, pp. 80ff. E. Gallacher and S. Worrall, *Christians in Ulster 1968–1980* (Oxford University Press, 1982).

20 *Journal* 7, 4 January 1985, p. 42; *BE* 23, p. 340; *Journal* 7, 8 January 1787, p. 235; 27 January 1787, p. 305. *Letters* 4, p. 266.

21 *Journal* 8, 14 March 1790, p. 49. J. Vickers (ed.), *Dictionary of Methodism* (Epworth Press, 2000), p. 339.

22 W. J. Warner, *The Wesleyan Movement in the Industrial Revolution* (Longmans, 1930), pp. 165ff. R. F. Wearmouth, *Methodism and the Common People of the Eighteenth Century* (Epworth Press, 1945) pp. 212ff.

23 John Walsh, 'John Wesley and the Community of Goods', in K. Robbins (ed.), *Protestant Evangelicalism 1750–1850* (Blackwell, 1990), pp. 25ff. M. Weber, *The Protestant Ethic and the Spirit of Capitalism* (Unwin, 1965), pp. 139ff., 177ff.

24 Walsh, 'John Wesley and the Community of Goods'.

25 *Works* 11, Part 5, *Thoughts on the Scarcity of Provisions* (1773). M. Edwards, *John Wesley and the Eighteenth Century* (Epworth Press, 1955). D. J. Jeremy (ed.), *Religion, Business and Wealth in Modern Britain* (Routledge, 1998), ch. 6, W. R. Ward. M. Marquart, *John Wesley's Social Ethics* (Abingdon Press, 1992). L. D. Hynson, *To*

Reform the Nation: The Foundation of Wesley's Ethics (Grand Rapids, 1984). P. R. Meadows (ed.), *Windows on Wesley* (Oxford, 1997), ch. 4, T. A. MacQuiban; ch. 5, D. Deeks. H. McLeod, *Religion and the People of Western Europe* (Oxford University Press, 1981), p. 39.

26 The phrase is from John Lawson (Lord Lawson).

27 Cf. E. R. Taylor, *Methodism and Politics 1791–1851* (Cambridge University Press, 1935). D. W. Lovegrove, *Established Church, Sectarian People* (Cambridge University Press, 1988). J. E. Bradley, *Religion, Revolution and English Radicalism* (Cambridge University Press, 1996). J. Kent, *The Age of Disunity* (Epworth Press, 1965), chs 2–5. M. Edwards, *After Wesley 1791–1849* (Epworth Press, 1935). D. Hempton, *Methodism and Politics in British Society 1750–1850* (Hutchinson, 1984). *HMGB* 4, p. 351 (Hazlitt).

28 B. Semmel, *The Methodist Revolution* (Heinemann, 1972).

29 D. W. Bebbington, *The Nonconformist Conscience* (Allen and Unwin, 1982), p. ii. C. Oldstone-Moore, *Hugh Price Hughes* (University of Wales, 1999). G. Kitson Clark, *The English Inheritance* (SCM Press, 1950), p. 128.

30 E. R. Norman, *Church and Society in England 1770–1970* (Oxford University Press, 1976).

31 C. Binfield, *So Down to Prayers: English Nonconformity 1780–1920* (Dent, 1977), p. 11. *HMGB* 3, chs by H. D. Rack and J. M. Turner for detail.

32 J. Garnett, 'Nonconformists, Economic Ethics and the Consumer Society in Mid Victorian Britain', in J. Shaw and A. Kreider (eds), *Culture and the Nonconformist Tradition* (University of Wales, 1999), pp. 95ff. G. Milburn, 'Piety, Profit and Paternalism', *PWHS* 44.3, pp. 45ff.; 'Big Business and Denominational Development in Methodism', *Epworth Review* 10.3 (September 1983).

33 *HMGB* 3, ch. 8, 'Education', by F. C. Pritchard. *Works* 13 parts 35, 36, 37, 54, 58. A. G. Ives, *Kingswood School* (Epworth Press, 1970). G. M. Best, *Continuity and Change: A History of Kingswood School* (Kingswood School, 1998). H. F. Mathews, *Methodism and the Education of the People 1781–1851* (Epworth Press, 1949). D. Baker, *Partners in Excellence* (The Leys School Cambridge, 1975). *Journal* 7, 18 July 1784, p. 3. *BE* 23, p. 323. J. C. Bowmer and J. A. Vickers (eds), *The Letters of John Pawson*, vol. 3, (World Methodist Historical Society, 1995), pp. 70ff.

34 T. W. Laqueur, *Religion and Respectability: Sunday Schools and Working Class Culture 1780–1850* (Yale University Press, 1976). *Journal* 7, pp. 155, 377.

35 J. T. Smith, *Methodism and Education: J. H. Rigg 1849–1902* (Oxford University Press, 1998). T. MacQuiban (ed.), *Issues in Education: Some Methodist Perspectives* (Westminster College, Oxford, 1996).

36 L. F. Church, *More About the Early Methodist People* (Epworth Press, 1949), ch. 4. P. Mack, 'Methodism and Motherhood', in J. Shaw and A. Kreider (eds), *Culture and Nonconformist Tradition* (University of Wales, 1999), pp. 26ff. D. Valenze, *Prophetic Sons and Daughters: Female Preachers and Popular Religion in Industrial England* (Princeton University Press, 1985). P. Chilcote, *John Wesley and the Women Preachers of Early Methodism* (Scarecrow Press, 1991); *She Offered Them Christ: The Legacy of Women Preachers in Early Methodism* (Abingdon Press, 1993). G. Milburn and M. Batty (eds), *Workaday Preachers* (Methodist Publishing House, 1995), pp. 165ff. *Letters* 4, 14 February 1761, p. 133. *Letters* 5, 18 March 1769, p. 130; 13 June 1771, p. 257. *Letters* 6, 2 December 1777, p. 290; 13 November 1778, p. 329. *Letters* 7, 25 March 1780, p. 9. *Letters* 8, 15 December 1789, p. 190.

37 D. Hempton, *The Religion of the People*, p. 190. Cf. D. Newsome, *The Victorian World Picture* (Fontana, 1997), pp. 191ff.

7 Did Methodism Prevent Revolution?

1 D. Martin, 'Faith, Flour and Jam', *Times Literary Supplement*, 1 April 1983.

2 Cf. R. Moore, *Pit-Men, Preachers and Politics* (Cambridge University Press, 1974). J. Rule, 'Methodism, Popular Beliefs and Village Culture in Cornwall', in R. D. Storch (ed.), *Popular Culture and Custom in Nineteenth-Century England* (London, 1982), pp. 48–70. N. Scotland, *Methodism and the Revolt of the Field* (Sutton, 1981). J. H. Wigger, *Taking Heaven by Storm: Methodism and the Rise of Popular Christianity in America* (Oxford University Press, 1998). L. Lyerly, *Methodism and the Southern Mind 1770–1810* (Oxford University Press, 1998).

3 J. H. Plumb, *England in the Eighteenth Century* (Penguin, 1950), pp. 93–4. Rupp, pp. 448–9. F. C. Mather, *High Church Prophet* (Oxford University Press, 1992).

4 D. Hempton, *Religion and Popular Culture in Britain and Ireland* (Cambridge University Press, 1996), p. 32. M. Watts, *The Dissenters* (Oxford University Press, 1995), vol. 2, pp. 367ff.

5 Hempton, *Religion*, p. 45.

6 J. D. Walsh, *John Wesley: A Bicentennial Tribute* (Dr Williams's Trust, 1994).

7 E. J. Hobsbawm, *Primitive Rebels* (Manchester, 1959); *Labouring Men* (Weidenfeld and Nicolson, 1974). F. C. Mather, *Public Order in the Age of the Chartists* (Manchester University Press, 1959). E. Royle, *Chartism* (Longmans, 1996).

8 D. Hempton, *The Religion of the People: Methodism and Popular Religion* (Routledge, 1996), ch. 6. Rupp, p. 449.

9 W. R. Ward, *Religion and Society in England 1790–1850* (Batsford, 1972), pp. 1, 94.

10 William Cobbett, *Rural Rides 1830* (Penguin, 1967), p. 188.

11 F. Maurice, *Life of F. D. Maurice*, vol. 11 (London, 1884), p. 14.

12 E. Troeltsch, *The Social Teaching of the Christian Churches*, ET, vol. 2 (London, 1931), p. 721.

13 J. L. and B. Hammond, *The Town Labourer*, vol. 2 (Longmans, Green, 1949), pp. 93ff.

14 R. F. Wearmouth, *Methodism and the Working Class Movements in England 1800–50* (Epworth Press, 1937).

15 E. Halévy, *The Birth of Methodism*, trans. B. Semmel (Chicago, 1971). J. Walsh, 'Elie Halévy and British Methodism', *Journal of the Royal Historical Society*, 5th Series (1975). G. W. Olsen (ed.), *Religion and Revolution in Early Industrial England* (University Press of America, 1990).

16 E. Halévy, *A History of the English People in 1815*, bk 3: *Religion and Culture* (Penguin, 1938), pp. 10, 47–8.

17 D. W. Bebbington, *Evangelicalism in Modern Britain* (Unwin Hyman, 1989). W. R. Ward, *The Protestant Evangelical Awakening* (Cambridge University Press, 1992).

18 This was the case even in the Anglican–Methodist Conversations in the 1960s.

19 D. Hempton, *Religion of the People*, p. 1, ch. 1. Cf. F. M. L. Thompson, *The Rise of Respectable Society* (Fontana, 1988).

20 M. Edwards, *Methodism and England* (Epworth Press, 1947), pp. 36ff. Cf. W. L. Burn, *The Age of Equipoise* (Unwin, 1964). Hempton, *Religion and Political Culture*, p. 43.

21 E. P. Thompson, *The Making of the English Working Class* (Penguin, 1968), pp. 13, 28–58, 358–410.

22 D. Hempton, *Religion of the People*, pp. 1, 26, 168–71. E. P. Thompson, *Customs in Common* (Penguin, 1991).

23 E. P. Thompson, *Witness Against the Beast: William Blake and the Moral Law* (Cambridge University Press, 1993).

24 J. C. Bowmer and J. A. Vickers (eds), *The Letters of John Pawson*, vol. 3 (Methodist Publishing House, 1995), p. 75.

25 P. Gay, *The Bourgeois Experience* (London, 1985).

26 W. R. Ward (ed.), *The Early Correspondence of Jabez Bunting 1820–29* (Royal History Society, 1972), p. 17.

27 Cited in J. A. Hargreaves, 'Methodism and Luddism in Yorkshire 1812–13' *Northern History* 26 (1990), p. 184.

28 John Kent, *The Age of Disunity* (Epworth Press, 1966), pp. x–xi. A. Pollard, 'Factory Discipline in the Early Nineteenth Century',

Economic History Review (December 1963). B. Jennings (ed.), *History of Nidderdale* (1967), p. 416. C. Aspin, *Lancashire: The First Industrial Society 1750–1850* (Carnegie Publishing, 1995). Watts, *The Dissenters*, vol. 2, pp. 75ff.

29 E. P. Thompson, *The Making*, pp. 381–2. L. Tyerman, *John Wesley*, vol. 3 (London, 1870), p. 499.

30 Ward, *Early Correspondence of Jabez Bunting*, pp. 61–2. R. Moore, *Wesleyan Methodism in Burnley and East Lancashire* (1899), p. 80. Watts, *The Dissenters*, vol. 2, pp. 402ff.

31 M. Batty, *Stages in the Development and Control of Wesleyan Lay Leadership 1791–1878* (Methodist Publishing House, 1992), p. 42. Ward, *Early Correspondence of Jabez Bunting*, p. 21.

32 E. P. Thompson, *The Making*, p. 47.

33 G. Crossick (ed.), *The Lower Middle Class in Britain* (Croom Helm, 1978), pp. 61–88.

34 R. Currie, 'A Micro-Theory of Methodist Growth', *PWHS* 36 (1967–8), pp. 65–73.

35 J. D. Walsh, *The Planting of Methodism in British Society* (World Methodist Historical Society, 1975), summary of lecture by J. A. Vickers. E. Royle, *Nonconformity in Nineteenth Century York* (St Anthony's Press, 1985). A. Everitt, *The Pattern of Rural Dissent: The Nineteenth Century* (Leicester University Press, 1972). J. Obelkevich, *Religion and Rural Society* (Oxford University Press, 1976). J. D. Gay, *The Geography of Religion in England* (Duckworth, 1971), p. 71.

36 C. D. Field, 'The Social Composition of Methodism', *Bulletin of the John Rylands Library* (1994), pp. 153–65; 'The Sociology of Methodism', *British Journal of Sociology* (July 1977), pp. 199–225. Watts, *The Dissenters*, vol. 2, pp. 718ff., very full statistics for the whole country.

37 A. D. Gilbert, 'Religion and Political Stability in Early Industrial England', in P. O'Brien and R. Quinault (eds), *The Industrial Revolution and British Society* (Cambridge University Press, 1993); *Religion and Society in Industrial England* (Longmans, 1976), pp. 60, 83ff.

38 T. W. Laqueur, *Religion and Responsibility: Sunday Schools and English Working Class Culture 1780–1850* (Yale University Press, 1976). Watts, *The Dissenters*, vol. 2, pp. 58–63, 290–303.

39 K. Parker, *Confidence in Mutual Aid* (Methodist Publishing House, 1998).

40 John Kent, *Holding the Fort* (Epworth Press, 1978), p. 41.

41 Cited in E. P. Thompson, *The Making*, p. 438.

42 R. Currie et al., *Churches and Churchgoers* (Oxford University Press, 1977).

43 E. Welbourne, *The Miners' Union of Northumberland and Durham* (Cambridge University Press, 1923), p. 57.

44 Cf. H. McLeod, *Religion and Society in England 1850–1914* (Macmillan, 1996).

45 H. Perkin, *The Origins of Modern English Society 1780–1880* (Routledge and Kegan Paul, 1969), pp. 176ff., 340ff.; *The Rise of Professional Society Britain Since 1880* (Routledge, 1988).

46 D. Blunkett, *On a Clear Day* (M. O'Mea Books, 1995), pp. 57–76.

47 D. Frost, *An Autobiography* (Collins, 1993), pp. 3–9. M. Thatcher, *The Path to Power* (HarperCollins, 1995), pp. 36–40.

48 S. T. D. Green, *Religion in the Age of Decline: Organisations and Experience in Industrial Yorkshire 1870–1970* (Cambridge University Press, 1996). Cf. D. R. Pugh, 'The Strength of English Religion in the Nineties: Some Evidence from the North West', *Journal of Religious History* 12 (1983), pp. 250–65.

49 C. Ford et al., *The Church in Cottonopolis* (Lancashire and Cheshire Antiquarian Society, 1997). M. Smith, *Religion in Industrial Society: Oldham and Saddleworth 1760–1865* (Oxford University Press, 1994).

50 F. M. L. Thompson, *The Rise of Respectable Society*, pp. 196ff. P. Joyce, *Visions of the People: Industrial England and the Question of Class 1848–1914* (Cambridge University Press, 1991); *Democratic Subjects: The Self and the Social in Nineteenth Century England* (Cambridge University Press, 1995). D. Cannadine, *Class in Britain* (Yale University Press, 1998). P. Taylor, *Popular Politics in Early Industrial Britain: Bolton 1825–1850* (Keele University Press, 1995).

51 R. Colls, *The Pitmen of the Northern Coalfield* (Manchester, 1987).

52 Jack Lawson, *A Man's Life* (London, 1932), pp. 111–13.

53 George Edwards, *From Crow Scaring to Westminster* (Labour Publishing, 1922), p. 240.

54 M. K. Ashby, *Joseph Ashby of Tysoe 1859–1919* (Cambridge University Press, 1961), pp. 205–6.

55 Norman Nicholson, *Wednesday Early Closing* (Faber, 1975), pp. 82ff.

56 J. S. Habgood, *Faith and Uncertainty* (Darton, Longman and Todd, 1997), p. 198.

57 F. Hoggart, *The Uses of Literacy* (Penguin, 1958); *A Local Habitation: Life and Times 1918–40* (Chatto and Windus, 1988), an account of Primitive Methodist background in Leeds.

58 C. G. Brown, *The Death of Christian Britain: Understanding Secularisation 1800–2000* (Routledge, 2001). G. Davie, *Religion in Britain Since 1945* (Blackwell, 1994). But cf. S. Bruce, *Religion in Modern Britain* (Oxford University Press, 1995); *Religion in the Modern World: From Cathedrals to Cults* (Oxford University Press, 1996). S. C. Williams, *Religious Belief and Popular Culture: Southwark c.1880–1939* (Oxford University Press, 1999).

8 *Church of the People: Primitive Methodism*

1 J. H. Plumb, *England in the Eighteenth Century* (Penguin, 1950), p. 94. E. P. Thompson, *The Making*, p. 41. R. Colls, 'Primitive Methodism in the Northern Coalfield', in J. Obelkevich (ed.), *Disciplines of Faith* (Routledge and Kegan Paul, 1987), pp. 321ff.; *The Colliers Rant* (Croom Helm, 1977); *The Pitmen of the Northern Coalfield* (Manchester University Press, 1987).

2 H. McLeod, *Religion and Society: England 1850–1914* (Macmillan, 1996), p. 25; *Religion and Irreligion in Victorian England* (Headstart History, 1993). Cf. J. Obelkevich, *Religion and Rural Society: South Lindsey 1825–75* (Oxford University Press, 1976). R. W. Ambler, *Ranters, Revivalists and Reformers* (Hull University Press, 1989). J. G. Rule, *The Labouring Classes in Early Industrial England 1750–1850* (Longmans, 1986).

3 H. R. Niebuhr, *Christ and Culture* (Faber, 1952), pp. 58–92, 192–228.

4 J. Kent, *Holding the Fort* (Epworth Press, 1978), pp. 41–2. A. Wilkinson, *Christian Socialism: Scott Holland to Tony Blair* (SCM Press, 1988), pp. 206-7.

5 M. A. Noll, *A History of Christianity in the United States and Canada* (SPCK, 1992), pp. 165ff.

6 J. Baxter, 'The Great Yorkshire Revival 1792–6', in M. Hill (ed.), *Sociological Year Book of Religion in Britain*, vol. 7 (SCM Press, 1974), pp. 46ff.

7 R. Carwardine, *Transatlantic Revivalism and Popular Evangelicalism in Britain and America 1790–1850* (Greenwood Press, 1978), p. 104. But cf. J. Vickers, *Thomas Coke* (Epworth Press, 1969), p. 217.

8 R. Richey, *Early American Methodism* (Indiana University Press, 1991). R. Richey and K. E. Rowe (eds), *Rethinking Methodist History 1780–1830* (Abingdon Press, 1985). W. J. Townsend (ed.), *A New History of Methodism*, vol. 2 (Hodder and Stoughton, 1909), p. 70. N. Hatch, *The Democratization of American Christianity* (Yale University Press, 1989). J. H. Wigger, *Taking Heaven by Storm* (Oxford University Press, 1998). C. L. Lyerly, *Methodism and the Southern Mind* (Oxford University Press, 1998).

9 R. Richey, 'The Chesapeake Coloration of American Methodism', in T. MacQuiban (ed.), *Methodism in its Cultural Milieu* (Applied Theology Press, 1994), p. 119.

10 P. H. Kaufman, *'Logical' Luther Lee and the Methodist War against Slavery* (Scarecrow Press, 2000).

11 Cited in W. A. Visser't Hooft, *The Genesis and Formation of the WCC* (World Council of Churches, 1983).

12 *HMGB* 2, ch. 7, J. T. Wilkinson. J. T. Wilkinson, *Hugh Bourne 1772–1852* (Epworth Press, 1952); *William Clowes 1780–1851*

(Epworth Press, 1951). J. S. Werner, *The Primitive Methodist Connexion* (University of Wisconsin Press, 1984). H. D. Rack, *How Primitive was Primitive Methodism?* Chapel Aid Lecture, 1996.

13 J. F. C. Harrison, *The Second Coming: Popular Millenarianism 1780–1850* (Routledge and Kegan Paul, 1979). E. P. Thompson, *Witness Against the Beast: William Blake and the Moral Law* (Cambridge University Press, 1993).

14 Whitney R. Cross, *The Burned Over District* (Harper, 1965).

15 G. F. Nuttall, *The Puritan Spirit* (Epworth Press, 1967), ch. 20.

16 Carwardine, *Transatlantic Revivalism*, p. 106.

17 J. Vickers, *History of Independent Methodists* (Independent Methodist Bookroom, 1920).

18 W. R. Ward, *Religion and Society in England* (Batsford, 1972), p. 52.

19 Cf. M. Batty, *Stages in the Development and Control of Wesleyan Lay Leadership 1791–1878* (Methodist Publishing House, 1993), pp. 41ff. D. Hempton, *The Religion of the People*, ch. 6. B. L. Manning, *The Protestant Dissenting Deputies* (Cambridge University Press, 1952), pp. 130ff.

20 Hempton, *The Religion of the People*, ch. 5.

21 D. Graham, 'Chosen by God', *PWHS* 49.2 (October 1993).

22 C. Aplin, *Horwich Moor Methodist Church 1906–1994*.

23 P. Stubley, *A House Divided: Evangelicals and the Establishment in Hull 1770–1914* (University of Hull Press, 1995).

24 Wilkinson, *Clowes*, pp. 85ff. Cf. William Clowes, *Journal* (Hatcher, 1980).

25 H. B. Kendall, *The Origins and History of the Primitive Methodist Church*, 2 vols (Dalton, 1906).

26 E. J. Hobsbawm, *Primitive Rebels* (Manchester, 1974), ch. 8.

27 *HMGB* 2, ch. 1, W. R. Ward, p. 45.

28 H. McLeod, *Religion and the People of Western Europe 1789–1970* (Oxford University Press, 1981), pp. 29ff.

29 E. Welbourne, *The Miners' Union of Northumberland and Durham* (Cambridge University Press, 1923), p. 51.

30 E. P. Thompson, *The Making*, p. 451.

31 'Wesley Perrins Remembers', *Proceedings of the West Midlands Branch of the Wesley Historical Society* (1979–80). *Bulletin for the Study of Labour History* (Autumn 1970).

32 Cf. J. Lawson, *A Man's Life* (London, 1932), pp. 111–13. E. Armstrong, *Address to the Methodist Conference*, 1972.

33 D. Valenze, *Sons and Daughters of Prophecy* (Princeton University Press, 1985). Cf. Graham, *Chosen by God*.

34 Cf. Valenze, *Sons and Daughters*.

35 B. Harrison, *Drink and the Victorians 1815–72* (Faber and Faber, 1977). L. Billington, 'Popular Religion and Social Reform: A Study of

Teetotalism and Revivalism 1830–50', *Journal of Religious History* 10 (1978–9).

36 R. Moore, *Pit-men, Preachers and Politics* (Cambridge University Press, 1974).

37 Cf. Obelkevich, *Religion*, for a perceptive account. M. Douglas, *Purity and Danger* (Routledge & Kegan Paul, 1966)

38 J. Petty, *The History of the Primitive Methodist Connexion* (London, 1864), pp. 419–20. Kendall, *Origin and History*, p. 452.

39 Obelkevich, *Religion*, p. 258.

40 P. Horn, *Joseph Arch* (Roundwood Press, 1971); *PWHS* 37.3 (October 1969), pp. 69–72, Oxfordshire in the 1870s.

41 Turner, *Conflict and Reconciliation*, pp. 86, 168.

42 N. Scotland. *Methodism and the Revolt of the Field* (Sutton, 1981).

43 G. Edwards, *From Crow Scaring to Westminster* (Labour Publishing, 1922), p. 36.

44 C. P. Griffin, *PWHS* 39.3 (October 1973), pp. 62–71, Leicestershire and Derbyshire. A. R. Griffin, *PWHS* 37.1 (February, 1969), pp. 2–9, Nottinghamshire and Derbyshire. S. Y. Richardson, 'John Skevington of Loughborough', in C. Dews, *Primitive Methodism*, pp. 47ff.

45 J. Kent, *The Age of Disunity* (Epworth Press, 1966), p. 137.

46 R. F. Wearmouth, *Methodism and Working Class Movement in England 1800–1850* (Epworth Press, 1977), pp. 173, 213ff.

47 B. Wilson, *The Struggle of an Old Chartist* (Halifax, 1887), p. 3.

48 P. Joyce, *Visions of the People: Industrial England and the Question of Class 1848–1914* (Cambridge University Press, 1994).

49 I. Sellers, *The Hymnody of Primitive Methodism*, Chapel Aid Lecture, 1993.

50 J. Briggs and I. Sellers, *Victorian Nonconformity* (Arnold, 1973), pp. 35ff., from *Primitive Methodist Magazine* (1896), pp. 830–1.

51 G. Milburn, *Church and Chapel in Sunderland 1830–1914* (University of Sunderland, 1988); *The Christian Lay Churches* (Sunderland, 1977); *A School for Prophets* (Hartley Victoria College, 1981).

52 *Proceedings of the West Midlands Branch of the Wesley Historical Society* (1979–80).

53 A. Wilkinson, *Dissent or Conform? War, Peace and the English Churches 1900–1965* (SCM Press, 1986), pp. 61ff.

54 *HMGB* 3, ch. 3, J. T. Wilkinson. Cf. G. Milburn, 'Piety, Profit and Paternalism', *PWHS* 44.3, pp. 45ff.; 'Big Business and Denominational Development', *Epworth Review* 10.3 (September 1983).

55 A. S. Peake, *The Life of Sir William Hartley* (Hodder and Stoughton, 1926).

56 M. Hooker, 'Ministerial Training: The Contribution of A. S. Peake', *Epworth Review* (1985). I. Sellers, 'A. S. Peake Remembered', *Epworth Review* (October 1997).

57 S. Mews, 'John Day Thompson and the New Evangelism in Primitive Methodism', in S. Mews (ed.), *Modern Religious Rebels* (Epworth Press, 1993), pp. 206ff.

58 D. Graham, 'Bourne College: A Primitive Methodist Educational Venture', in A. P. F. Sell (ed.), *Protestant Nonconformity and the West Midlands of England* (Keele University Press, 1996), ch. 7, pp. 135ff.

59 *HMGB* 3, ch. 3, J. T. Wilkinson; ch. 9, J. M. Turner, pp. 328–33.

60 G. Milburn, *Unique in Methodism: 100 Years of Chapel Aid* (Methodist Chapel Aid Association, 1990).

61 *Primitive Methodist Leader* (April 1920), pp. 273. J. T. Wilkinson, *A. S. Peake: Essays and Collected Writings* (Epworth Press, 1958), pp. 143–59. *Holborn Review* (1930), pp. 32ff.

62 D. B. Clark, 'Local and Cosmopolitan Aspects of Religious Activity in a Northern Suburb', in D. Martin and M. Hill (eds), *A Sociological Year Book of Religion in Britain*, vol. 3 (SCM Press, 1970), pp. 45ff.; vol. 4 (SCM Press, 1971), pp. 42ff.

Select Bibliography

Primary sources

Bicentennial Edition of the Works of John Wesley, Clarendon Press and Abingdon Press USA. By 2000 vols 1–4 (Sermons); 7, 9, 11, 18–24 (Journals and Diaries); and 25–26 (Letters) were available.

Works of John Wesley, 14 vols, ed. Thomas Jackson, London, 1829–32.

Journal of the Rev John Wesley, 8 vols, ed. N. Curnock, Epworth Press, 1906–16.

Letters of the Rev John Wesley, 8 vols, ed. J. Telford, Epworth Press, 1931.

Wesley's Standard Sermons, ed. E. H. Sugden, Epworth Press, 1931.

Lives of the Early Methodist Preachers, ed. Thomas Jackson, Wesleyan-Methodist Book Room, 1865; 4th edn, Tentmaker, 1998.

The Poetical Works of John and Charles Wesley, 13 vols, ed. G. Osborn, Wesleyan Conference, 1868–72.

Secondary sources

J. S. Simon, *John Wesley*, 5 vols, Epworth Press, 1921–34.

V. H. H. Green, *The Young Mr Wesley*, Arnold, 1961; Epworth Press, 1964.

V. H. H. Green, *John Wesley*, Nelson, 1964.

M. Schmidt, *John Wesley: A Theological Biography*, 3 vols, Epworth Press, 1966–72.

E. G. Rupp, *Religion in England 1688–1791*, Oxford University Press, 1986.

R. E. Davies and E. G. Rupp (eds), *A History of the Methodist Church in Great Britain*, 4 vols, Epworth Press, 1965–88.

F. Baker, *John Wesley and the Church of England*, Epworth Press, 1970, 2000.

H. D. Rack, *Reasonable Enthusiast: John Wesley and the Rise of Methodism*, Epworth Press, 1989, 2002.

H. P. Heitzenrater, *The Elusive Mr Wesley*, 2 vols, Abingdon Press, 1984.

H. P. Heitzenrater, *Wesley and the People Called Methodists*, Abingdon Press, 1995.
The Proceedings of the Wesley Historical Society.
J. A. Vickers (ed.), *A Dictionary of Methodism in Britain and Ireland*, Epworth Press, 2000.

By the author

'Methodist Religion 1791–1850', in R. E. Davies (ed.), *A History of the Methodist Church in Great Britain*, vol. 2, Epworth Press, 1978, pp. 97–112.
'John Wesley: People's Theologian', *One in Christ* 14.4 (1978), pp. 328–9.
'Primitive Methodism from Mow Cop to Peake's Commentary', in C. Dews (ed.), *Primitive Methodism*, Wesley Historical Society, 1982, pp. 1–13.
Religion and Capitalism: A Continuing Debate, Epworth Press, 1982, pp. 57–65.
'Methodism in England 1900–1032', in R. E. Davies (ed.), *A History of the Methodist Church in Great Britain*, vol. 3, Epworth Press, 1983, pp. 309–61.
Conflict and Reconciliation: Studies in Methodism and Ecumenism in England 1740–1982, Epworth Press, 1985.
'John Wesley: Theologian for the People', *Proceedings of the United Reformed Church History Society* 3.8 (May 1986), pp. 320–8.
'Victorian Values, or Whatever Happened to John Wesley's Scriptural Holiness', *PWHS* 46 (October 1988), pp. 165–84.
After Thompson: Methodism and the English Working Class, Halifax Antiquarian Society, 1989, pp. 57–72.
'People's Church: Primitive Methodism', Chapel Aid Lecture, 1994.
'Years of Tension and Conflict 1796–1850', in G. Milburn and M. Batty (eds), *Workaday Preachers*, Methodist Publishing House, 1995, pp. 35–56, 310–13.
'Wesley's Pragmatic Theology', in R. P. Meadows (ed.), *Windows on Wesley*, Oxford, 1997, pp. 1–19.
'The Long Eighteenth Century', *PWHS* 51 (February 1997), pp. 4–10.
Modern Methodism in England 1922–1998, Epworth Press, 1998.
'Preaching, Theology and Spirituality in Twentieth Century Methodism', *Expository Times*, January 2000, pp. 112–17.

I am grateful for permission from the named publishers to quote from and use these articles, chapters and books.

Index